at swim around ...
whenever I attempt to think
nice thoughts about The
...cle Works.

But upon entering their
world I find I'm in for a big
surprise. It pains me to have
to tell the truth about such
matters, but McNabb and
company are splendid. They
trash the memories of all
those podgy would-be hit
singles and turn their long-
thought-of-as-flabby tunes
into bright, booming
anthems.

Trapped on vinyl, the
group seem to always be
straining; going nowhere
fast. But 'Love Is A
Wonderful Colour' and 'Wh...
Do You Want For Your
Love', both of which are
and irritating in their
recorded formats, tonight
burst open like cocoons
being shed by new
butterflies. You get the
impression they've never
really breathed before now
unless it's always like this,
which case I'll be back in
...rry.

...ook at McNabb go,
relishing every second
...cheekily recreating
Towns... 'I Can See F...
Miles' power chords
whenever he can get away
with it, clearly a man of
taste. He'd love to be
breaking up the equipment.
You can tell, it's in his eyes,
and Chris Sharrock too — he's
virtually drumming his kit
...o the ground.
...m already transfixed by
...e time 'Evangeline' comes
along and does me in
completely, and before one
can blurt out the word
'Orgasmic', these Icicle
Works have pulled off the
impossible — a devout cynic
...has been converted. Who'd
...have believed it?

SPENCE...

CONCERTS

JLP CONCERTS

...Works change their pop soc...
...and obscenely good

...Working... ...he rank...

...er cringing...
...requests! We're...
...reet's less salu...
...es here and no b...
...g. It's real. It's ap...
...list/guitarist Ian McNa...
...orks have always, it would s...
...cceptable behaviour which indicates that a...
...t. Both socially and musically they are a ba...
...ne and have even been known to flirt with n...
...shrewd gaze of fame itself!
It all happened in '83 when the Icies had their big...
Wonderful Colour which reached slot 15 in the natio...
— well, nothing much. It was just confirmation for...
who talks delight in sniffing out the latest one-hit wor...
Now it's almost 1988 and they may just happen ag...
under I'd say that this could be their most powerful...
Icicle Works' new 45, High Time, has all the blata...
with the added angst and urgency which complete...
...giant.
...na: "I always thought it was quite catchy but it w...
...out to promote and an album to follow in the s...
...pare to talk sho_p, and discuss the total-pop-c...
...al hazards that are part and parcel of life a...
cupational Hazard No.1 — The D...
..."We dread those!"
..."The trouble is that the industry thrives...
...n our trendiest jacket and make the best of...
...runk, then we leave early and everyone us...

The Small Price Of A Bicycle

PAiST...

...YMBALS SOUND...

THE ICICLE

...to be nice to...
...that I really say that and you don't...
...m!"

...you have a hit you have to go on chat shows and do all sorts of horrible
...it happened to us with Love is a Wonderful Colour. I keep thinking that if
...y awful Night Network thing and pass comment like I was some sort of oracle
...a hit we'll have to go through all this again. I mean — I could never go on
kids' stuff. You're just doing a job so why should you be held up as a voice of

...The thing is they're only interested in you until someone else comes along.
...now that some people think we're being deliberately awkward but we're not and
...that I come over as an incredibly world-weary at times ...... we're still excited
...being in the band and we still want to be successful."
"It's just that we've learned an awful lot about the music industry and most of it is
...superficial."
"We're a band, not a performing circus act!"

3 — The Press (naturally!)

Icicle Works have never catered to the press — at least not in recent
...sequentially, they'll never be good copy and although that's bad, it's good for
...ous reasons.

..."Most bands will tell you that they're God's gift to popular music. Obviously we
...nk we're good but we're not going to turn around and tell you we're the best band in
...world because there's no such thing."
Chris: "It's just that it's an attitude that comes from living in Liverpool but we weren't always
...this way. We used to be really cool 'cause everyone else was! We used to say, 'don't
...say blah blah blah 'cause they won't like it and don't do this or that 'cause they'll say
...that about us,' and then we suddenly realised that it didn't matter anyway. Whatever
...anyway says about us doesn't make the slightest bit of difference in the long run — at
...the end of the day it's how many records you sell that the Icicle Works have always defied satisfac-
...confuses the issue."

No.4 — Categorisation

Whilst we're on the subject of confusion, The Icicle Works can't see the problem!
tory categorisation but Ian and Chris can't see the problem!
Ian: "I never understand why the press have so much difficulty categorising us. I think
they should just see us as a er . . . a group! A group who write songs — it's as simple
as that."

...The Icicle Works never stand still long enough to tell! They disagree that they...
...play Americanised music:
...steen or Bon Jovi. I suppose I sing in an American accent a bit but not like say, The
Ian: "It depends what you mean by 'Americanised' — I always think of Bruce Spring...
...fact I think that some of what we do is incredibly English."
Waterboys — It doesn't offend me but I don't really think that we're Americanised
And whilst their eponymous debut LP was pure pop counterbalanced with a lyrical
obscurity, The Small Price Of A Bicycle was a rougher-edged affair. Following the
compilation album, Seven Singles Deep, came the third PROPER album, If You Want
To Defeat Your Enemy Sing His Song, which seemed to embrace all sides of the band.
Whilst reflective of past styles it was by no means retrospective and glanced in a
direction that would indicate that the forthcoming LP, at present entitled Blind, would
logically be a more definitive work. Thankfully not so. True to form the band have
essentially more beautiful and diverse than ever. Thankfully once again and this album is more frivolous,
thrown the proverbial icicle in the works.

Ian: "I know you'd have expected a more 'they've settled down now' type of album but
what's the point? If something isn't going to evolve and change what's the point in
doing it?"
Still, it must be said, something is emerging — be prepared for an album which is
more confident and, dare I say it, more ICICLE WORKS?
Chris: "Yes, well that's because we produced it ourselves this time and also we are a lot
good at what we do. I know it sounds big-headed but we're not kids anymore, we've
been together a long time now and it all gets so much easier these days."
It's always been an issue but even more evident than ever is the odd coupling of
subjects within the album itself. 223, a mouthpiece for a new McNabb persona — a
sleazeball with a lust that would shame Mr. Mindwarp's warbling antics into impotence
is found to be juxtaposed with the aching pathos of Starry Blue-Eyed Wonder.
Ian: "Well, people do it in books and films, don't they? Why should an album have one
kind of image or personality? Starry Blue-Eyed Wonder is a more reflective song and 223
is a dirty blues song, but why shouldn't you do that?"
Indeed. And why not have optimism posted on some kind of duty opposite pessimism
where do the harrowing images of social injustice things that he knows aren't right in
Ian: "Well, Blind is about someone who sees things and is prepared to do anything to change them?
issue is too big for him — he isn't prepared to do anything to change them?
a bit like me I suppose ."
And what of the sentiments of unrequited love in Little Girl Lost and Hurt? Little girl...
Are they from?
Ian: "Well, my lyrics are usually other people's lyrics! Little girl...
because I Liked The Doors song Lost Little Girl! I'm not very good...
— I like them to be half-realised so that I can make them be...
indirect...
Ian: "The minute you starting bowing down to what's expected...
...numbered beginning your heart's not in it."
The magic word. I'm suitably confused and reassured...
things never change and never stay the same...

The Icicle Works have no
credibility or cool at all. What they
have are the kind of tunes most
young, male guitar groups (cute or
grubby) would die for. 'When It All
Comes Down', 'Evangeline', 'Ho...
Springs Eternal' . . . all sound fab...
gear and marvy tonight. Passionate...
invigorating, a good crack. 'Up Her...
In The North Of England' is boss,
but then I'm biased. Any song that
asserts the racial and genetic
superiority of northerners is oka...

Love is A
. nothing
usic press
The Icicle

really gone
. say that the
an Evangeline
crafted chart

single.' With a
quet, the Icicles
ending occupa-
g demi-gods!
Part

MerseyBeast is published by :

Trinity Mirror North West & North Wales
PO Box 48
Old Hall Street,
Liverpool L69 3EB

Produced by Trinity Mirror Sport Media

MerseyBeast design:
Lee Ashun

Executive Editor:
Ken Rogers

Editor: Steve Hanrahan

Book Editor Peter Grant

Production Editor: Paul Dove
Art Editor: Rick Cooke

Sales and marketing manager: Elizabeth Morgan

© Pictures provided by author and Trinity Mirror NW2

Cover image:
Paul Slattery

ISBN 978-1-905266-88-3

Mersey Beast

A musical memoir

by
Ian McNabb

 # Foreword
by Janice Long

Ian's a mate, always will be.

We met at BBC Radio Merseyside in 1981. I presented a show called *Streetlife*. I wanted to showcase Liverpool's new bands and talk about the stuff that was crucial to the 'alternative' scene. So sandwiched between The Cherry Boys and The Pale Fountains would be a phone-in on how to come out of the closet. You get my drift.

The show went out on a Sunday night between eight and ten. The budget was a tenner! I asked the Icicle Works to come on *Streetlife* because I had heard their stuff and loved what they were doing. My brother Jeff was also a huge fan and was hell bent on signing them up for a publishing deal. Anyway, Ian, Chris and Chris turned up armed with a single and ready for the interview. I vividly remember asking a question I have never asked any band since. "Where did you get your name from?" The look on Ian's face. He thought I was a dozy cow, I thought he was a cock. A friendship was born.

I call him McNabb. Is that a Scouse thing? Is it because there are Ians a plenty in bands in Liverpool?

I have lost count of the times I have seen McNabb perform as an Icicle Work and solo. I can honestly say that I have never had to worry about post-gig dressing room chats. He gives everything and more. I saw him in Birmingham when I was

squashed down at the front of the sold-out Academy.

What a night.

We all sang our hearts out knowing the words to every song. It was such a rush and very emotional.

I also remember going to the launch of *Head Like A Rock* at a studio in Primrose Hill. Ian sat at the piano and played Beatles songs for hours. Another sing-a-long. I had to do a photo shoot and had *Truth and Beauty* playing to relax me.

Ian was brilliant after the Liverpool City of Culture Concert at the new arena. There was a party at the Albert Dock and Ian took to the stage with a few members of Amsterdam and Starsailor. They raised the roof and got the whole thing going.

We've done so many things together, gigs, telly, judging. Actually the judging was not a pleasant experience. We were asked to judge a band competition. We chose a winner but it didn't go down well with another band's fans and we had to be rushed out of the back door.

We've hung out at his place and my place. He is one of the funniest people I know and I love his stories. He is a fantastic mimic. He is great to be around. I have met all of his girlfriends and none of them have been over twenty two!!

Enjoy the book. I have.

Love you, Ian.

A Concert Report From The Stables, Milton Keynes.
Ian McNabb Concert
22/04/06
DTM: Rhea Perkins

'During the Ian McNabb concert there were a number of problematic factors: Firstly, once clearance had been given to Lynn Andrews in the green room there was a further five minute wait whilst Ian had to wait for his technician to give him the go ahead.

During this time the technician was pouring Ian's Guinness into a pint glass on the stage.

A member of the audience had consumed a little too much alcohol and started to heckle Ian. This turned into him using bad language as he shouted from C block. To which Ian swore back at him.

Ian also swore at another member of the public when he got up and stood at the side of the auditorium and started to dance, shouting 'Sit the f*ck down!' The drunken member of the audience lit up a cigarette in the auditorium.

I had become aware of the situation and was on my way to escort him out of the building when I met Noeleen coming through the door marching the young gentlemen in question towards the exit.

The young man was no problem on a one to one basis and very apologetic to us about his behaviour.

Another member of the audience had become agitated by the drunken member and came out offering to hit him for us, to which we calmed him down, replying that the Stables was a peaceful venue and we never had cause for such actions, whilst also making sure that he was alright and able to enjoy the rest of his evening.

Towards the end of the concert, Ian had drunk two bottles of wine, four cans of Guinness, and the audience were buying him single shots of Jameson's.

Ian at this point then invited the whole of the audience to join him on stage.

At that point the whole of the audience ran at the stage, with drinks in their hands, and circled Ian dancing and singing. Ian then invited them to sing as he played.

Ian was supposed to be performing a forty-five minute second set but after one hour and ten minutes and a dangerous situation on the stage, we called for house lights to prompt Ian to finish the concert.

Ian then came up into the foyer and proceeded to be inappropriate with every female he came into contact with.

The evening's events culminated in an extremely worrying event, where I tried to maintain order as best I could.'

CHAPTER ONE

(I go)
my OWN way

I've pretty much always known what I've wanted.

I feel sorry for people who seem to drift through life without any real aim or purpose. They vote for whoever hasn't had a go for a while. Many of them don't really have a passionate interest in anything they either control or have effect thereon. They tick over. They bemoan the lack of quality in modern entertainment as they fart their way through reality TV shows like *Big Brother*. They buy three record albums a year. Quiet, loud, and the one nearest the checkout.

They tell you there's got to be something better than this, but they don't try to make it better. They experience excitement vicariously by supporting football teams who are largely comprised of individuals that have no concern for anything but their own pay packets.

"We did it!" Cry the fans. Who? You? Think again! Some of them may drink and/or take drugs to make themselves more exciting to themselves alone - whilst boring those around them to death. Many of them do jobs they hate. They're trying to be happy but somehow never really succeed because they don't know what it is. Some claim to be free but ultimately do what they are told.

The lucky ones find their twin and breed merrily while the rest seem to fall into relationships and have kids because - that's what everybody else does. Very few marriages or partnerships seem to last the distance it seems because people race or stumble into them. Most of the friends I have who've gone down this route now see their kids at the weekend and are skint. How many men leave their families when they meet a younger woman, breed again and shower their new offspring with more attention than the children from their first marriage? You can set your watch to it. They were too young and selfish to appreciate it all first time around they say. Tell that to the previous wife and children. A lot of women seem to get to their early thirties and start panicking if they haven't reproduced yet.

They ruled the roost from the age of sixteen until this time and now they feel threatened by the younger models of their species. At this stage, if still single, they may be prone to select someone, sometimes seemingly at random, in order to breed. Many men come into their own when they get older.

Men can have women twenty or thirty years younger than them at almost any stage of the game provided they possess power and money. If they don't, well they're gonna stick with what they've got and make the best of it.

Maybe. Whenever a sexy young woman hooks up with a wrinkly old geezer and they're asked about the age difference, the lady in question will usually bang on about how age doesn't mean anything and love is all. If this were true how come she's going out with a millionaire and not a plumber? You could argue that in the circles these lithe creatures operate in they are more likely to meet a property magnate than a builder, and you may be right. You're probably not gonna meet this year's girl in the Dog and Amoeba (although I did get to meet last year's girl in there once).

Many women are turned on by power and position, standing and place. Some of them of course are genuinely loving and sincere. Some of them. If you meet one, try to hold onto them! I was having some fun with a lass not too long ago who told me this - if she didn't get where she wanted to be through her own merits soon, she'd simply bag some bloke with loads of cash and a hard-on and lay back and think of England. Anything to avoid a struggle. I don't blame her - I think - but it's a little disappointing to hear this kind of thing from one so young. Why should they strive for greatness for years when all they believe they have to do is look cute to land in luxury? They have a name for them now - WAGS (wives and girlfriends - usually of football players - the biggest catch - young, fit, rich and full of cum). Most of the youth of today (not all) believe that fame and wealth are all - irrespective of how it is acquired. Not all females are like the one I mention, but I seem to meet a lot of them. That's probably due to the nature of my work, and the circles I move in. There's no business like show business. I guess it's where you look. I'm only telling you what I have seen through these wise old eyes.

Sometimes these old eyes are not so wise. Due to my like-the-company-but-couldn't-eat-a-whole-one attitude towards the opposite sex over the years, I've spent many an evening trying to coax certain women of beauty - but questionable motives - into bed for a brief liaison, who weren't that crazy about me for my winning personality or boyish good looks alone. God knows what they thought I had to offer them (apart from a night of red-hot sleep and a couple of free tickets to the N.M.E. tour). Carrots were often dangled of course to ensure safe passage to my lair and to minimalise flight risk. Foolish really - but perfect sense at the time.

It isn't difficult believe me. You'll probably never have their undying love but you'll get to perform the most natural act with someone you actually fancy on a fairly regular basis.

Usually at weekends. Who wants undying love? It's a pain in the arse. It stops you focusing on the important stuff. It's more trouble than it's worth. Falling in love sucks and doesn't swallow. You came in alone, you're going out alone. Deal with it.

You're lucky to be here. I choose to be single most of the time. Most of the time.

Being partnered isn't really my style. I've done it. It's rather boring. I'm not very good at it.

I tend to smother or ignore. I go out to socialise, have a few drinks, watch a band, get somethin' to eat, entertain myself and hopefully those around me. I have a laugh and maybe get laid that night. Doesn't matter if I don't - it's not that important. I'm comfortable going home to my king-sized bed alone.

I've been lucky enough to travel around the world with my mates many times and there's always been people standing at the edge of the stage who've paid to see me (sometimes that's the only place they're standing). People think I'm a hopeless romantic because of my lyrics.

I'm not. I'm a grumpy old cynic with a gift for prose. I've been in love about four times in my life. Purely for research purposes. There've been maybe two women I've met who I've thought about making babies with - but for one reason or another it never came to pass. A realist, I'm a musician by trade. I don't live by the same rules as Joe Blow. I'm an artist(e). A poet. A visionary. A restless boarder. I'm honest. Sometimes too honest. I don't want to sit in a fuckin' pub eatin' peanuts whilst trying to think of something new and interesting to say to someone I see all the time. I don't want to see someone fall apart in front of my eyes over the years. I'm sure they'd feel exactly the same underneath it all. Get comfortable in your own skin. Kill your own snakes.

Don't look for your own happiness in others, you won't find it, matey. They don't know where it is either. Trust me. The reason why I succeed a lot of the time in my various chosen pursuits is because I'm not bothered if I fail. Failure is more important than success. You learn a lot more about yourself. People who win generally lose a lot, but you don't hear about that. There are more important things than being with someone, like what drives you for instance.

What drives me is music. Excitement. Adventure. Passion. Soul.

Danger. Yes danger! The unknown. The not knowing.

Peace and quiet is good too - in small doses.

By the way, as I write this, I live with my dear mother, Pat. Or should I say she lives with me. I lived alone in a castle which my good fortune had brought me, and in the absence of any female appearing in my life whom I felt was suitable as a full time companion, I invited my mother to share the fruits of my labour/luck. People often find this amusing, me being an alleged wild-eyed loner and all that, but she's the best person I ever met in the world. Your mother always is. Elvis Presley - The King Of Rock'n'Roll? Well, his mother Gladys lived with him too - and - fuck me - how bad did he lose it when she passed?

I worry about that.

Worrying is good, too.

Gives you an edge, la.

Mmm.

Look after your mother, she bore you. One day she be gone.

And then she bore you no more.

Since the age of twelve, music has been my religion. It was - what I wanted. It's always there for me, I'm good at playing, writing and singing it, and it never lets me down. I've made some duff records over the years, but I've made some amazing ones too. I've done some wonderful shows - and quite a few dreadful ones. It's organic. We're not robots. I could've made a lot more money if I had been more ambitious, but success is a by-product of what I do, not a pre-requisite. As long as I can pay my bills, make another record, do another gig, have some cash to throw around on what I see fit - I'm alright Jack. You can't know what it's like to walk out on stage to a thousand people (hell a hundred will do! Fifty!) and hear them cheer your every move - unless it's actually happened to you. They love you. For a little while anyway.

What can be better than that? Whenever I get down, and of course I do sometimes - yes, even me - I read the fan letters and realise as fucked-up as I might feel at that particular moment in time, someone, somewhere, is listening to 'You Must Be Prepared To Dream' and it's making them feel good for a time.

And that makes me feel good.

I was reasonably smart at school. In the top three in my class before I lost interest. A child of the Apollo generation, I, like many others around me, fancied myself as an astronaut, but sadly found the concepts of mathematics, physics and chemistry rather hard to master. Also, being English didn't help - you had to sound like a Texas wrangler to bounce around convincingly on the Sea Of Tranquility. Right? The only reason why I passed certain exams at the time was because I memorised everything I was supposed to - regardless of whether or not I actually understood it. It all went out the window when I saw T. Rex on *Top Of The Pops*.

It was like the doorway to another world, which I was more than ready to walk through. Marc Bolan had corkscrew hair, a satin jacket and a Gibson Flying V guitar. What the fuck? He was telling me to "Get it on!" And, er, "Bang a gong!" OK then.

My mum and dad bought me a second-hand classical guitar, sent me to music lessons and that was it. No turning back. I had an idyllic childhood. An only child, doted on by my father who drove a taxi, and my mother who worked at United Biscuits, Ogdens, and then did bar work for years to help support us until she had a terrible accident and fell down some stairs when she was going to change a beer barrel. We never had much money but they gave me whatever I wanted - eventually - and encouraged me in whatever I wanted to do.

That's good parenting.

I'm sure if I'd have wanted to join the Mafia they would've

bought me a gun. God bless them.

So - I decided to write a book about my experiences. I thought I'd get it all down before I forget it all or something bad happens to me. It's a pop book. It's written by someone who never made it that big but still has an interesting story to tell. I've read a lot of pop books by very rich and famous people and the male, hetero version usually goes something like this:

Shitty childhood (maybe a bit of abuse), teen dreams of stardom, discovery of the opposite sex, discovery of music, alcohol, bit of soft drug dabbling, Cocaine, HEROIN. Bad marriage, bad parent, career nose-dive. Recovery, remorse, new young wife, new family, comeback album. Autobiography (usually ghost-written), media blitz.

My story isn't quite like this. If you want that kind of stuff buy Slash's or Nikki Sixx's tomes.

And if you want to be bored to death, buy Eric Clapton's volume of endless, witless whitterings.

Shaddup and play yer guitar.

My story isn't as extreme, but a lot of it is funny. Some of it is quite sad. It's the story of my life. I aim to corner the market in 'moderately successful' rock star memoirs.

Perhaps that's where they'll file it in your local bookstore.

I hope you enjoy reading it and kills some time for you on a long journey, a rainy day, or a beach somewhere. You can view it as a cautionary tale, or an invitation to the dance.

Anyway, thanks for looking in.

My name's Ian.

I've pretty much always known what I've wanted.

Lucky bastard.

How about you?

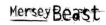Mersey Beast

CHAPTER TWO

Born to Boogie

My father's name was Robert Gerard McNabb.

His parents died before I was born and I don't recall anyone ever telling me their names or what they did for a living.

My mother certainly doesn't remember, although she remembers meeting her future mother-in-law just once briefly, when the lady in question opened the door to her, muttered something, and then scurried away hurriedly to fetch my dad.

Dad - Bob - had a younger brother, Hal, and an older sister, Kay. The family home was an end terrace, 44 Morden Street, off Boaler Street, Fairfield, Liverpool 6. Approximately three miles from the city centre.

A tall, handsome, quietly spoken, gentle man, everybody who met Bob seemed to like him a great deal, and his company was keenly sought, although he liked being on his own well enough. Being of optimum age to enter the services at the start of WW2, his military career was short but exemplary.

By the end of the conflict he had risen to the rank of sergeant, fighting Rommel's Afrika Korps in the North African Desert, and managing to return home without injury.

In later years, apparently due to his exposure to the constant blazing sunlight on his flesh during the war, Dad contracted a form of non-life threatening skin cancer which caused ugly sores to appear.

He would then have to visit the hospital periodically to have them zapped by radiation.

For some reason he took me to a couple of these sessions and I would watch in horror as he lay on a bed with this frightening contraption above him making scary noises.

It used to terrify me.

A succession of unsteady jobs followed the war years, one being a credit draper... basically a money lender.

However, my dad was not a muscle man and quickly became unstuck in this employ due to his kind nature. He would let people pay back so slowly that he was eventually fired.

In and out of various jobs which nobody who knew him at the time can seem to recollect due to their mundanity, he eventually met my mother, Patricia Mavis Forsyth, at a local dance.

Pat was a good twenty years younger than Bob which seemed to bother neither party and they married soon after.

My mum's parents were May and Tom, and she had a younger brother, also called Tom. Dad's parents both passed away in the mid-1950s. His brother Hal, became a great hero in the war, flying sorties in Lancaster bombers above night-time Germany.

He soon became a Squadron Leader, took part in the Berlin Airlift, and was eventually awarded the Distinguished Flying Cross. After the war he moved to Blackheath, London, where he married a woman called Marie.

They adopted two children, a boy and a girl - Ian and Barbara-Ann.

Nobody liked Marie except Uncle Hal, and we lost contact with them in the late sixties.

We went to stay with them once and it was awful. They spoke to me like I was a child.

My parents never spoke to me like I was a child, they spoke to me like I was a person. There were horrible arguments. Marie was the matron from hell.

I'm sorry I have nothing nicer to say about this.

I only ever saw her once again, when my dad was dying and she came to see him in the hospital.

Dad's sister Kay, married a man called Jim Atkinson and moved to Manchester. Mum and Dad moved into the family home in Morden Street.

My mum's dad had recently become a taxi driver and persuaded my father to do the same. He saved up enough money to put a down payment on a black cab, loved the work, and would do such until the end of his life.

Somewhere amidst all of this activity Bob and Pat found time to make me, and I was born on November 3rd, 1960 at Lourdes Hospital, Greenbank Road, Liverpool. (In the early eighties my record plugger Kim Glover told me to shave a couple of years off my age as it looked better on my biography, the British music scene being continually, myopically, youth-obsessed.

I was still only twenty-two years old but complied.

It's caused confusion down the years for those who care about such things, and sometimes for a laugh in these later years I've knocked a couple more digits off - usually when trying to convince somebody much younger than myself to sleep with me. For the record, I've found that usually around the early forties mark is acceptable).

My mother has told me that the birth was so painful, and so reluctant was I to leave the womb, that she swore she would never have another child.

A promise that she kept.

My first memory is of a large shape above me blocking out the light and making high-pitched noises, baby talk.

I'm told I was a good-natured child, hardly ever cried, and seemed content in my own company.

At eighteen months old I caught pneumonia, which nearly killed me and left me with a weak left lung.

Around the age of three, so cute was I allegedly that my dad's friend, Daily Mirror photographer Bill Mealey, convinced my parents that I should be a child model, which I briefly became.

I have a vague recollection of modelling slippers in the local paper for a city centre department store.

I don't know if it's better to be an only child or not. I don't know the difference.

I never felt lonely, always had plenty of friends to play with, and was never left feeling needy in any way. I usually got whatever I wanted, even if I had to wait a time, and most of my memories of early childhood are all fairly wonderful.

My dad smoked a pipe, and when this curious object was in his mouth all seemed good with the world. It meant everything was calm because he didn't touch it when things were not good. I would always say "Dad put your pipe in your mouth!" Because his face looked kinder and more handsome that way.

He looked more relaxed.The scent of pipe tobacco still puts me at ease, but I've never gotten around to smoking one myself, perhaps because I can't think of any significant rock 'n' roller who has done so yet (not a tobacco pipe anyway). Perhaps I should become the first!

Perhaps not.

I have snapshots of my early days. I know it's all in there somewhere but I have trouble accessing it. Sometimes I remember things vividly.

Smells, places, and then they're gone again, to return God knows when.

I do wonder if alcohol and drug abuse have affected my brain sometimes. It's the price you pay. Short term memory loss is definitely a casualty of a hedonistic lifestyle.

I can remember exactly how I felt standing in the schoolyard one day about forty years ago, but I can't remember who I'm supposed to call today, despite the fact that I made a mental note before I went to bed last night. I can't remember where I put a CD an hour ago.

I walk into another room and then can't figure out why I did.

I get halfway up the stairs, and wonder why I'm there. I'm told this happens with age, but I think it may be a little premature sometimes.

It gets harder to learn my own lyrics. I look at a familiar face, and no name comes up. Sometimes it's a blessing to forget things.

One vivid memory I have and would rather not is of running around the mini-market on Boaler Street pushing a shopping trolley.

I was about five. I had a bad fall and crashed into a wall. My head crashed against the wire of the trolley with such force I was lucky not to put my left eye out.

I had to go to hospital for a few days and was so hysterical they strapped me in the bed. I still have a large scar underneath my left eyebrow to prove it. I got a train set for that.

I REMEMBER...

...coming down a slide the wrong way round in Sheil Park playground and landing on my chest and not being able to breathe for about a minute.

...digging up the muck in the gutters using lolly ice sticks with John Thornley who lived a few doors down from me... 'Blackberry Haunted' and 'Greenberry Funny.' Two slagheaps next to the car park in Sheil Park, so named by John and me.

Sheil Park was the place which housed three huge blocks of flats that towered over Morden Street like sentinels.

...riding my mustard coloured Chopper bike around Newsham Park.

...my dad getting me out of bed at four in the morning to watch the first Moon landing.

...crying when Arsenal's Charlie George scored the winning goal against Liverpool in the 1971 FA Cup Final, and then lay flat on his back with his arms aloft. Bastard.

...being punched in the face at secondary school and running along the road panicking, feeling the side of my face blow up to the size of a tennis ball. I trust I will witness every event again in digital quality as I draw my terminal breath.

My mum worked initially at United Biscuits in Lockerby Road in Liverpool 6, and my first school was St. Sebastian's - in the same road. She would drop me off and then walk up the road to work, and pick me up again at the end of the day.

She was a comptometer operator (a form of adding machine), totting up company accounts and the like, always good with numbers my mum (she still does my accounts).

My dad always seemed calm except for when my mum got up on Sunday mornings and he would put his pipe down and busy himself making tea, nervously fumbling with the toaster while I watched *Space:1999*.

He seemed scared of her sometimes and she always seemed to wake up in a bad mood. Something which she still does to this day.

I liked my school.

I liked English and Science (despite the fact I never understood any of the latter). I was very good at art. My hobby interests were limited to Johnny 7 plastic machine guns (they fired white plastic bullets and grenades), war in general, and Action Man (a plastic toy soldier with 'realistic hair' which also had a string you could pull which would elicit pre-recorded vocal samples the like of which "Mortar attack! Dig in!" became my favourite), until Dad took me to see Stanley Kubrick's *2001: A Space Odyssey* at the Abbey Cinerama, opposite Picton clock, in 1968.

I was seven years old and it blew my fucking head apart. I didn't have a clue what was going on but... Christ, the future looked exciting (we was robbed... It's 2008 as I write this. Where's my lunar holiday?)

A bit later on I got hooked on *Star Trek* and decided space really was the place. I vowed to free myself of these earthly bonds as soon as possible.

Girls didn't figure yet.

Home was my favourite place to be. The original house had no kitchen so my dad built one himself from tarpaulin, wood and hardboard in the back yard, which connected to the outside toilet.

We had no bathroom and we washed ourselves by standing in a bowl in the kitchen a couple of nights a week (not all together).

It was no hardship - we didn't know anything else.

My mum took me out of St. Sebastian's when she got a new office job at Ogden's tobacco factory on West Derby Road.

My new school was St. Michael's which was opposite the factory and thus convenient for her to drop me off in the morning.

When I got to being around nine or ten I started having funny feelings and noticing girls. I fell in love with a beautiful blonde called Sharon Roberts, who was in my class. I was tall but quite chubby and she never noticed me.

I had braces on my teeth which didn't help either. She crossed my best mate Steven Murray's pin (an early form of bonding) but laughed at me when I asked her to do the same for me.

I cried myself to sleep a few times.

I saw Jane Fonda in the soft-porn psychedelic sci-fi flick *Barbarella* and my tiny penis became hard for no apparent reason.

Destiny Angel in Gerry Anderson's *Captain Scarlet* also brought about a similar reaction - despite the fact she was made of wood. I discovered the only way I could relieve this burdening tension was to rub myself against my pillow until a curious feeling of deep pleasure came over me and I suddenly felt fantastic and then completely relaxed.

Later on my willy would produce a sticky white liquid every time I did this (which was becoming more frequent) and I would think there was something wrong with me and feel terribly guilty. I thought I'd broken it.

I was a football fanatic around this time (briefly an Evertonian and then a lifelong Liverpool follower) and my (limited) ability at the game gained me a place in the school team.

I was not a particularly skillful player, lacking in ball control, but my specialty was defence as I had weight, height and speed and would usually scare the shit out of approaching strikers by smashing the ball away from them with such ferocity that it would usually end up at the other end of the pitch near the opposing team's goalmouth. I was a fast runner over short distances but would regularly collapse after ten minutes on any given marathon.

I had a friend called Robin Reeves who lived around the corner from me on Halisbury Road.

We discovered music together. He worshipped Gary Glitter and David Bowie (later on I would learn that he was gay - this had nothing to do with his choice of music I stress, although it did go some way to explaining some of the activities he suggested we should take part in together - which I declined).

I loved Marc Bolan and not much else. It was the glam era.

The Beatles were passe. I'd loved 'She Loves You' and 'Ticket To Ride' when I was five, but this was a new era.

Our time.

We went to see David Essex in *That'll Be The Day* in a double bill with T.Rex's *Born To Boogie*. Both films changed my life there and then.

The Essex movie portrayed a young man who begins a family but quickly becomes bored, buys a guitar and decides to try his hand at being a rock 'n' roll star. I decided to skip the family bit and get straight to the good stuff. I persuaded my folks to send me to guitar lessons and... that was it.

Every Saturday morning I would go to a little school above a butcher's shop on Penny Lane to learn how to master this six-string phenomenon.

We weren't messing about, so I'd go to a little old French guy's house just off Green Lane every Tuesday night as well. His name was Pierre Bethel and he must have been eighty years old. My guru. My dad insisted I should do it absolutely properly so I started taking classical theory also. I was going to learn to read music as well as play it.

Dad bought me a gut-string guitar for five pounds for my twelfth birthday to replace the piece of shit I'd found somewhere which I'd been miming to T.Rex records to, and I was away.

Everything else went out the window.

It cost my folks a fair bit of money to make all this happen for me for which I'm eternally grateful.

> *'Baby baby, I was born to boogie,*
> *baby baby, I was born to boogie,*
> *spent some time with you,*
> *I'm gonna do what I wanna do.'*

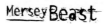

CHAPTER THREE

Fairfield
Conservative Club

My mum wasn't particularly political, but my dad was a Tory.

His best mate George Hesketh was a local councillor and we often posted flyers for him at local elections.

For the record, I'm apolitical.

They're all the same to me. We live in a capitalist society and they're all out to make money and a name for themselves. Don't trust them, they will steal your shorts as they kiss your baby.

I detest politicians.

They are the opposite of artists. The anathema.

I have never voted for anyone in my life - nor will I. George Hesketh seemed alright though.

Anyway...

My dad's right into the local Tory party and my mum works behind the bar at the Fairfield Conservative Club.

Our club.

My dad got his sister Kay's daughter Susan and her husband Eddie the job of being the club's licensees when they fell on tough times. They are living in the vast apartment on the top floor above the club with their young children, my second cousins Amanda and Michael.

They have entertainment on there seven nights a week.

My dad asks the band that plays there every Saturday night if I can get up and do a number with them one night.

Of course they say yes.

I'm going to get up and perform 'You're Sixteen', a recent hit for Ringo Starr.

The moment arrives. I'm nervous, but not terrified.

I'm a natural show-off - even at this stage.

I get up on the small stage.

There is an organist and drummer. The drummer tells me he will click his sticks together four times. On the first beat of the bar I am to commence singing and playing my guitar.

I play a C chord.

This is the key the song is in. I find my starting note.

The clicks come.

I start playing and singing where I am supposed to.

The performance is good. I play and sing in time. I smile at the audience a lot. I tap my foot in time with the song.

The song ends.

Loud applause.

Everyone pats me on the back all night and tells me how good I was.

It's the easiest thing I've ever done in my life up to this point.

What took me so long?

CHAPTER FOUR

Liverpool
1975

I'm fourteen years old.

I'm in the town centre with my mother on a Saturday afternoon. It's summertime.

It's hot.

I want to go home. We've been trailing around the shops all day and now I'm bored.

My dad dropped us off about three hours ago in the cab. I used to love that cab.

It was a limo to me.

I can still remember the registration: SKA 583G. Dad's working for the rest of the day and so we'll be getting the bus home. I want to go home NOW.

Wait a minute - we're walking down Whitechapel and we come to the corner of Stanley Street.

I see Frank Hessey's music store next to the Kardomah Cafe and suddenly become animated. This is a place I visit from time to time to drool over guitars my parents can't afford, ever since I started playing.

"Can I just have a quick look?" – Me.

"Go on then," – Mum.

We cross the street and I look through the window and survey the delights on offer. Gibson Les Pauls, Gibson SGs, Fender Stratocasters. Fender Telecasters. A Gibson Hummingbird acoustic.

Marine Band harmonicas. An accordion (lots of folk music in the 'pool). A drum set.

Pictures of the Beatles with Jim Gretty (local legend, great guitar player, the man who will sell me my first decent amplifier a couple of years later, a Jensen AC40. Jim sold the Beatles their first gear too).

Everything's really expensive in this window apart from a Saxon Les Paul copy (£70), the model of electric guitar I currently own, which Jim sold to me about two months ago. I am currently playing it through a Woolworth's amplifier (£14), which makes it sound very similar to the sound John Lennon has on the song 'I Found Out' on his *Plastic Ono Band* album. i.e. shit - but full of character.

I've had my little fix of one day you will be mine and I'm ready to go now, but my mother has other ideas. She's looking the other way at a notice board which features all these little cards which say things like:

> *VOCALIST/DRUMMER/GUITAR PLAYER REQUIRED*
> *FOR SEMI-PRO CABARET GROUP WITH OWN P.A.*
> *AND TRANSIT VAN. FULL DATE SHEET.*
> *GOOD PROSPECTS. NO TIME WASTERS. MUST BE*
> *INTO 10CC, STEELY DAN, SUTHERLAND BROS*
> *AND QUIVER, EAGLES, SMOKIE, QUO.*
> *CALL BILLY WINTERS ON 709 3765 AFTER 6.00PM.*

Plumber by day, Don Henley by night, I'm not interested in any of these wanted ads. I don't consider myself to be of a sufficient standard to play music with others. I want to go home. "Look at this one, Ian."

And so I look.

> *LEAD GUITARIST WANTED FOR YOUNG*
> *VOCAL/INSTRUMENTAL GROUP. MUST*
> *BE BETWEEN AGES 15 TO 20. WORK WAITING.*
> *CALL ROD NEWALL ON 489 7690.*

I don't think my mother understands, I am not a lead guitarist. Jimmy Page is a lead guitarist. George Harrison is a lead guitarist. Eric Clapton is a lead guitarist. Even the bloke out of the Bay City Rollers is a fuckin' lead guitarist.

With regards to the electric guitar, I'm a strummer who can play a few licks I've copped off T.Rex records and I'm reluctant to let anyone hear them.

This is despite the fact that I've been studying classical guitar and learning to read music for a couple of years now, largely under the tutorage of the Yoda-like Mr. Pierre Bethel, but what these cats are after is a different world. They don't want some ponce sitting with his legs apart playing a classical piece (the only one he knows) written by someone who died three-hundred years ago, on a five pound nylon-strung guitar.

"I'm going to ring this man up and you should go and audition for them."

No way!...I think to myself.

Anyway she'll forget when we get home as she'll have to make my dinner, bacon and eggs tonight I believe. She forgets until the next day and calls the number as soon as she gets up. I hear her on the phone and I'm frantic.

"I am not a lead guitar player!" I cry aloud, but she motions me to be quiet as she speaks in her best telephone voice.

"Hello... I'm ringing up with regards to the advert for a guitar player in Hessey's window. My son is a brilliant guitar player (lie), he's fifteen (lie) and he's had a bit of experience (another lie). He also sings."

(What?!!).

She jangles on for another minute or so and then hangs up. The person on the other end of the line has suggested that my audition take place on this very eve if convenient, as the gang are all there and there's no time like the present. Turn up about 7.30pm.

Shit.

After Sunday dinner we drive to a Liverpool suburb called Page Moss, a place generally regarded as somewhere where the natives play tick with hatchets, but to us it is posh as people around here seem to at least have gardens and indoor toilets.

We park the family yellow Ford Cortina up and are kindly ushered inside Mr. and Mrs. Newall's semi-detached home and led into their back room where there is an array of amplifiers, a couple of guitars (a bass! - never seen one of those outside a shop window before) and, erm, a ukulele.

They make us tea and introduce us to their two sons, Peter (seventeen), David (nine), and their daughter Lynn (eight). Here's the deal. The band is called Daybreak. Peter plays rhythm guitar and sings, Lynn plays the bass and sings, too.

David is the front man (freshly squeezed out of another young Liverpool act called Our Kid, who will go on to win the national *New Faces* TV talent show and have a hit with a tune called 'You Just Might See Me Cry.').

David is also a superb ukulele player. He is fat and looks like Jimmy Osmond. Apparently the latter characteristic is a big selling point.

I wonder where the drummer is?

I concede he is still in the womb.

They ask me what kind of music I like. I think for a second. The album I've been playing a lot recently is *Bandolier* by a hard rock trio from Wales called Budgie.

I tell them this and they try not to look too disheartened.

Guitars, bass and ukulele are brought to arms, and after a few run throughs of 'You're Sixteen', 'From Me To You', 'Una Paloma Blanca', 'Beautiful Sunday', 'Jesus Christ Superstar' (honestly) and 'Breaking All The House Rules' by Budgie (just kidding), another round of teas are consumed, there is more chit chat, and me and my mum and dad are informed that they will let me know the outcome of my audition on the following Monday afternoon.

I get home from school at four-fifteen the next day, whereupon I'm informed by my parents that I have passed the audition and have been offered the job of lead guitarist in the Newalls' family cabaret outfit.

The first gig will be a showcase at Ernie Mac's Broadway social club three weeks hence.

I was in the business.

Roll over Beethoven.

…And tell Tchaikovsky the news while you're at it.

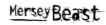

CHAPTER FIVE

Young World

You've gotta start somewhere.

Young World was my start. My first group. Originally called Daybreak, the new name (decided upon without my consent) came from a Jerry Fuller song recorded by Ricky Nelson in 1962.

Here we are then, that line-up in full now: Lynn Newall on bass, brother Peter on rhythm guitar, brother David on ukulele, Cheryl Potter (fourteen) on ukulele (two ukuleles!), me on lead guitar.

We all sang. No drummer. Cheryl was enlisted just after me, despite my profound disapproval - but I didn't have a full say, as the Newalls' dad, Rod, managed the group and ran it with an iron hand. I was the new boy after all. We played in working men's clubs in and around the north west of England. It was the mid-seventies.

We had a local agent, Dave Cullen, who attempted to get us dates every weekend.

Week nights were a bit of a no-no as we were all at school, besides the fact that midweek generally meant pub gigs which were a little rough, less money, and the clientele less likely to be impressed with our cuteness. We wore cream crimpeline waistcoats with matching flares; red shirts open to the breastbone with optional medallion, and white moccasins.

Later on we got pale blue matching suits. What can I tell you? It was the seventies. You should've seen what everyone else was wearing. Our choice of songs was fairly obvious, popular tunes of the day (the easier ones), and a selection of favourites from the fifties and sixties.

It was hard sometimes keeping time without a drummer and we relied heavily on Lynn's counter-bass parts to keep it together. Sometimes the resident drummer in a club we were playing would tap along if he was feeling particularly benevolent, which often caused unintentionally hilarious results.

Sometimes the resident organist would play along too.

Christ, what a racket that was.

We sounded like the Partridge family bus crashing into Blackpool Tower.

It was exciting. I was fifteen now. You got to perform in front of people who were not always particularly attentive, learn the dynamics of your instrument and voice, and get to understand how a crowd works. I did this for years before I even attempted to go professional.

Many artists these days are signed to a major recording contract before they've played half a dozen gigs.

Their debut record comes out, the company spends a fortune on marketing them, they have a hit if they're lucky, they're then placed halfway up the bill at a festival, and then everybody wonders why they can't deliver the goods live. They simply don't know how. It's one thing to write a catchy tune, throw out snazzy sound bites in interviews and look cool in a video, but His Majesty The Punter needs a lot more than that when he's been standing in a field for three days caked in mud waiting to hear you put your worth across. It takes years to become a good stage performer.

If you rehearse a lot you become good at rehearsing. There was no thought at this stage of our career of making a record, the most you could aspire to was to get a week's residency at the Wooky Hollow club on Breck Road on the outskirts of town (Tom O'Connor, legendary comedian - who had actually been on the telly – played there! Regularly!). The She club on Victoria Street was another hallowed engagement.

The Shakespeare club with local D.J./M.C. Pete Price hosting was seen as the cream of the crop. The best chance you had of stardom was to audition for *New Faces* on ITV, famous for the Simon-Cowell-of-his-day hatchet man, Tony Hatch (really!), who famously co-wrote 'Downtown' with his missus for Petula Clark, but later went on to hit true pay dirt with the theme music to endless Aussie soap *Neighbours*.

He also wrote the theme music to *Crossroads*. A teatime drama about a fictitious B-road hotel in Birmingham, famed for its wobbly sets and poor acting.

Young World never got an audition for *New Faces*, but we managed to get one for *Opportunity Knocks* - hosted by Canadian star-spotter Hughie Green.

We offered 'Octopus's Garden', 'Tequila Sunrise' and 'I Should've Known Better'.

I'm still waiting to hear if we got through.

We would travel in two cars to gigs. Rod Newall's Ford Fiesta Estate packed to the max with the bulk of the gear, Cheryl, David and Peter in the back, Rod driving, me in the front as I had the longest legs, usually with Lynn sitting on my knee. Highly illegal on both counts (Lynn and I developed something of a crush on each other). Mum and Dad following up the rear in the family jalopy stuffed with the rest of the kit. There were lots of arguments, usually amongst the parents. Cheryl's mother, Maureen, was a particularly vociferous pushy showbiz mum. "Smile! Smile! Project!" There would be other grumblings. "David's hogging it!"

"Lynn shouldn't be singing lyrics like that, she's only nine!" ("...and I've had so many men before...in oh so many ways..."). It was an experience. It was around this time I started trying to write my first song. After much trial and error I came up with a fairly decent effort called 'Apologise (I Will)'.

Everyone seemed to like it (apart from Rod Newall who regarded it as some kind of threat - I might gain more status than his offspring if I was to flower in this creative area). We would shoehorn it into the second spot of our show, the 'dance' spot as it was known (in the cabaret world you don't perform 'sets,' you do 'spots'), and usually it went over pretty good, generally placed somewhere between 'Una Paloma Blanca' or 'Ten guitars'.

After about six months of being in this band I started getting itchy feet - I hated Cheryl - with her fuckin' wringlets and permagrin, strumming that bastard ukulele (I would later have a brief affair with her after she straightened her hair and dyed it blonde), and I threatened to walk unless we became a proper band and got a drummer.

Rod grudgingly put the word out that we were looking for one - I was after all clearly the most talented member of the band and he didn't want to lose me. In time we got word that there was a fine young drummer from 'over the water' (a scouse expression meaning across the River Mersey, on the Wirral peninsular) looking for a gig, so Rod went over to Bebington (posh!) to audition a young lad by the name of Chris Sharrock who was just nine at the time.

Apparently this kid was a prodigy - and he was in before I even got to hear him play. His mum and dad, Glenys and Richard, owned the local family butcher's just down the road from where they lived on Stanton Road.

He had an older brother, Phil. They all loved music more than anything. They were lovely.

They were brilliant.

We didn't have a rehearsal but he heard a tape of our show and learnt it perfectly. The first time I met him was at Netherton and Sefton British Legion when the band and he played a spot together. At one stage he knocked a cymbal off its stand and his dad ran on and stuck a screwdriver through the top of the cymbal into its mount to hold it in place.

Chris was terrific and I fell in love with him instantly.

Everyone did.

My schoolwork was beginning to suffer around this time. I was now at Campion (formerly S.F.X), on Shaw Street, just north of the city centre. A bilateral school of learning (they took brains and brawn); A Catholic Education.

We were right across the road from the Collegiate which was full of Protestants. We tried to murder each other at every opportunity.

Hatred of other religions was programmed into us from an early age (when I was seven years old, a Catholic priest shoved a tasteless piece of circular thin white bread into my mouth and told me it was the body of Jesus Christ - who'd lived and died for my sins.

What the fuck had I done?

I was only seven. I was always suspicious that they got wined-up while we got the bread. Praise the Lord). We were told that Catholicism was the true path and everyone else had it wrong.

I was always very tired on Monday mornings due to the average three shows per weekend we were doing, and I didn't really get any livelier in the week. I was earning decent money for a lad of my age and got fed up of teachers telling me that if I didn't get my shit together and get some results I would end up on the dole. I was more frightened of ending up a fuckin' teacher.

Some of the teachers crept me out. There was one guy who used to give some boys a lift home every night and even took them camping some weekends.

You could smoke in his car.

Nice.

He offered me a lift home one night and I told him to go fuck himself. For this he duly caned me.

I started becoming a bit belligerent and getting into trouble. There'd been a short piece on the band in the Liverpool Echo and I was having my first taste of notoriety.

Teachers and students started treating me a little differently. I'd always kept to myself beforehand as I tended to get picked on a lot due to my alleged posh speaking voice (Dad drove a cab but spoke like a Spitfire pilot, and always pulled me up if I spoke quickly or with a scouse slur), the fact that I was taller than most, and was a chubby lad until I was about sixteen ("McFlab! Come 'ere!").

It also used to wind fellow students up that I would be dropped off at school in a black cab on a regular basis. The fact that my dad was driving it did not deter some of the jumped up little twats who would administer a brief beating every time this happened. I was getting a little cocky and began showing signs of early rock star behaviour.

One time I grabbed hold of the Geography teacher's arse as I brushed passed her and copped a feel for a laugh (she was gorgeous - short blonde hair and tiny little tits with nipples like football studs that poked through her sweater on cold mornings), and nearly got caned to death by the deputy headmaster.

This, of course, ingratiated me to my classmates and I grew in stature in time and subsequently a few of the hard cases started hanging out with me (if you can't fight the bad guys make 'em laugh).

Gradually I was no longer a target. I joined the school string quartet on cello - which I learned to play fairly poorly fairly quickly. Whenever we would do a short recital in front of an audience, I would always deliberately play certain notes hilariously off-key at opportune moments in order to elicit uncontrollable laughter from my fellow players to which end the piece would rapidly descend in to farce.

It got you through.

I was outgrowing Young World and wanted to get into something a bit more substantial and less cheesy. It had been a great education but I'd had enough. I didn't want to be in a band with any fuckin' birds in it for a kick off.

My O levels were coming up and I wasn't too confident I was going to get through them. Time to get into a higher gear. I realised the music wasn't going to be a passing fad as predicted by my teachers.

I started looking around.

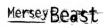

CHAPTER SIX

City lights

Autumn 1976.

I found an advert in the Liverpool Echo for somebody looking for a guitar player/singer.

A band who had been working the club circuit for a while had just lost their singer and guitar player, and were looking to replace two people with one. I called them up and arranged to meet up at a house in Alexandra Drive in Litherland, North Liverpool.

When I got there I met Jimmy Sangster (seventeen) bass/vocals, Jimmy Hughes (sixteen) guitar/vocals, and Mark Cowley (sixteen) drums.

The house we were in was the Sangster family residence where Jimmy lived with his mum and dad - Mary and Lenny - his brother Paul (twelve), and his sister Lyn (fourteen). Also living at the house - curiously - in my opinion, was the manager of the band, Norman Lane. Norman was in his early forties and hailed from Derby.

Everyone was incredibly friendly and we hit it off right away. We played some Beatle tunes, Everly Brothers, some rock 'n' roll, the usual stuff. Everyone could sing really well, Jimmy S had a Hofner Violin bass - the first one I'd seen in real life.

What I was excited about was being in a four-piece band with guys my own age. I wanted to escape the vaudeville of

Young World. They said they'd be in touch and the next day I got the word that I was in. I called up the Newalls to tell them the bad news, and then called the Sharrocks and told Chris personally.

This was the only part I felt bad about - but he was fine about it. They eventually replaced me with Chris's brother, Phil.

I started going to proper gigs at the Empire Theatre in Liverpool around here. I'd only seen bands play in clubs and pubs before and the difference of seeing something in a concert hall freaked me out.

It was so loud and the lights looked amazing.

I saw Barclay James Harvest, AC/DC, Dr. Feelgood, Budgie, Be Bop Deluxe, Squeeze, Steve Gibbons Band, all in rapid succession. It was fuckin' brilliant and gig tickets were seventy-five pence.

We started rehearsing a couple of nights a week at the local church hall, and then I was told that Mark Cowley wouldn't be in the band any longer as he'd had a few personal problems.

We later heard that he was backing an Elvis impersonator called Billy 'Elvis' Helm. Jimmy S quickly remedied the problem by asking a mate of his, Howie Minns (nineteen), who lived just around the corner, to sit in on drums with us until such time we found a permanent replacement for Mark. Howie was fantastic.

A Keith Moon devotee - he had the biggest drum kit I'd ever seen in my short life. He also had a bizarre fascination with bowel movement and would weigh his stools everytime he had an evacuation. He kept a 'log' of such things and informed me that Tuesdays produced the weightiest turds. This information was greatly appreciated.

He hung by a thread to sanity. He lived to play drums and was at the time in a proper rock band called Flight. Flight had supported the likes of Nutz on the university circuit and were all grown up and didn't do social clubs. They wore what they wanted on stage and played their own material in places like the

Moonstone pub in St. John's Precinct in town.

They'd done gigs in the city centre. This was heady stuff.

Howie made sure we knew that he would do a few gigs with us on a temporary basis, but we would have to find somebody else soon - as he was headed for bigger stuff apparently. He was doing us a favour and we should be grateful.

We were!

Howie lived with his mum Lil and his sister Hilary who we all fancied like mad, as she undoubtedly had the best arse this side of Bootle which she thoughtfully presented in extremely tight jeans. She also had a lovely, petite face and a Chrissie Hynde hairdo.

I still had no great aspirations to be in a band that wrote and played its own material at this time - I didn't really know anyone who did it, and besides that, whenever any scouse band ventured outside the city boundaries trying to get someone's attention in London for instance, they usually failed - and everybody just went on about the Beatles all the time.

"No band from Liverpool will ever make it again, Merseybeat's gone!"

It was the era of the supergroup. Gatefold sleeves, concept albums, side-long tracks, lightshows and stadia.

Howie's band Flight were playing their own material but didn't seem to be getting anywhere just yet - Liverpool Express had had a couple of hits recently (fronted by Billy Kinsley, ex-Merseybeats - they specialised in McCartney-esque pop tunes and ballads), and that was it.

We started getting regular work and having a great time. I started seeing Hilary and one night while her mum was in bed and Howie was over at his girlfriend Pauline's house, she relieved me of my burdening virginity.

I couldn't believe how great it felt.

Having my engorged member emasculated within the hot sticky walls of a young, firm, wet vagina was something I was never going to forget (or if I was lucky, or became rich, or famous, or all of the above, would ever have to).

The experience was other-worldly and I decided I would pursue this activity with great enthusiasm from that day forward.

Norman - the manager - was an oddity.

The fact that he shared a room with Jimmy in Jimmy's house seemed strange, but I never though about it too much.

I was naive.

The way I understood it, Norman was down on his luck and was lodging at the Sangster abode until things perked up a bit. Jimmy told me that Norman had snuck into bed with him one night while he was asleep. Jimmy woke up, flattened him, and went back to sleep.

No big deal.

Norman got us a lot of work and was very professional in the eyes of the outside world, but would cause us many problems.

He was a seasoned attention-seeker amongst embryonic attention-seekers. On a number of occasions he pulled his favourite party trick. We would be driving back from a gig in Warrington or somewhere and Norman would start an argument with Jimmy.

We'd all be in the back of a Ford Transit, sitting on the amps. We would tell him to shut up and we'd then carry on drinking beer. Norman would then open the door and throw himself out on the motorway - on to the hard shoulder - at seventy miles per hour plus.

He did this several times and never perished. Amazing really. More than once we'd returned to Liverpool, started unloading the gear, when Norman would rush out of the house and greet everyone with a smile. He would pick himself up off the motorway, get to a telephone somehow, ring himself a cab - and get home before us. Sometimes he was bloodied and went to A&E before he came home. Jimmy would attack Norman occasionally for various reasons, usually because Norman knew how to press Jimmy's buttons.

After one particularly savage attack, Norman handed over an envelope to Howie containing the night's fee. He'd taken each note out individually and rubbed it against a cut. The money was covered in blood. Blood money.

Eventually everyone had had enough and Norman was told he was no longer our manager and ejected from the house.

We employed a driver called Jazza. A small, toothless, bald fifty-something who wore thick glasses and drove a three-ton truck which all the gear all fitted into the corner of. He was as bent as they come despite the fact that he had a wife and family.

He would regale us with stories of his 'chickens' (game young lads who will fuck for cash) and how he loved to bathe them and perform unspeakable acts. We all thought this was hilarious.

What the hell - they were all of legal age and consenting. It's a sad and beautiful world. Howie would encourage him to go into great detail regarding his exploits and cackle with every lurid detail. I learnt more about the ways of man in these formative years than I did travelling around the world in a successful pop group many years later. Jazza never tried it on with any of us, and was to all intents and purposes a lovely fella who never hurt anyone knowingly. It was all a bit fuckin' weird though to say the least.

I was still only seventeen.

One time we came home from a gig and were unloading Jimmy Hughes' gear at his mum's house in Lewisham Road in Norris Green. Jimmy S was bursting for a pee and walked over the road to a hedge opposite. We finished unloading and we couldn't find Jimmy anywhere.

We searched the length and breadth of the road for about half an hour and gave up.

The next day we found out that a Black Maria had screamed

up the street after arresting a load of scallies who had been scrapping about a hundred yards away - the coppers saw Jimmy in the street taking a leak - and assumed he was part of the gang.

They threw him in the clink with the other miscreants for the night. The next morning, realising he wasn't with the gang, they didn't know what to do with him - so they charged him with indecent exposure - showing his dick to a hedge on a darkened street at two o'clock in the morning.

Bad luck plagued Jimmy Sangster.

One night, some guy who he'd been drinking with asked him if he needed a lift home. Jimmy only lived around the corner but the guy insisted.

Jimmy was so pissed he didn't notice that the guy was actually breaking into the car outside the pub - he hot-wired it and they sped off. Jimmy and his new pal ended up in a high-speed car chase across Liverpool.

A few other random things that befell luckless Jimmy in later life:

He was sitting in his basement flat on Canning Street eating his breakfast in the kitchen one evening when a car crashed through the window and landed on his table, nearly killing Jimmy. The driver crawled from the wreckage and asked Jimmy if he had a phone he could use.

He had the most hideous dog I've ever seen in my life. It was the size of a small donkey, covered with thick matted fur, and stank to high heaven. One night somebody broke into his flat and stole it.

One night I was giving Jimmy a lift to a party in my Opel Manta GTE. I pulled up and parked with the kerb to the driver's side. Jimmy opens the passenger door just as some scallies in a stolen car being chased by the police scream around the corner and take the door off its hinges at eighty m.p.h. The door flew about twenty feet down the road with Jimmy still attached to it.

* He walked out of his flat one night and somebody, a complete stranger, just walked up to him and punched him flat out in the face. Reason? Unknown.

At one stage Jimmy thought of suing the council for bad luck.

The bane of our lives was bingo. Bingo was more important in any social club than any musical entertainment, even as luminous as ours.

One particular concert secretary at Rainhill Ex-Servicemen's Club got on the wrong side of Howie one night, so he decided to remove the spring that caught the bingo balls as they shot up the tube. When everyone had their eyes down for a line - any line - the geezer turned his machine on, only for all the balls to fly out into the audience, landing in pints everywhere. We were all in the dressing room gasping for air.

One time we were doing a gig in Leeds when the concert secretary rang a bell in the middle of our first spot - I was lost in a rousing performance of 'Nights In White Satin' (my big number) when the power was turned off. "Sorry lads - emergency!" Came a distorted, thick-Yorkshire-accented voice over the club's ancient P.A. system.

We took our guitars off quickly and got ready to leg it with as much of our kit as we could carry - we thought there was a fire. "Ladies and gentleman... Harry, you all know Harry who is meant to be delivering the pies toneet, has broken down on the Snake Pass and we need somebody to go and get him or there'll be nay pies nor peas toneet!"

This kind of thing happened all the time.

We auditioned for *New Faces* (Yay! At last!). We drove all the way to Birmingham for the audition. The guy in charge was called Albert Stephenson, a cantankerous, nasty, old fat bastard in a suit with white hair and glasses.

We played our ace first - a modern, beaty arrangement of 'Strangers In The Night' which we were particularly enamoured with.

"Well, now that you've got that out of the way what else d' you do?" Thus Spake Albert.

When we were dismissed we went into his dressing room (which was next to ours) and pissed in his shower in concert.

I'd left school at this point (English Literature C.S.E. - Grade 1, English Language O Level - A. And fuck all else - I never went to pick the certificates up) and Jimmy Hughes and I had decided to attend Mabel Fletcher Music College in order to avoid getting jobs.

Mabel's was OK, but I'd studied classical guitar and theory privately for years anyway, so I already knew what they thought they were teaching me. I played dumb so they wouldn't suss me out and I'd be left in peace to claim my grant. One time I stayed away for two months and turned up for an exam. I got one hundred per cent.

My tutor Earl Howarth called me to his desk, congratulated me on my result and told me not to bother turning up for class again.

"I wouldn't like to be eighteen again," he intoned.

Jimmy and I would loaf about and play pool in the pub opposite the college most afternoons.

Our prospects seemed to be diminishing by the day.

My dad started complaining that he was having trouble going to the bathroom. He was constipated all the time and he was starting to get fed up with it. He made a joke about it and me and Mum told him told him to get some roughage inside him. We stocked up on bran flakes and hoped nature would do its thing.

One night I was watching Granada TV - our local station, when a weird band came on.

They were from Liverpool and they were called Echo And The Bunnymen. They looked as odd as their name. The lead singer had the strangest hair I'd ever seen. It looked like a busby crossed with Ronnie Spector's beehive. He was tall and skinny and you couldn't see his eyes for his fringe. He sang in a baritone, Bowie-esque style. The guitar player looked at his fingers and not much else. He wasn't technically a great player, but the notes he played conjured up mystery. The bass player looked like James Dean. They didn't have a drummer, they used a drum machine, and they called it Echo.

I couldn't decide whether or not they were brilliant or rubbish, but they were on my mind. Something was happening.

City Lights was becoming a drag. We'd started writing songs but we weren't getting anywhere with them.

We were earning good money playing other people's songs. We'd had a little interest and had even met with a couple of small labels in London, but nothing was happening.

The most worrying development recently was that we'd begun doing a bit of comedy - and it was going over well. We'd finish our first spot with the Shadows' 'Apache' – doing the whole step routine with our white kipper ties tied around our heads. It was very funny.

Howie would do a thunderous drum solo in the middle (by this time he had a huge double bass drum kit with a gong behind him - a kit worthy of Wembley Stadium which he would dutifully set up night after night in British Legions across the North West).

It brought the house down usually but none of us got into the business to elicit laughs from our audience.

Our agent encouraged us to start bringing more of it into the show, promising better money. We were on course to become the new Grumbleweeds. Howie could be the new Russ Abbott

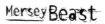

if he played his cards right (Howie never returned to his 'proper' band - instead he'd got a new girlfriend and started working at the Giro in Bootle).

Chris Sharrock had left Young World and had joined a group that eschewed the cabaret circuit. Featuring a fine guitarist/writer by the name of John Byrne and singer/bassist Keith Gunson, they called themselves the Cherry Boys.

They played original material only, and had recently recorded a demo tape at Open Eye studios in town, produced by a guy called Noddy Knowler. I went to see them play at Lincoln's Inn, a hip new venue just off Mathew Street, and was transfixed. I was in a cabaret band still - making OK money but headed nowhere (except maybe the Talk Of The North - we did actually eventually get a residency at the She club), and these guys had prospects. Since being exposed to the Bunnymen, I started hearing about local bands with names like the Teardrop Explodes, Orchestral Manoeuvres In The Dark, and Dalek I.

I was in danger of being left out. I would be twenty soon and I had to get a move on.

I'd been treading the boards for nearly five years, playing the same songs in the same places. I was stuck in a rut. I had to stop doing this cabaret shit, and form a band that played new, exciting original music.

Dad's problem wasn't going away. He'd been to the doctor who had then referred him to a specialist. He had a swollen stomach and they wanted him to have exploratory surgery to find out what was going on.

It was February 1980.

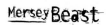

CHAPTER SEVEN

A Beginning
& an Ending

I had a vision.

I was well and truly immersed in the music of the time.

I was listening to debut albums by Joy Division, the Cure, Echo And The Bunnymen and the Teardrop Explodes.

John Peel was guiding me and an entire generation through this exciting new musical wonderland. Anything new was worth a listen. Anything old was gone. It was the new age.

It was after all a new decade. I told the lads in City Lights I was quitting the band – everyone knew the fun times were behind us. We got together at my house and had a last meeting where everybody agreed it was probably the right time to stop.

Jimmy Sangster was mournful but saw the sense. Jimmy Hughes didn't really say anything - as usual. We had a little party in our usual fashion. We got in Jazza's truck and had one last trip to Knutsford services to eat bacon and eggs in the middle of the night, play the machines and cram ourselves into the photo booth to make stupid faces one more time.

We were so innocent it was almost cute.

Howie was the most pained at my decision as he was still immersed in the classics and thought I was mad getting into this new rubbish. He was only a couple of years older than me but sometimes it felt like ten.

My relationship with his sister had also naturally put a strain

on our working together.

Hilary and I had a very fiery time together. There was a lot of fighting and she ruled the roost. She was older than me and I was scared of her. She beat me up on a number of occasions and once bit so hard into my hand that I couldn't feel my thumb for eight months.

Chris Sharrock was still playing in the Cherry Boys but they were hitting a wall.

Also, good and fresh as they were, they were definitely retro. Aping the Jam on many levels, who were aping sixties bands themselves. Chris and I loved the new music - we'd been to the Futurama festival in Leeds and watched a grand parade of fabulous new artists. The statues were being kicked over.

Our favourites of the new crop were Soft Cell and the Bunnymen. We also loved early Human League.

I asked Chris if he'd like to be in my new band and he replied in the affirmative.

The Cherry Boys still needed him so we'd keep it quiet for a bit - I needed to write the appropriate songs after all, and we still had to find at least one other member. I had some basic recording equipment at home and every day I would try to come up with something interesting.

It was difficult - I was very learned in the ways of yore and I had to rip it up and start again. I'd been playing and singing in so many styles over the past five years it was hard for me to find my own sound.

Most of the artists we were into could hardly play their instruments, but they had their own identity.

I'd been learning how to play other people's material almost every day of my musical life. I could impersonate many guitar players but didn't have my own style. Vocally it was a lot easier - I certainly didn't sound like anyone else in that department.

I was coming up with all kinds of experimental stuff that was pretty shit, but it gave me a starting point. At least it didn't sound like 10cc, ELO, the Eagles or Wings - which is what my efforts in City Lights reminded people of. Song titles - 'All In The Gleam Of A Scientist's Eye', 'Are We Dreamers', 'A Cure for Something'. None made the final cut but were grand experiments.

Dad had been in hospital. He'd had his operation and we had to go in and see the surgeon to see what was going on. He took us into his office and we sat down, naturally nervous.

We just didn't expect it. No-one does. We were told that my dad had been having trouble because he had bowel cancer.

The cancer was very advanced and had also spread to his liver, lungs and kidneys. My mum looked at me like she'd already known. I felt like a huge, black weight had just been placed on my soul. I couldn't move. I couldn't think. I couldn't breathe. I tried to ask a question.

"What can you do about it?"

The guy was very quick and forthright. No emotion.

"It's far too advanced for us to do anything now, we can make him comfortable."

"How long?" Mum asked.

"About six months."

"Does he know?"

"No, no. That's up to you."

We decided not to tell him. I'll always regret it. We found out years later off his old friend, George Hesketh, that he knew anyway. What a fuckin' great man my father was.

He didn't bring the subject of his own death up once in his remaining time - because he didn't want anyone to be upset. I aspire to be as strong as that.

If we'd have spoken about it, maybe more could have been said about certain things. Did we make the most of our remaining time anyway?

You bet. I loved my dad. He was brilliant. He told me to stand up straight and push my chest out.

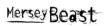

"Walk tall son... walk tall."

So the main breadwinner of the family is dying and can't work anymore. This is when I decide to give up a reasonable wage playing the clubs and enter into a game where you usually didn't make any money at all - unless you are incredibly lucky. The timing couldn't have been worse. This catastrophic news achieved one positive thing - I threw myself into the task of writing great songs like someone who was goin' to the chair.

I had to find another musician who would join Chris and I on our journey, so I put an ad in the local paper.

I think only one guy came forward, his name was Chris Layhe. An academic who was studying a variety of lofty subjects at Mott College in Prescot, Liverpool.

I can't say I ever liked Chris L much - I don't think he ever liked me either. You couldn't have two more different guys. But we had the same vision - we were hungry for success on our own terms, and I was aware that a good collaborator was what I needed - and not a new mate.

He looked kind of odd - six feet and three inches, skinny as a rake, with an owlish face (photos were always a problem - I was six feet tall but looked small next to Chris L - while diddy Chris S barely got his head into the shot).

Anyway, the three of us met at my house, went for fish and chips and decided we were a band. We worked hard at rehearsals and the songs slowly started to come together.

My dad was great when he came home from hospital. The major upset for him was that he'd be using a Colostomy bag from now on - not as horrific as it sounds I promise.

Life carried on as before - the only difference now being that Dad didn't go to work. We kept up the facade that he was going to get better all the way, and it was fine.

It was strange to think that he wasn't going to be here much longer, but you always think a miracle might come along and this case will be the one that shocks them all.

I cried all night the time they told me my daddy was going to die soon - and then I never cried about it again - until his funeral, and even then I had to force it a bit. I was numb. I didn't think it looked right not shedding a tear at the crematorium and everyone was waiting for it so I obliged.

One evening Dad was fed up and frustrated about being housebound. He wanted to go out for a walk. We walked around the streets at a sturdy pace alone in the dark and chatted. All of a sudden he started throwing up so violently it shocked me to my core. I barely got him home again without carrying him. He was so thin. It's so hard to watch someone you love disintegrating before your eyes. I wouldn't wish it on anyone.

I met a cool guy who was part of the social circle my mum was weaving in and out of at the time. She was working every night in the Balmoral club (formerly the Conservative Club, it had now been taken over by a new owner) in order to keep us alive.

Tony Barwood was a part-time mobile DJ. He worked as a sales rep for Whitford Plastics out of Runcorn. He was divorced, had two kids and lived with his girlfriend Alison on Staplands Road, Broadgreen, just by the hospital. He had a van and offered to drive us to rehearsals every Sunday for a few quid. It wasn't about the money - it was about the craic. He was into what we were doing and watched us intently every week.

After a while he asked if he could help out in a management capacity - if no-one else was doing it of course. No-one had any objections and we needed all he help we could get - Tony seemed genuinely into the music - so we gave him a chance. He would be the best manager I ever had. Tony suggested we do some cabaret work (groan) to generate some cash to float the band through its birth pangs.

None of us were eager to do this, but we had no choice. We needed a small PA system to do it, which we couldn't afford. My mum pleaded with her dad to lend us the four hundred and fifty quid to buy one. He did - God bless his soul.

After knocking band names around for quite a long while, it was me that eventually came up with something that everybody liked. I was an avid science-fiction fan and had just finished reading a short story by Frederik Pohl written in 1959 called *The Day The Icicle Works Closed*.

The Icicle Works as a band name fitted with the time, and could be interpreted as a noun followed by an adjective - as in the Teardrop Explodes.

Anyway, it stuck and no-one objected.

Dad took a really bad turn after a few months and was re-admitted to hospital. He recovered for about a week and it was marvellous. We spent all of this time together at home and it was all really upbeat. Then he faltered again and the ambulance took him away. One night my mum came home and told me he was gone. "Good," I said. He hadn't suffered too much.

The doctor's estimate of how long he had was right on the money. It was a few days after my twentieth birthday and I decided I'd had his best years. He was sixty-seven years old when he died (an ancient age to a twenty year old, but not old at all to me now of course). He was a great man. I've never been to visit his resting place - I don't need to - he's not there - he's here.

In me.

Thanks Dad.

I don't know if we'll ever be together again somewhere, it'd be fucking great if we were though. I've got about a hundred million things to ask you. I've made a list. I'm sure you've got a few things to ask me - if you've been watching...

I wonder what he'd think of how I've lived my life?

'My dad died when I was twenty, I didn't cry but it tore me up inside,

I got a band and wrote some music, it wasn't bad and we went on a long ride...'

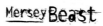

CHAPTER EIGHT

Brookside
Ricky Tomlinson
& The Russian Ballet

It's 1981.

The band is rehearsing every Sunday afternoon from eleven-thirty am to four pm at the Ministry Rehearsal Rooms in central Liverpool. We are subsidising ourselves by playing Saturday cabaret shows as, ahem...Current Affairs - much to the chagrin of Chris Layhe who considers this type of work to be below him.

We're not allowed to play on Fridays or indeed any other night of the working week as he wants to spend them with his girlfriend. Money is therefore scarce. In order to combat this problem I decide I will attempt to get some 'extra' work.

Extras are those people who you see in movies, on TV and in the theatre, who are in shot but don't speak. I've had an actor's union card at this time for a few years now due to the amount of theatres I've played in as a musician on the pies and peas circuit. This qualifies you to be an actor somehow.

The extras you see (but never look at) are generally comedians, singers, musicians etc. who have all come by these Equity memberships in the same way as me.

At the time you got paid around seventy pounds a day to wait around, drink tea, eat bacon and egg sandwiches, and at some point be called into shot. It was boring as hell but it was money. Somebody gave me the number of an agent who could get me

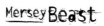

some work. I went to meet him in a tiny office off London Road, have a chat and give him some mugshots.

His name was Ricky Tomlinson. Ricky would go on in later years to become a much loved actor. He would play a long-running character by the name of Bobby Grant in Channel Four's *Brookside*, star in *The Royle Family* as nose-picking couch-potato Jim Royle, and even co-star with Samuel L. muthafuckin' Jackson in the Liverpool-filmed feature *51st State*.

But this was back in the day when Ricky was just starting off.

He said he was always looking for new blood and promised to get me plenty of work. He was true to his word. I can be seen lurking in and around the scenery in *Boys From The Black Stuff*, I got to throw a cabbage at Jeremy Irons in a mob scene in *Brideshead Revisited* as well as walk past the camera in many other television programmes for Granada and Yorkshire TV that have now vanished from our collective memory.

Ricky liked me. He decided to send me for a speaking role audition for Channel Four's newly commissioned soap. The soap was to be called *Brookside*.

I wasn't that keen as I was only interested in earning a bit of cash to keep myself and the band going, and had no aspirations to become an actor. However, Ricky was persuasive and assured me it wouldn't do any harm just to audition.

I went and read for the part of Barry Grant (Ricky would get the role of Barry's father sometime later).

Also at the audition was a mate of mine, Paul Usher, who I'd known for years, as his parents had a cabaret duo that played all the same joints as Young World.

As part of the audition, Phil Redmond - the show's creator - gave myself, Paul and a couple of other hopefuls an improvisational situation where we had to interact.

Everyone spoke in really thick Liverpudlian accents which I thought was horrible, so I tried to communicate with the speaking voice my dad always encouraged - non-dialectic King's

English. I thought I'd land the role easily, as everyone else had bad grammar. I found out sometime later that Paul had won the role. When I eventually saw the first episode of *Brookside* I understood why I didn't win the part.

Everybody spoke with thick Liverpool accents. Phil Redmond obviously thought me too much of a toff.

Paul made the role his and enjoyed many years of success in the show, the irony being that what he really wanted was to be a successful musician.

A couple of weeks later Ricky called me up and asked if I fancied a week's work at a theatrical production at the Liverpool Empire.

"The money's great lad...there's a bloody gang of us doing it."

"Sounds good." I retort. "What is it?"

"It's the Russian Ballet Company's production of *Romeo And Juliet.*"

"Eh? You're jokin' aren't you?"

"It'll be sound lad...get yer arse down to rehearsals at the Empire. Ten am on Wednesday!"

I was extremely sceptical about this one.

Ballet? Jesus.

He was right about the money though, fifty quid a day plus meals for rehearsals, one hundred quid per show. The first morning I realised it was easy money with a large embarrassment factor. All we extras had to do in the production was stand around the stage in ridiculous costumes at various points during the performance and try not to get in the way of the dancers.

I got to get incredibly close to some gorgeous petite Ruskie ballerinas, but alas, dragging them off to the pub post-gig for a few lagers was a non-starter as none of them spoke a word of English, comrade.

To be backstage with this motley crew of social club entertainers chatting away about their various experiences on the pies and peas circuit was an experience I must say.

We were kitted out in the fashion of the R&J era - tights, cod-piece, waistcoats and silly hats. We were pissing ourselves laughing constantly. The sight of Ricky Tomlinson in this get-up is something I still think about to this day.

I looked at myself in the mirror and nearly went into convulsions. I had a problem with the footwear. Robin Hood style pointy boots. None of them would fit me. They were all too small. The wardrobe department were very concerned. I told them not to worry, I had the perfect solution.

The opening night on the Monday was a full house and a very serious concern to be sure.

The first time we were required was in a market scene. My job was to walk across the stage carrying a bag, presumably full of fruit and veg (it was actually full of rolled up newspapers).

I was sat side-stage with Ricky, smoking a fag and listening to him prattle on about the workers when I received my cue. I duly threw my bag of swag over my shoulder, extinguished my Marlboro, and got into character. There were about ten dancers doing their thing at the front of the stage as I made my entrance.

And so it was that the hi-brow ballet-going aristocrats of the Merseyside area's attention was momentarily diverted from the beautiful poetic display of lithe, tender nymphs and nymphets gliding gracefully across the Empire's vast stage, as they pointed their gaze at a six-foot scouser stomping across the ersatz market square looking slightly embarrassed, wearing high-heeled Beatle boots with pink tights and lime green cod-piece.

My ballet career has been on hold since that night.

DAYBREAK
CABARET, RADIO & T.V.

051 - 489 -

Manager:
R. NEWA
9 PAGE M
LIVERPO

AND IN THE BEGINNING,
THERE WAS
DAYBREAK.
IAN, PETER, LYNN
& DAVID.

THE FIRST GIG.

Jan

Cheryl

Peter

Lynn

David

SOLE AGENT:
MARY WILLS
(051) 526-0202
526-9090

YOUNG WORLD
CABARET
RADIO & T.V.

MANAGER:
R. NEWALL
(051) ___ ____

Right: One of my
doodles for my first
Scrapbook.

Extracts from
the
YOUNG WORLD
Phenomenon.

CITY LIGHTS (4 Piece Group)
Cabaret - Radio - Television
051-263

Above: Clockwise
Jimmy S, Jimmy H,
Howie Minns and me.

ON THE 22ND OF NOVEMBER 1975, ROBERT IAN McNABB PLAYED HIS FIRST CONCERT WITH YOUNG WORLD (THEN KNOWN AS DAYBREAK).
ON THE 22ND OF JANUARY 1977, HE PLAYED HIS LAST.
HE WAS REPLACED BY PHILLIP SHARROCKS, BROTHER OF CHRISTOPHER SHARROCKS, YW'ᵣ DRUMMER.

Above: Photo session for Liverpool Echo.

Left: First Holy Communion.

Above: Ian as
Batman in front of
Dad's taxi in
Morden Street
approx 1965.

Left: Sleeve to
eponymous album
2001.

Left: Ian with teddy and racing car.

Below: Video shoot to 'You Must Be Prepared To Dream' Mojave desert 1994.

Above: Bob McNabb with my first Fender Stratocaster.

Left: The cellar. Be afraid, be very afraid.

Left: Destined for the stage from a young age... an early modelling job.

ALL SHOTS FROM THE FIRST GIG.

CHAPTER NINE

Birds Fly
(Whisper to a scream)

We did our first gig at Brady's.

We were co-headlining the former Eric's venue with fellow local hopefuls Cook Da Books, on Mathew Street in April 1981.

We had about eight or nine songs including 'Are We Dreamers', 'A Cure For Something', 'When Winter Lasted Forever' and set closer - Dobie Gray's 'The In Crowd', recently re-vamped by Bryan Ferry. We had only one song at this time which would survive until the first album, 'As The Dragonfly Flies'. We were terribly nervous.

We went down reasonably well with the sparse, curious crowd and - very slowly - began to grow in confidence.

We played at the Masonic on Berry Street. We opened for John Cooper Clarke and Alberto's Y Los Paranoias at Liverpool University, thanks to the patronage of the social secretary there, Chris Turrill, who would later become our road manager.

We played at Brady's again in the summer where local promoter Dave C saw fit to put us on a bill with the Cherry Boys, the band that Chris Sharrock had just left. In a development typical of the Liverpool scene, Howie Minns from City Lights was now the drummer with the 'Cherries'. This of course caused much tension backstage.

There was a lot of bad blood between us as I had nicked Chris Sharrock from them, and the Cherries sought to throw us off

our guard and ruin our night by stealing my precious Korg synthesizer when we went for something to eat after soundcheck.

They protested their innocence but I knew they'd done it.

It was my word against theirs so I was fucked. We went next door where Orchestral Manoeuvres In The Dark had a studio and they took pity on us and lent us a synth to get us through the gig. We had to do many cabaret shows to replace that keyboard and I never forgot how I'd been stabbed in the back by jealous and bitter young men.

I vowed that I would avenge this treachery by becoming successful and leaving the Cherry Boys in their retro dust.

We proceeded with steely determination. We worked hard on songs and by the new year we had many interesting new ideas. We did a half-hour live lunchtime TV show for Granada from outside St. Nicholas's Church by the docks. After a mis-fire attempt at recording a single for Shepperton-based company Rock City who seemed anxious to acquire a token Liverpool band in the growing climate, we decided to record our own self-financed first single at Square One studios, just off Stanley Street in Liverpool (now the site of Crash rehearsal rooms, which I still use to this day). It was February 1982.

The little four-track was owned by an old school spiv called Alan Peters who had a weird blues/jazz combo called the Lawnmower. Pete Coleman was the engineer. We cut three tracks, 'Nirvana', 'Lovehunt' and 'Sirocco', all written by me. 'Nirvana' would be the A side. 'Nirvana' was a funny little ditty with lots of drums and daft lyrics which conveyed little more than youthful energy and sixth form poetry, but it was the best thing we had at the time.

We put it out on our own label *Troll Kitchen* and Geoff Davis from *Probe* records agreed to distribute it for us.

It sold pretty well locally - we were gradually building up a good following.

Tony used his array of disco lamps at our shows in a clever, inventive way so we always had a good light show even in shit-holes.

We would dangle tinfoil across the stage which caught the light in strange, interesting ways.

Well, we thought so anyway. We tried to put on a show - even with a tiny budget. We actually got a few plays on John Peel thanks to Tony stomping into Broadcasting House (the BBC) in Portland Place in London, and actually putting it into his hand.

We got a much-needed Peel session out of it and a gig or two in London. The first place we played was the Hope and Anchor in Islington.

Thus began a lengthy period whereby various, curious A&R men (record company scouts) would come to see us play, told us they enjoyed it - and then become unavailable anytime Tony called them. This was/is common practice and we learnt not to be too disappointed.

After much deliberation we had decided to remain a three-piece. Chris was a very busy drummer, I played guitar with one hand a lot of the time (in open tunings) and played pads on my Logan String Machine and weird drones on my (new) Korg synthesizer, whilst singing into a head-mounted microphone. I was a busy little bee.

Chris Layhe played melodic, twangy bass lines high up the neck a lot of the time - we figured we made enough noise and anyone else would have trouble finding a space.

It was round about here that I first took L.S.D. Acid. Howie Minns passed me some one night after a party at the Warehouse, a venue which we played at frequently, which mysteriously burned down when the owners failed to cough up protection money (Craig Charles - local 'punk' poet - a kind of bargain basement scouse version of John Cooper Clarke - later to become a popular actor in *Red Dwarf* and *Coronation Street* - hounded me to death every time I saw him about a support

slot at one of our upcoming shows. Eventually I capitulated. I thought he was going to turn up alone and perform some of his mildy-amusing rhymes: 'Fuckin' Go 'Ead Ged!' is one chortlesome ditty I recall - however he turned up with a full band - Shades Of Grey - all wearing comedic straw hats, and proceeded to scare half the audience to the bar).

I started eating acid on a fairly regular basis. One night Chris Turrell and I knecked some round at Tony Barwood's flat and insisted he take us out onto the M62 and drive at illegal speeds. We were out of our minds listening to *Notorious Byrd Brothers* by the Byrds.

I saw God in the middle of 'I Wasn't Born To Follow' (I didn't - it just sounds good - but I laughed until I thought I would expire). I wondered if it would ever wear off. We went back to Tony's and I set fire to the Bunnymen's *Shine So Hard* E.P. His copy, not mine.

One day I cycled to the dole when I was still tripping from the night before. It was very weird, I couldn't stop giggling - and I decided to leave it alone for a little bit (I'd also had a little incident when I'd tried to board a bus home from town wearing an original Gestapo jacket I'd bought from Callan's Military Clothing Store. The driver told me I couldn't get on displaying a swastika. The acid made me think it was hilarious to wear this type of apparel).

I was still seeing Hilary - which had put a big distance between me and my mother who thought I was being thought-controlled and manipulated most of the time. In retrospect, I was, but it was the first proper relationship I'd had, and I'd handed the power over early on - which I'd never get back.

I was pale and thin around this time. Still recovering from my dad's passing, and most recently from a terrible bout of chicken-pox which I caught from Hilary's niece Louise. It was incredibly painful, left holes in my face and nearly killed me - or so it felt.

We were rehearsing two or three times a week now, and the

songs were getting better. One night, at a disused police station off Duke Street (you set up in the cells!), I showed the chaps something I'd just written. I asked Chris S to play a drum part similar in many ways to 'Nirvana' but with the backbeat in a different place.

I showed Chris L the chords which were basically C to F major 7th most of the time, and counted it off. Before I'd started singing it sounded amazing. When I did start singing we all looked at each other and had to stop.

It sounded like a number one record and we hadn't even worked out an arrangement.

Dick Sharrock, Chris's dad, had just turned up to get Chris. He stood in the doorway with a look of amazement on his face. "Play that again!" We did.

"That's a hit! It's fantastic!"

He ran outside to tell his wife Glenys who was waiting in the car. Chris Layhe came over to me with a grin on his face.

"Have you got a title for it?"

"Er...yeah...sort of."

"What's it called then?"

"It's called 'Birds Fly'."

We got a session for David 'Kid' Jensen's programme at the BBC for Radio One. It was the one that changed everything for us.

These were the best songs we'd recorded to that point, with a great engineer (Dale 'Buffin' Griffin - formerly the drummer in the brilliant Mott The Hoople).

We recorded 'Birds Fly (Whisper To a Scream)', 'Lover's Day', 'As The Dragonfly Flies' and 'Lovehunt'. As soon as the session was broadcast there was a buzz about it.

Suddenly everyone was interested - largely due to 'Birds Fly'. It was an out-of-the-box hit record, and we hadn't even recorded it properly yet. It was a undeniable song that you just couldn't ignore.

People who'd previously written us off now had to take notice. We were now in the right place at the right time, and it was only a matter of time before someone offered us a record/publishing deal.

Situation Two (the independent wing of Beggar's Banquet records, located in Wandsworth) came up with an offer for us. They would pay for us to record a single, pay for the manufacturing, artwork and distribution, put a press officer and radio plugger on it, and if it was a success, they would offer us an album deal.

It was a great opportunity.

If the single wasn't a success, we wouldn't be bound to them in any way - we'd have had a great craic out there, and lost nothing. It was all their risk. Publishers started chasing us.

EMI and Chappell were the forerunners. One day I was sitting at home when the phone started ringing off the hook with offers (they couldn't get hold of Tony).

It was all happening.

We recorded 'Birds Fly' with producer Hugh Jones, who had worked with our heroes the Bunnymen and the Teardrops, at the Producer's Workshop in Fulham, and then went to R.G. Jones in Wimbledon to mix it. The B sides would be 'Reverie Girl' and 'Gunboys' (my tongue-in-cheek little comment on the recent Falkland Islands conflict. Argentina had invaded this small piece of British territory in the South Atlantic - forcing then prime minister Margaret Thatcher to send the army in - it was a strange time and we all thought we'd be drafted).

Everybody loved the record. It got loads of airplay and got to number two in the indie chart (independent). Jeff Chegwin at Chappell Music signed us after a silly bidding war with EMI.

We were hot.

We headlined a show at the Rock Garden in Covent Garden in London and Billy Bragg opened the show for us. We had the same publisher in Chappell and Billy recorded his classic first album in the demo studio there. Billy did many other shows with us around this time and became a good mate.

We used to go to the park and shovel up loads of leaves, bag them, then scatter them all over the stage and amps, much to the annoyance of the venues we played in.

One time Billy was opening for us at the Polytechnic in Liverpool. At the climax of our set, Bill came out dressed in a gorilla suit and threw leaves all over the band and the audience.

What we didn't realise was there was quite a bit of dogshit mixed in with all these leaves. We were never asked to play at the Poly again.

I liked Bill a lot. He was too lefty for me but realised early on that I didn't give a shit and never brought it up around me unless I was trying to get a rise out of him.

He was very clever and, I felt - more interested in money and success than he actually let on.

Ian McCulloch once asked him if he'd ever heard of over-exposure. Bill asked Mac if he'd ever heard of millionaires.

We toured Europe a couple of years later with him. There is a soundboard recording of us jamming on 'Louie Louie' in Dortmund during an encore that you shall never hear.

Word came back from the record company that there was a great deal of excitement about 'Birds Fly' building up in the U.S.A. We would record another single, and then commence work on our debut album.

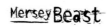

CHAPTER TEN

Love is...
A hit single

We'd made giant leaps with the second single.

Now the pressure was on to break into the mainstream.

We needed a proper hit record. I came up with two good new songs. 'Chop The Tree' and 'Love Is A Wonderful Colour' were both contenders for a follow-up. I got the idea for the title of the latter from a Pale Fountains song called 'Love Is Such A Beautiful Place'.

I nicked a few ideas off Paleys/Shack songwriter Mick Head - I also was 'inspired' by the title of his song 'Jean's Not Happening' to write a song later on called 'Melanie Still Hurts'.

I think I also stole most of the guitar solo. Cheers Mick. It was decided that LIAWC would be the shot at the big time.

We went to Crescent studios in Bath to work with producer David Lord whose work with Peter Gabriel we admired greatly (Hugh Jones wasn't available - he was working with Echo And The Bunnymen on 'Never Stop').

The track sounded funny when we'd finished it.

We were using Chris Sharrock's drum performance to trigger a Linn Drum, the new piece of kit which everyone was excited about all of a sudden (basically an early version of a sampler, it can be heard to full effect on many records of the time - check out the Human League's *Dare* or Prince's *Purple Rain*).

We weren't so sure - and as soon as Hugh Jones heard it, he

demanded to remix it. We did a long overnight session in John Foxx's Garden studio in East London where Hugh brought Chris's drums back into the track. I then went straight to the cutting room with it.

I was so tired I couldn't tell if it was any good anymore. It was also four minutes and ten seconds long - a bit lengthy for an attempted hit single.

The record came out in October and failed to get in the top hundred. This was a crushing blow and we started to think maybe our time was over before it had begun. We got a slot on Channel Four's new pop show *The Tube* where we got to meet Chrissie Hynde of the Pretenders (who I'd developed a hopeless crush on - just like everybody else).

Chris Layhe got talking to her and she said we could support the Pretenders in the U.S.A. the following year if we wanted to as she liked what she heard - an amazing thing for her to do.

The performance turned the record around and it began to climb the charts slowly. Radio started to play it.

We headed off to Rockfield studios in South Wales with Hugh Jones to start work on the album.

It was the first time any of us had been to a residential studio and it was at times very exciting and others a bit depressing. Stuck in the middle of nowhere in the winter working long days and sporadically getting on each others' nerves. I had a lot of trouble with my voice and recall spending a lot of my time with my head over a bowl breathing in mentholated steam.

We took a break for Christmas. The record was still getting played and climbed the charts - at an agonisingly slow pace.

You couldn't tell if it was going to stall or keep moving.

In January - when all the Christmas deck stopped getting airtime, LIAWC started getting a tremendous amount of support.

We got word that the midweek sales would give us an estimated chart position of twenty-eight.

The BBC's *Top Of The Pops* had been in touch with the record company for all of our relevant details. If the record continued to sell as predicted, we would be beamed in to millions of homes the following week.

A dream was about to become reality.

We did *Top Of The Pops*.

All I'd ever wanted was to get on this show and here I was. The day was actually a bit boring as they made you run through the track about eight times till you were sick of it.

However, It was an amazing feeling. Success. I was a bit pissed off about the other acts who were on the same week as us - Roland Rat, Snowy White, Shakin' Stevens and Bonnie Tyler, and the geezer who sang the theme tune to TV comedy drama *Auf Wiedersehen Pet* - I was hoping for slightly more exciting company but hey, what can you do?

Anyway, we were here and it just made us look better.

I've never understood those pretentious fucks who refuse to appear on programmes 'cos they think they're too cool. Why don't you do the show and make it cool then?

The Cocteau Twins were on Beggar's sister label 4AD and they pulled this number. Just plain silly. Sell yourself! Educate people! Maybe they'll buy your record instead of Bananarama's!

(I once reduced Liz Frazer to tears when we did a gig at the ICA with the Cocteaus. I told her I was going out to get a burger).

Top Of The Pops.

Everyone who'd ever doubted my talent or ability could now eat their words.

After the recording we didn't hit the top London nightspots and grab a page three bird each, we had an argument about who wanted a curry and who didn't, and in the end we just drove back to Rockfield in stoney silence. *Top Of The Pops*!

I'd done it.
I'd hit the jackpot.
I was a pop star.
At last. It had taken nine years.
Everybody watched TOTP.
Girls swooned and men envied.
Friends and relatives beamed with pride.
The top of the mountain as far as I was concerned.
Bliss.
For now.

CHAPTER ELEVEN

R.E.M.

R.E.M. were a new, as yet unknown band from Athens, Georgia.

I shared the same publisher in Chappell Music. Someone from the company sent me a copy of R.E.M's first album *Murmur*.

It was a classic.

The Icicle Works started playing 'Radio Free Europe' as an encore.

Just after our first album came out we played at the Venue in Victoria, London. R.E.M. were in town to play some shows themselves, and someone at Chappell's told them that there was an English band playing in London that night who covered one of their songs.

They were amazed and two of the band came to our show.

After the gig Mike Mills and Michael Stipe came backstage. Mike Mills was very sociable and friendly and had a great interest in British humour, his favourite being the Morecambe and Wise Show - which he could reel off sketches from ad finitum complete with their English dialect.

Michael Stipe walked in the dressing room and immediately pressed himself into a corner, his long curly hair covering the whole of his face as he surveyed the dressing room carpet with great interest through thick glasses.

He stood like this for about a minute when I thought I'd introduce myself.

"Hi, I'm Ian, how are doing Michael?"

"Oh hi...thank you very much for covering our song Ian... It was a great version."

"Well, it's a great song mate."

He pushed his hair out of his eyes.

"Where did you get the words?" He asked me.

"Well I couldn't really make them out, so I just learnt them phonetically."

"Oh that's really great 'cos there aren't any."

"What d'you mean?"

"The song doesn't have any words."

"Oh...OK."

Thank God for that, I thought I was going deaf.

(When R.E.M. played at the Royal Court in Liverpool later that year they dedicated the song to us).

CHAPTER TWELVE

Sausalito
1984

We're on our way to the U.S.A.

Our debut single over there - 'Birds Fly (Whisper To A Scream)' - is causing quite a stir we are informed. There is a new sensation sweeping the nation. It's called MTV. Music Television. The concept being a nationwide TV channel that shows nothing but video clips of artists miming to their latest single release.

This idea being revolutionary may seem funny to folk who are too young to remember a world before the internet, stacked twenty-four hour satellite or cable channels and cellphones, but this is how it was.

This was a very exciting new development. We'd made just two video clips at this point, cheaply and cheerfully over the course of two days in Shoreditch and London.

One for 'Love Is A Wonderful Colour', which had just been a top twenty hit in Britain (it climbed to number fifteen after our TOTP appearance) and another for 'Birds'.

The yanks retitled the track 'Whisper To A Scream (Birds Fly)' presumably as the lyrics 'Whisper to a scream' were repeated ad infinitum in the track whereas 'Birds fly' appeared but once.

They also insisted we remove the cheesy voice-over (my idea originally) which had appeared at the head of the UK version, and shorten our handle to Icicle Works. They also changed the

artwork to our debut album and re-jigged the running order, even substituting one track for another.

I protested this interference at every step but was shouted down and assured that I was a very small piece in a very big puzzle and don't blow it kid.

MTV had added our clip to its playlist, and we were currently on medium rotation. No mean feat I was assured. The record company - Arista - were 'hyping' it to fuck (this means payola - money for airtime - but we were oblivious to all of this stuff - we were still kids - we thought people played records on the radio and telly because they were good. Ha ha ha).

Anyway, here we are.

We're getting on a plane. A big plane. A 747 Jumbo jet. I look out of the window nervously at the huge nose of the aircraft as we begin boarding. It says Pan American - 'Clipper Of The Seas'.

Pan Am would go bust sometime soon after. I'm glad I didn't know this then. The plane looks old. I've only been on an aircraft once before and that was a shuttle flight from Liverpool to London to meet a producer.

I haven't yet decided if I like flying or not (I still haven't - ignorance is bliss - if you don't understand how something works it gives you less insight as to how many things can go wrong). I'm sitting next to Chris Sharrock as we take off and we both plug our headphones into his Walkman on which the Byrds' 'Eight Miles High' is playing (airlines had no problem with personal stereos back then - you could also light up as soon as the plane levelled off - imagine!).

Paul 'Wherever I Lay My Hat' Young and his band are on the flight and we make conversation throughout the long journey to the west coast of America.

I don't like it when people who are more famous than me are on my flight. You just know that they'll get the headlines when it falls into the drink and you'll be an afterthought (showbiz kids think this way - shame on me).

Two things happen on my debut transatlantic flight to break up the monotony:

1) Violent turbulence - which causes me great stress, I think I am going to die, not helped by the fact that everyone else in our party sleeps through the whole thing.

2) The guy sitting in front of me, actually does, die. I don't know what he died of, there was no dramatic yelp or exhalation of breath, he just slipped away. Perhaps it was boredom.

Fact: It is a ruling on any aircraft that if someone pops their clogs inflight they cannot be removed from their seat due to the theory that flyers may be distressed to see a real-life corpse being carried down the aisle of the aircraft while they are eating or watching Eddie Murphy's latest hilarious offering.

You can see the point.

However this is of scant consolation to me, who has to sit looking at the top of a dead man's head for the best part of a day. The recently deceased individual is given a scrape of dignity by having an orange blanket thrown over him by a startled looking flight attendant. Somehow it doesn't put me off my food.

The journey passes without further incident, and our (seriously delayed) bird touches down in San Francisco at three a.m. local time.

After the regulation age-long entry through U.S Immigration (it takes even longer these days) we emerge intact, dog-tired and excited to finally be in the land that we'd only ever seen in movies.

A Long Black Limousine appears out of the darkness to take the band (everyone else - Tony Barwood our manager, Geoff

Muir our sound engineer, and Karen Kirsch our U.S tour manager - is in a people carrier along with our guitars) to the location of our hotel, the Alta Mira in Sausalito. We have a cheerful black driver who winds his window down to greet us.

I ask him if we can lock the doors as I'm a bit spun out from jet lag and have become suddenly paranoid that I am going to be shot, as that is what Americans do to musicians from Liverpool.

He assures me this will not happen and I sink back into the leather upholstery to contemplate the enormity of what is happening to me. He then inquires if we "Wanna get high?"

I do not know what he means. Higher than I've just been? What's he talking about?

He then proceeds to offer us Cocaine. We've been in the country approximately one hour.

We politely decline. Isn't that the stuff you put up your nose? Fuck that.

Who wants a blocked nose?

We arrive at the hotel around forty-five minutes later, still undercover of darkness.

The Alta Mira is a luscious retreat built into the side of a huge mountain which overlooks the bay.

I feel the warm air around me, hear the crickets chirping and smell the sweet early morning breeze.

It smells like... victory. I'm living the life of a British rock star in California and we haven't sold a single record yet.

The following morning I awoke at around seven due to jet lag.

I opened the curtains and looked out on the sun-kissed bay. It looked like I'd arrived in paradise. I did a ring-round to see who was awake. Jeff Muir was the only taker. We met in the lobby and decided to stroll down the hill towards the water.

We came to a seafood restaurant with many expensive looking boats moored alongside it. As we approached the entrance a guy with long hair was sitting on the steps petting his dog. I looked over at him and he smiled. I smiled back.

"Hey, how ya doin?" He offered.

Very friendly. I'm not used to this.

"Good... good. Er... how are you doin'?" I retort chirpily. I feel spaced out still. Nothing feels real.

"Yeah great. Just great thank you."

I recognised him. I thought I knew him, and then I realised it was the actor Michael Douglas.

Mersey Beast

CHAPTER THIRTEEN

I NEVER saw
my hometown
'til I went around the WORLD

Our first show was at the Stone Club on Broadway, downtown San Francisco.

It was awful.

We had decided to rent amplifiers rather than bring our own in order to keep costs down. I turned up to find the Fender Deluxe amplifier I'd ordered sounded like a piece of shit.

The gear came from a company called S.I.R. (disdainfully referred to in the biz as 'Sorry I Rented'). I ended up trying out half a dozen other set-ups and none of them sounded right.

This was a mistake I would never make again. There was hardly anybody at the gig as the record had only just been serviced to radio. It seemed our timing was off, but it turned out the show had been put in at the last minute to coincide with promotional work and our slot on the Pretenders tour (Chrissie came good).

The mixing desk kept sparking out and Jeff couldn't figure out what was happening. Eventually two cockroaches crawled from inside it. It was a nightmare. We were all devastated that our first ever gig in America was an embarrassment.

Things could only get better.

They did.

We flew to Los Angeles and did three great shows opening for the Pretenders at the Universal Amphitheatre.

The after-show bash was a gas.

I met Linda Gray (Sue Ellen in mega popular T.V. show *Dallas*). Steve Jones from the Sex Pistols was there. I told him I wanted my picture taken with Sue Ellen - he told me he wanted a picture of her "Wiv me cock in 'er mauf."

I asked him why he lived in L.A. - he told me he liked a bit of sunshine in the morning with his cup of tea.

What a great guitar player. What a great rock star. What a shame he never lived up to his initial promise.

His aura dying away the further he got from 1977.

Anyway, our album came out to some great reviews.

Here's one.

ROLLING STONE:

'Icicle Works are a young Liverpudlian group whose first album is like an aural rummage through a Haight-Ashbury head shop. It's all here: cosmic particles of thought afloat in an ether of backward guitar solos, sitarlike drones, squealing feedback and a recorder piping breathily along in a manner redolent of drugs and Donovan.

And that's just one song

("Nirvana, we adore you," goes the chorus).

The Icicles bring a fresh urgency to the psychedelic-pop formula, interrupting their craniumbending reality detours ("Culling time.../In the camp of unused dreams") with double-time choruses, Antmusic-style snare-drum rolls and minor-key melodies that hit like the first blast of autumn's chill.

The band seems fixated on elemental, outdoors thing - trees, seasons, birds, deserts, dragonflies - seeing in the natural world a paradigm for the matter of living. Within a song, Icicle Works build, by addition, from mantralike calm to gale-force climax.

The thrilling choruses and rollicking psych-pop punch of "A Factory In The Desert."

"Whisper To A Scream (Birds Fly)" and "Chop The Tree," to

name but a few, will shake you into a state not unlike ecstasy.
Tune in and turn on.' (RS 423).

The yanks were gettin' it. Wow.

The single was starting to pick up a lot of radio. We were staying at the Tropicana Motel on Santa Monica Boulevard and eating breakfast at Duke's coffee shop everyday. I was thrilled because I was walking in the footsteps of Jim Morrison and Tom Waits, who had both lived at the 'Trop.'

It was a great time. I lay by the pool between interviews and got very red.

We did a show in Long Beach and a beautiful girl by the name of Michelle came backstage to say hi.

She looked like the young Victoria Principal (I was big on *Dallas* - my mum was taping it for me while I was away).

I was gob-smacked. I'd never actually seen anyone that gorgeous in real life. We were in the promised land. I told her we were going to Disneyland the following day and asked her if she'd like to come (I was still very much going out with Hilary - but the world was opening up in front of me. Fast).

A young scouse painter and decorator came to see us called Mick Winder. He'd been married to some troublesome woman over there recently in a whirlwind romance and she eventually flipped him over. He was licking his wounds.

He seemed happy to be around folk from back home and started spending time with us around L.A. I eventually offered him a job as my guitar roadie - he came back to England later that year where I put him on a wage and introduced him to the music biz.

"Waifs and strays... you love 'em."

That's my mum.

I copped off with a girl who worked for Arista one night and took her back to my room. I froze in the middle of drunken passion when I could only find one breast. I freaked out. I told her I had to get up in a few hours and called her a cab. I told the guys over breakfast and much laughter ensued.

Not as much laughter however as when she turned up a couple of days later at a show. She fought her way to the front of the stage where she clearly displayed two magnificent mammaries. Either she'd had a drive-thru boob job or I'd been too walloped to find titty number two.

Nobody could breathe for laughing.

"You must've felt a right tit," declared Geoff Muir - following his quip with a raspy cackle.

We performed the single and 'In The Cauldron Of Love' on Dick Clark's *American Bandstand* while gorgeous young things danced around us in very little.

Dick interviewed us. "What is it about Liverpool that produces so much great music?" he asked.

"It's something in the water," said Chris L.

We were living the dream. We went to watch our new mates R.E.M. opening for the Human League at the Hollywood Palace and then slipped backstage to re-acquaint ourselves.

We'd hung out with them one more time since the Venue show in London - in Colchester, when they played at the university. We went back to someone's house after the gig where Peter Buck talked the ear off me all night. At one point he took me to the bathroom and offered me a small mountain of speed (amphetamine) on a plectrum.

"Ah! That's way you talk so fast!" I remarked.

"Oh shit no, I'm like this all the time," he said.

We went to Hawaii for a week's residency at a club in Waikiki. I pined over Michelle, my Disneyland date. Tony Barwood and I got badly sunburned through riding motorbikes across the island without wearing enough sunblock.

We were covered in blisters. Mad dogs and Englishmen.

I recall most of our party being bombed on Maui-wowi. Super-strength weed.

Somebody thought it would be a good idea for us to open for David Gilmour of Pink Floyd on his solo Canadian/U.S. tour (our album and single were becoming a great success in Canada).

We didn't think the idea was that sound ourselves, we didn't really want to play on the same bill as some old hippy - we were punks! - but the brass at Arista and Polygram (our Canadian label) wanted it, so it came to pass. We flew to Quebec and jumped on the opening night.

I was being grouchy but Tony insisted I shake hands with Mr. Gilmour.

I said: "Pleased to meet you, fuckin' hippy!"

He said: "Wait a minute I'll just go and get my headband!"

He took it well and was very friendly. We had to soundcheck in front of ten thousand people as Dave (you could call him that then) didn't leave the stage until fifteen minutes before the doors opened.

We did Neil Young's 'Sugar Mountain'. Well, what the hell - we were in Canada.

The applause was immense when we finished our set - we were ecstatic - until we realised they were applauding the fact that we'd finished and they'd soon be in Floyd world.

Crushing.

David Gilmour was a nice bloke. The Conservative MP for Cambridge. His second solo record, *About Face* was out and he was determined to prove himself outside of Roger Waters' orbit. We got to hang out a bit. One night in the hotel bar I got to talking about Roger's current record *The Pros And Cons Of Hitchhiking* - they both had solo records out at the same time on the same label. He pretended not to be interested in it but eventually couldn't help asking if I'd listened to it properly, and if so what it was like? I thought for a bit and told him it wasn't as good as Pink Floyd. This seemed a measured response to me.

One night we all went to a club somewhere and I was waiting to use the men's toilet.

Whoever was in there took ages. Eventually Diamond Dave bounced out and started singing 'You've Really Got a Hold On Me'. He looked like he'd been consuming something slightly stronger than a fine Chardonnay. Very funny.

The tour was hard. I remember walking out on stage at the Beacon Theatre in New York to see the entire front row holding up the opened gatefold sleeve of *Dark Side Of The Moon* above their heads so the prism ran the whole length of the row. What a welcome. We discovered that Pink Floyd fans don't like much else apart from Pink Floyd. Maybe the Australian Pink Floyd.

They certainly didn't like us much. At one gig some twat was shouting "Gilmour! Gilmour! Gilmour!" all the way through 'Out Of Season'. I'd had enough.

"Listen, shit-for-brains... we may not be David Gilmour but we're much, much better than you are!"

Wild applause. We went down a storm after that. All those nights on the pies and peas circuit had to count for something.

Gilmour's crew really took to us from that point on.

One night after a show at the Veteran's Memorial Arena in Philadelphia, Tony came into the dressing room looking ashen and asked Chris S if he could have a private word.

After about five minutes, Chris walked back into the room without looking up, grabbed his stuff and exited quickly.

His dad Richard had died from a heart attack while doing some decorating in the front room of their house in Bebington.

We were all devastated. We all loved Richard and he had always been a great supporter of Chris and the band.

When we got back to the hotel I called Chris to give him my shoulder, and tell him I knew what he felt like.

He said a quiet "Thanks" and put the receiver down. We never spoke about it again, ever. I always felt something changed after that night. I'd lost a bit of him for good. Somehow I felt guilty.

I felt that Chris was out here working his arse off for me - not really enjoying it - and I took him away from the place he loved to be most, which was at home with his family and friends, stoned to the bone and high on the hooch.

He was always a homebody - I could never get him out.

Except to play music. Eventually I wouldn't even be able to get him to do that.

We decided to cancel the rest of the tour. Mr. Gilmour was very gracious and came into our dressing room to thank us for doing the shows with him, and personally give his condolences to young Chris (David Gilmour's solo album/tour tanked and many fans complained about having to shell out to hear two Pink Floyd songs. Three years later the Floyd were back on the road selling out stadia, without Roger Waters).

After the funeral we'd pick up where we'd left off.

A lengthy, head-lining club tour was booked for the States and Canada. We would hit all the places we'd not yet been to.

The album and single were top forty now - north and south of the border - and it was time to attack.

We had a couple of weeks off before we flew out again and it was also time for me to face Hilary. I'd been having a wild old time out there on tour and I came back with a dose of the clap.

Those days were pre-AIDS and I never wore my wellies. Naughty boy (It seemed the only girl I hadn't fucked yet in America was the lovely Michelle - whom I had high hopes for and wouldn't sully with a mere shag).

I'd managed to get out of having sex with Hilary for a week or so but now she was starting to get suspicious. I sat her on my bed and told her the grim news, which she took remarkably well. She was clearly upset but was the model of adult composure. She went home and I left her to deal with the situation. I felt bad but it had been nearly five years and I was ready to move on.

I had the fucking world on a string at twenty-three and was going to enjoy it.

A few days later she called me up and asked if she could come and see me. Before the band made its first trip Stateside I'd decided to leave my recently-acquired orange Gretsch Tennessean semi-acoustic guitar at Hilary's mum's house, as I was paranoid that it would be stolen from my own (we'd had a recent burglary), and felt it was too precious to fly with me.

Hilary turned up with my guitar. She was so calm! She told me to open the guitar case.

She had smashed it to bits.

My precious, beautiful, vintage instrument.

Did a fuckin' Pete Townshend on it she did.

The first thing I'd bought with my advance, along with my Rickenbacker twelve-string. It was like looking at your best mate's dead body. I ran out of the house and ran around Newsham Park for half an hour to displace my anger.

If I would've stayed in her presence I would've hit her.

That was the end for Hilary.

She also erased my vast collection of rare music clips on VHS which I had patiently compiled over the years, not destroyed, but erased.

Hell hath no fury etc.

(I had the guitar rebuilt and it has featured on many of my records ever since. It is now black in colour and its finest recorded moment is probably the solo on 'Love's Young Dream' off the 1996 album *Merseybeast*.

I still haven't found all the clips I had recorded - some twenty five years later).

You can't kill a squadron.

You can't kill a squadron!!!

CHAPTER FOURTEEN

The White Stuff

I'd been offered cocaine a few times in the States but had always refused.

Drugs were bad stuff apart from acid and a bit of pot - oh how the young mind works.

One of our roadies over there kept borrowing money off everyone all the time and we couldn't work out why he was always broke when we fed him every day and he was being paid well enough.

We were so naive.

One time he borrowed sixty dollars off Chris L to "buy a belt." Drugs make liars. One night after a show in Toronto I was sitting on the bus having a drink with Karen Kirsch. She seemed full of energy despite the fact that we'd had a long day and everyone else was pooped.

She pulled out a vial and showed it to me.

"Ian, somebody at the show had some of this for sale so I thought I'd get some in case you guys needed a pick-me-up at any point."

I was a bit drunk and curious.

"What does it do then?"

"Well it just makes you feel good y'know? Nothin' heavy."

She passed it to me. It was gonna happen at some time so it might as well be now. I tipped a little onto a cassette box, chopped it into a little line, rolled up a dollar bill (I'd seen it done enough times by now), blocked one nostril and had a good sniff with the other one.

It was bloody amazing. I felt a great rush of euphoria, and wanted to dance in the street. I ran off the bus and went into the hotel, banged on Chris Sharrock's door, woke him up, and frantically relayed my experience to him.

I dragged him to the bus, got him tooted up, and we stayed up partying most of the night thanks to our new friend.

We were in the club.

Chris L would never touch drugs. He was scared of them. I wish I could've been.

In the eighties coke was more exclusive than it is now. You would get a gram in a wrap for about seventy quid.

"Cocaine is God's way of letting you know you're making too much money!" Was a popular saying at the time. Coke kept you awake, made you feel sexy, and put you in a private members club that was easier to get into than it was to get out. Anyone who wasn't carrying was excluded. There would be secret little gangs ("They haven't got any! Keep schtum!").

Coke made you feel like a new man, and the new man wanted a line as well.

The biggest problem with coke is there's never enough of it - and frequently too much. A lot of girls like to hang out with guys who've got coke on them. It's party time - but timing is everything.

If you do too much, your equipment won't work anymore - but if you don't do enough you'll lose your buzz and the young lady may start thinking about leaving (often enough to find more coke) - or fall asleep.

A lot of guys I know snort Viagra with the coke so they can buzz and fuck all night.

I've never tried it myself. I feel I'm getting too old to start finding new drug cocktails.

Half the time the buzz is knowing that you've got plenty more coke left to do. When it runs out you're screwed and you've got a comedown to look forward to.

The best way to deal with this is to have sex until you've tuckered yourself out (with or without a partner) - more booze, marijuana, downers or sleeping pills will help stave off the quick descent into hell. But you have to be careful.

The self-medicator has trouble remembering how much medicine they've taken.

You can toss and turn for hours, sleep a little bit and get so frustrated that you drink more booze and pop more pills just to obliterate the fast ride down. This can send you to sleep permanently if you're not careful. It happens all the time.

Many so-called overdoses were just silly accidents. Silly or not, they are irreversible.

I know a lot of people who've suffered suicidal comedowns... I've had a couple myself.

Most of the time you tell yourself it's chemically induced and you really don't need to hate yourself - honestly.

When I was living in London in the late eighties the early part of any given evening was spent ordering, and then going somewhere to score. This could take up to two hours, depending on the dealer.

"First thing you learn is that you always got to wait". Lou Reed told us.

Too fuckin' right.

It's a seller's market - he's got the shit you want and he'll get to you when he can. He doesn't even have to turn up - you'll forgive him of course, and the arrangement goes on. The only time you'll stop calling a dealer is when he gets lifted - which he probably will at some point.

You'll get fed up with him when he starts turning up too late (i.e. the next day), and then you'll move on to someone else. It's easy. The only dealer who survives is the one who is truly

paranoid, doesn't get high on his own supply, never sells anything to a cop, doesn't get caught on camera, and doesn't get on anyone else's turf.

If he does this he'll be either killed, deterred - in a dramatic way - from continuing this avenue of employment, or someone will make sure he has an unexpected rendezvous with the feds. There's a lot of money to be made in this game, and the bag you buy will have been stepped on a couple of times, reducing the kick but expanding the profit.

Unless you know the right people.

Music people usually know the right people. We take drugs for a living. Not just on bank holiday weekends.

We're great customers.

Coke went out of fashion briefly for a couple of years when Ecstasy first made an appearance, but it came back more popular than ever. Once the bastion of the successful businessman, model, rock star or movie star, or just person-in-a-hurry with money to spend - cocaine is now available to all citizens at a reasonable price.

Well that's progress I guess.

As for trying to stamp hard drugs out, forget it. The supply will always find a way provided there is a demand.

And there will always, as long as human beings roam the earth, be a demand for drugs.

A suggestion? Make them all legal, sell them in Tesco, tax us on them, and vast criminal empires shall fall.

What government fails to realise is that what makes drugs cool and sexy to people (particularly young people) is that they're told not to do them from the age they are able to absorb information.

Everybody looks into the dark corner of the room more than they look at the light. If you could buy them over the counter with aspirin and condoms most of the allure would vanish. I mean, making condoms so easily available and presenting them without stigma or shame stopped everybody using condoms didn't it?

If you're waiting for the big, sanctimonious don't-do-drugs message from a reformed user, you won't find it here. I don't condone drugs but I don't criticise people who take them.

That would be hypocritical. "Do what thou wilt shall be the whole of the law". The reason why drugs are as popular as ever is because people love to take them. There's always a fresh crop of eager youngsters coming up who want to do drugs. For many of them this will lead to misery but there's plenty who can handle all the twists and turns of a chemical relationship.

I don't think rehab works in the long term because the only way to really kick a habit is to do it yourself.

That says you're serious about it.

A famous friend of mine once told me he got the best coke he'd ever had in his life in a well known recovery residence. A cautionary tale falls deaf on the young.

It may have all been done before but - they've never done it before.

From a personal point of view I've always viewed the situation as a question of balance.

For everything bad you do to yourself you have to do something good. If you go through a period of heavy abuse you have to go through a period of equal abstinence. This is difficult to do if you have a circle of friends who all use.

Dopers stick together.

Half my friends have used and the other half haven't.

Balance.

Don't hang out with A if you want an easy night, go and see B instead.

B won't really like hanging out with A so you won't be torn. Use your loaf. If you eat and drink a lot you have to exercise and drink water a lot. It'd be great if drugs weren't around, it really would – but they always will be.

If you tell a child not do do something they'll want to do it, and let's face it - we're all still children.

Karen Kirsch had introduced me to Cocaine. If she hadn't have done it, somebody else would have eventually. Mick Fleetwood once said:

"Cocaine is an intelligence test, if you take it - you fail."

I don't agree with this - many clever people failed the test. The real test of intelligence with regard to this substance - as with any toxin - is to be able to use it in moderation if you have to have it at all. The drugs came with the territory in my chosen profession.

Over the next twenty years I would be offered it on a regular basis in any given situation. I would even deal it at certain points (the next step). I would spend a colossal amount of money on it.

Almost everybody I knew was using it on a regular basis - almost everyone abstained from it for periods of time and then binged on it for a weekend as a little reward to their self-control.

Most of them are still here.

Most of them...

I've sampled most of the drugs available over the years. I've taken Heroin a couple of times. Both times were accidents as the bastards who gave it to me told me it was coke. Heroin is just too fucking good.

You're not supposed to feel that way all of the time. It removes all desire and ambition and replaces it with heaven.

That is not life - it is death. Reward without toil.

Which is no reward at all (and toil doesn't mean waiting for your fucking dealer all night either).

Junkies like to get as many people on the same wavelength as themselves and occasionally will find it amusing to dose you with smack when you think you're in for a toot. The reason why I stayed away from smack was that I was scared of it. Whenever anyone I knew got into it (and there weren't that many), you'd stop seeing them as they stopped socialising.

Smack makes you retreat into yourself, and I'm a social person.

Junkies are the most boring fuckers in the world.

Cokeheads run a close second.

Cocaine found me and everything changed.

That's what it does.

'Back at home I lost some good friends,
people change and something pure ends,
soon enough a broken heart mends,
got drunk every night,
got an achin' head,
and a fire inside my soul...'

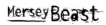

CHAPTER FIFTEEN

Hollow
Horse

America is a vast place.

Just when you think you've toured it you realise you haven't even scratched the surface and it's time to start again. Most British bands who go out there hit all the hot spots - New York, Philly, Boston, D.C. Chicago, Minneapolis, San Fran, L.A. etc.

They work hard, party harder, see themselves climbing up the charts and think the place is as good as conquered.

In reality what is happening is the record company is paying vast amounts of money to get them on the radio.

Hopefully, they may get some good reviews in the press (not too difficult if the radio is behind you and the right hacks are suitably schmoozed) which then creates a buzz around the band.

The English record company will pay for British journalists to fly out to an important showcase at a hip venue in a hip town, take a few snaps of the band underneath the Hollywood sign ..."The Shitwipes take on the U.S.A!" and everyone (except the people in the know) slaps each other on the back, snorts a celebratory line and heads to the bar.

We were guilty of this.

We saw our records climb the album and single charts and wondered when the money would start rolling in.

It never did, really.

We were on wages and I, as main songwriter, started getting fairly substantial publishing money through eventually.

I was OK but hardly wealthy. I was making more than anyone else in our gang however, which would be the cause of much consternation later on. There's so much outlay to break a place like America you only really start to see the green stuff if you sell a million units.

If you get that far, the record company will bankroll you even further to get it to two million. And so on.

You're always in hock to your label.

AND they own your masters. Crazy.

We were getting tired after about a month of playing clubs and most of the towns aren't sexy like the places you first flew in to.

I distinctly remember sitting in my room in the Brooke Cadillac Hotel in Detroit one Sunday afternoon and crying myself to sleep because I was so fed up playing the same show in an identikit town every night (I was also pining for my L.A. woman, Michelle, whom I'd developed a weighty crush on).

You can drive a thousand miles in America and when you get to the next town it looks the same as the one you just left.

The hotel room looks the same. There is a feeling of inertia. Everything I wanted to be doing in my life I was doing - and I still wasn't fucking happy.

It gets tedious just like any job does if you do it all the time. The initial buzz soon wears off.

This is when you start doing too many drugs, drinking too much, and taking anyone who's around to bed with you just to get you through the night (this was also before transatlantic cellphones or the internet - just calling home was a big deal and could take half an hour to arrange in some of the places we were staying).

We didn't have laptops wired up to the interweb to keep up with our friends back home. Nowadays of course I'd probably appreciate it more. Savour the moment - as one learns to do with age. However I was still a snotty-nosed kid and I was bored and a little disillusioned.

One of the main reasons for my mild depression was the realisation of the fact that the dream I'd worked for all these years was little more than that - a dream.

Pop stardom was not the panacea, and I would have to find my spiritual contentment within and not without.

This was a hard lesson.

We started getting the vibe that the record company was losing its initial thrill also. It was getting more and more difficult to get them to pick up the tab.

We met the then head of Arista in New York - Clive Davies (a legend in the business who'd signed the likes of Janis Joplin, Santana etc - he was also famously ejected from the head chair at CBS for getting caught with his hands in the till) the day after a show he didn't attend, and it was like getting an audience with the Pope.

All of his drones were scuttling around with their heads bowed which we thought was funny. We weren't impressed with suits - most artists aren't, they're bean-counters who only really impress their own kind. I sat in his office and looked at the black and white shots of him with all of these legendary acts he's been involved with over the years (and the Thompson Twins) as he reeled out his default speech-to-young-bucks and wondered if we were gonna get a dinner out of him.

We didn't (he did send us some flowers once though). His big piece of advice was that we should open our set with our current hit single, play it again in the middle and then reprise it at the end.

Genius.

We were only playing for an hour most nights (in all fairness, Clive Davies is an A&R genius with a great skill at matching talent with material and ideas, and has made himself and many of his artists wealthy beyond belief. Just not us).

One afternoon I jumped into the lift at the Mayflower Hotel in New York. There was a little girl of about eight or nine standing in there with a woman. I smiled at them and turned to face the door.

"Hi there. How are you?" It was the girl.

I turned around.

"I'm great thanks! How are you?"

"Are you a singer? I'm sure I've seen you on MTV."

"Er yeah, we've got a record out at the moment called 'Whisper To A Scream'. My band's called Icicle Works."

"Oh my God, is that the one with all the wind and leaves?"

"Ha...yeah, that's the one!"

"Oh wow. Could you sign something for me? I love that song!"

"Sure, no problem."

The woman with her tore off a piece of paper from a legal pad and handed it to me along with a pen.

"Who's it to?"

"Er that's Drew. D-R-E-W. Thank you soooo much."

"You're welcome! Take care."

I got out on the fifth floor.

Later that evening Karen Kirsch told me that Drew Barrymore was staying at the hotel.

We were invited to an MTV lunch to launch one of their new programmes, whereby we found ourselves sitting at the same table as Joey Ramone.

After a couple of gratis beverages I plucked up the courage to talk to him. He was an avid viewer of MTV in its infancy and was familiar with our tune, which he told me he liked a great deal. He was a charming fellow.

I was staggered how far one song I'd written had brought me to date, changed my life, and put me in the company of so many people I admired. Amazing. I promised myself I must write more of these type of songs. I didn't know just then how hard this would be.

We flew home a few weeks later for a rest and to re-group in a sane environment.

Arista waved us goodbye with the promise that they would consider which track to release next from the album and contact us.

We suggested 'Love Is A Wonderful Colour' which had, after all been a big song in our homeland - they said they'd be in touch.

As soon as I came home I carried on partying.

I was single for the first time in years and started making the most of it. I was out every night, usually at the Mardi Gras club on Bold Street or Macmillan's on Concert Street.

Speed (Amphetamine Sulphate) had now become my little tipple of choice - cheap, nasty and easy to find up north.

I'd had a little fling with the promotions girl at Beggar's Banquet, a beautiful, petite, blonde, brown-eyed seventeen year old by the name of Karen Protheroe.

She started coming up to Liverpool as much as I was hanging around in London and we became an (slightly covert) item.

She was amazing - and a bit mad (I was still in touch with the lovely Michelle but she was an awful long way away. I was discovering that I was not the faithful type and had the inherent ability to put the phone down on one lass and then pick up to another without pausing for breath. A trait I was not particularly proud of but one which I continued to allow). Karen was my type - everybody fancied her, and I pursued her with my usual vigour.

Beggar's re-released 'Birds Fly' backed with 'In The Cauldron Of Love' to announce our return to British shores and to celebrate our Stateside success.

The single failed to garner much airplay and stalled outside the top fifty - a bit of a worry - we thought we'd made it! We'd spent too much time away and would now pay the price.

Michael Barrackman (our favourite guy at Arista) came over to England on some other business and then flew up to the 'pool to give us a pep talk and hear if we had any ideas for the second album.

I was still living in Morden Street and we all gathered there.

He was always optimistic and positive about the Icicle Works and it was good to see him. "Can I use your bathroom?" he enquired.

"Sure, it's just out the back there," I advised.

"What... you mean... outside?"

(The toilet - for that is what we Brits unashamedly refer to it as - Yanks prefer the term bathroom or restroom - was at the end of the back yard remember - handbuilt by enthusiastic but fairly hopeless D.I.Y. dabbler, R.G.McNabb).

"Yeah... just down there."

He looked horrified.

"What? You mean your bathroom is outside of your apartment?!"

(Muffled giggles).

He looked at me as if I was a character from a Dickens novel. Oh how we laughed.

Perhaps they would work harder for us in future if they thought we were destitute.

Arista had decided to stop work on the debut album as they felt there wasn't another single. Quite why they arrived at this decision now, and not before they signed us, was a mystery.

They had half-heartedly serviced LIAWC to radio (perhaps one station in Doorknob, Wisconsin) and were assured in no uncertain terms that this track was not for U.S. top forty radio - or so they told us. In essence the plan was now to press on with a follow-up album.

We had a little bit of money, a taste of the high life, a spring in our step, and took the situation accordingly.

I started writing songs and brushing up old ideas. We had a good number that we had even opened up a few gigs with in the States with a working title of 'Hollow Horse'.

It also had a nice chorus which went "We'll be as we are, when all the fools who doubt us fade away".

A little anthem.

It seemed like a new start. We decided we would record it as soon as possible and get it out in the approaching winter to see if we could regain some lost ground.

Hugh Jones became available again ('Never Stop' had been a huge hit for the Bunnymen), he liked the new tune, and we set out for Strawberry studios in Stockport to nail it.

Chris Layhe had met a young lady in L.A. as I had, so when the single was finished and we'd done the usual crap video clip to promote it (never enough money, never enough ideas, never enough time - it hurt us), we both decided to fly back out there for a little holiday and to spend some time with our new friends.

It was great to see Michelle again, I was treated like the returning prodigal.

We made glorious love every day in her little bedroom at her parents' house in Torrance, listened to the Psychedelic Furs, R.E.M and the Cure, went out on day excursions - and all was good with the world. We hung out at the mall and got pizza, dude.

She introduced me to her friends and I wanted to sleep with all of those too. It was like living in an episode of *Buffy The Vampire Slayer*, and I was the only vampire.

When Chris and I got back home we were told that 'Hollow Horse' backed with 'The Atheist' and a live version of 'Nirvana' - recorded at the Paradise Club in Boston on our second U.S. jaunt, had peaked at a frightening number ninety-two in the charts.

Shit. This was worse than we thought. Everybody started panicking.

The fickle pop audience had bought our single and album in a fit of pop impulse buying - but now seemed to care little for us.

They'd bought the vinyl, not the band.

A second appearance on *The Tube* a couple of weeks later failed to halt the downward plunge of the record, although we did have fun getting bongo'd with Ian McCulloch (promoting his first solo single) and the Stranglers, who were both on the same show.

If in doubt, drink more.

CHAPTER SIXTEEN

All the daughters
of her
father's house

We started looking around for a potential producer for the second album.

Hugh Jones had made the decision that he wouldn't be involved, largely due - I believe - to the fact that I had now become immovable in my choices.

I had very clear ideas about how I wanted the band to sound and we didn't really see eye to eye.

The two Chris' were now being sidelined as I seized the reins of power. Chris Layhe in particular seemed intent on niggling me at every opportunity.

He had a grand idea of sound and arrangement but couldn't write songs, or sing, to a standard I felt was competitive of myself. I began to look upon him as a hurdle to cross in everything I did. He'd come up with the bassline to 'Hollow Horse' which admittedly spurred me on to write one of our most enduring songs however, and clearly believed he had much to offer.

I wasn't convinced anymore. He'd come to practice with songs that seemed little more than inferior re-writes of mine.

This is only my opinion, and others may beg to differ.

I knew I had power over him and didn't have to worry about him leaving anytime soon.

Chris Sharrock didn't really have an opinion about anything. He played the drums brilliantly (although he did speed up all the time on stage which drove me nuts - but this I believe was helped no end by the drugs I gave him), laughed at my jokes, cracked some very funny ones of his own, and smoked pot from the minute he awoke to the minute he slept.

He wore the same clothes everyday and appeared slightly detached. He basically did as he was told - which was great for me.

He didn't take sides which I always admired him for. He had himself a nice little girlfriend from the Wirral who never spoke out of turn. It seemed as though we could carry on to the next stage, whatever that may be.

After a while we settled on an American dude by the name of Wally Brill to produce the record.

He had recently had a hit with a cover of a Doors tune - 'Riders On The Storm' - which he produced for his girlfriend Annabel Lamb.

Quite why this gave him the chops to make our second album eludes me now but Arista probably thought they could get closer to what they wanted if they had a yank at the helm (wrong - as it would turn out).

It was decided we would decamp to Miraval studios in the south of France in January to start work on our second opus.

First of all, though, I had to have a small operation to remove a sebaceous cist from my back which had occurred due to the constant rubbing from my guitar strap over the past months, along with my stubborn refusal to ever drag myself away from post-gig backstage shenanigans for long enough to shower.

It had grown to the size of a tennis ball after being with me for the best part of a year and it had to come off.

I went to a private clinic where the operation was performed under local anaesthetic. I didn't have any stitches - I couldn't return home anytime soon in order to have them removed.

I flew to France the next day to start the album. I still have a large circular scar there. Stupid sod.

We had some good songs - 'Perambulator', 'Seven Horses', 'Rapids', 'Conscience Of Kings', but it was a lot different from the vibe we had at Rockfield for album number one.

First of all the studio looked great in the brochure which featured pics of Duran Duran and Spandau Ballet lounging around by the pool, however we were there in January and it was like being held prisoner in Colditz POW camp. Chris Layhe had also decided to bring Lisa - his yank squeeze - along, which broke up the dynamic of the band.

When she eventually returned to the States I decided to invite Michelle over from L.A. just to achieve balance (I was also horny as fuck). She was soon bored shitless, only a day trip to Cannes broke up the monotony, and we argued for a fortnight until she got fed up and went home.

Everyone was miserable.

We struggled through the sessions - I nearly got into a fist fight with Wally Brill when he told me we couldn't have 'Hollow Horse' on the album as it had been a flop - and therefore wasn't any good.

The sessions broke up in late February with about twelve tunes in the can.

The most positive aspect of our stay in France was that I learnt to drive, albeit in a left-hand drive Citroen automatic, on the wrong side of the road of course. Everybody said goodbye to Wally except me and I've never laid eyes on him since (Richard Mainwaring engineered the sessions, who did a great job and I would work with him again a few years later on the *Permanent Damage* album).

When we got back we delivered the tapes to Beggar's and waited for about two weeks to hear anything.

They couldn't hear a single.

One track - 'Rapids' - which featured some stunning playing

from Miraval's owner, renowned French jazz pianist Jacques Loussier, sounded like the likeliest contender, and was pressed up as a promotional 7" single to gauge reaction out there in radioland.

The powers that be were unimpressed and the pressure was on to write and record another track.

After a few weeks I came up with something a bit sunnier than anything else on the album and we went to London to record the track with Geoff Muir, our live sound engineer (a vociferous critic of our records - having heard the power of our live sound for a long time).

'All The Daughters (Of Her Father's House)' was a slice of cod-Motown with a brass section and a catchy chorus. It was knocked off quickly and cheaply. The record company were desperate to get a new single out so they gave it the go-ahead for a release in May.

During a lay off I passed my driving test first time (in a right-hand drive stick-shift Ford Escort).

Tony Barwood arranged for us to do another video with Chris Dixon, our friend from Leeds who had done the 'Hollow Horse' film.

We went to a studio in Leeds to shoot it. The set-up was a mock sixties TV show to reflect the pastiche nature of the track. There were two gorgeous girls standing at the front of the stage who had been hired to dance for the day. I got talking to one of them during a break, and when the shoot was over she invited me and the boys to an underwear party which was being held at her flat that evening. We couldn't believe our luck.

Chris Layhe went home of course, but myself, Chris Sharrock and Mick Winder (who was now working for us on a full-term basis) jumped in my car and we set off for the party.

We got a load of booze in and sat there giggling, stoned as monkeys while the two birds from the shoot and about half a dozen of their mates tried on underwear and paraded around the flat, slightly drunk. After the show we went to the pub with them and got really steamed. Later, back at the flat, I made my move on the one I'd been flirting with all day. We found a corner and started snogging when she whispered in my ear...

"Ian, I don't know how you'll feel about this, but everything me and my friend have...we share."

"What do you mean?" I asked.

"Well, we like to do things... together."

Fucking get in.

I was going to have two women at once. I tried to be cool. It was hard.

Literally.

"Wow, OK! Like... whatever."

"Are you all right with that? D'you understand what I mean?"

"I think so."

Fuckin' 'ell. I thought. It's Christmas! (Actually, not a good analogy for me, I despise Christmas).

She told me we would have to go to her friend's house which was a short drive away.

I told Chris and Mick what was happening, there was plenty of action going on in the flat anyway and they would have to spare me for a few hours. I'd come and get them when I'd finished and we'd head home. They were so stoned they didn't seem to care.

Me and the two ladies drove for about twenty minutes to a little cottage just outside the city. We got inside, opened a couple of bottles, and the pair of them stripped off and got down to it in front of me. It was fantastic. After about ten minutes I was suitably fortified with wine and stripped off and joined in.

It's weird fucking someone while someone else is getting off behind you and it takes a while to get used to - like about three minutes. It was fantastic and I was starting to feel like a proper rock star.

About seven in the morning, girl number one and I gathered our things together, kissed our mutual lover goodbye, and headed back to the flat. I woke the lads up, grinning like a Cheshire cat, and we hit the highway.

'All The Daughters...' came out a few weeks later.

We launched it with a party on the famous Liverpool Royal Iris ferryboat which was moored on the Thames for a week to promote tourism back home.

A grand party was had by all. We opened with the Sex Pistols song 'Pretty Vacant' which I dedicated to absent friends (the Pistols had launched 'God Save The Queen' on a boat on the Thames eight years earlier) and the event went over extremely well.

Which is more than can be said about the single which - appropriately - sank without trace.

CHAPTER SEVENTEEN

The small price of a bicycle

I was still living in Morden Street with my mum.

Which was quite funny considering the rock pig I'd turned into.

I'd made some money and was wondering what to do next when we got word that we'd have to move out of the house anyway as we were in a regeneration area and all the tenants were being given grants to bring their homes into the modern era.

I decided to buy a house nearby, where we could both live until Pat's house was done, at such time she could move back in and I would be set up on my own not too far away.

I found a nice little place on Hampstead Road just across Sheil Road, right by Newsham Park, and Pat and I moved in the spring of 1985.

There was genuine worry starting to creep in around the band and record company right now, due to the fact that we hadn't had a hit for about a year.

We had an album in the can and nothing to promote it with.

It was decided that we would have to reclaim this annoying lost ground by touring continuously.

No town was off limits and no venue was too small.

We climbed into the Ford Transit and began our scorched earth policy.

We had a lot of fun. Amphetamine Sulphate, pot and alcohol

were the fuel. There was a lot of it.

We'd hit the road with Tom Waits' *Raindogs* ablast on the stereo and party on to the next town.

We were still kids and we were practically invincible. It didn't feel like a climbdown from jetting around the States as we just laughed all the time. We didn't care.

The Columbia hotel in Lancaster Gate was the base for all sorties. I was still seeing Karen on a fairly regular basis and was still in touch with Michelle but operated a strict no-monogamy policy.

I wasn't proud of it - it was just the way I was. I wanted the world and I wanted it now.

Now?

NOW!!!

Karen would usually come out to shows on the basis of being the band's promotions liaison, get us a few local interviews with radio stations and then we'd get stuck into the fun stuff.

She was well fit and I was a lucky laddie. Chris Sharrock had found himself a new lady called Jo whom he met after a show in Bristol and they became a serious item very quickly. They made plans to shack up together soon in Liverpool.

Chris Layhe was also deep into his relationship with his girfriend Linda. The girls were becoming more important and things started to feel a little different.

Beggar's Banquet issued a new single in July with a huge advertising campaign in a bid to give the upcoming album its flagship and capitalise on the roadwork that was being done.

'Seven Horses' was released in multi-format 7", 12" and double gatefold EP editions in order to lure the faithful into securing us a decent chart position. Once again the record failed to catch fire and left us far from the reach of the top forty. Heads were now being scratched.

Beggar's stuck with us however - record companies did that back in the days when they were being run by people who had a passion for music - who had also learnt how to do good business.

These days it's common knowledge that the industry is run by finance robots who care not for their artists or music, but for themselves alone.

We pounded the streets and did show after show after show. Both myself and Chris Layhe recorded some solo sessions which were left in the can for now, for fear such activity would weaken the band's identity. They would eventually make their way onto B sides.

Album number two *The Small Price Of A Bicycle* was released in September and pleased us all by gaining some very positive reviews from the music press, who seemed to slowly start realizing we were not a throwaway pop band, but had substance, something to say, and would not be getting proper jobs anytime soon.

Arista rejected the new album as unsuitable for their needs.

A major blow all told.

They'd let us down big time. All that effort of getting us on the first rung of the ladder and now they didn't consider us a good bet for more success. We were so cocksure of ourselves at the time that this didn't hit us that badly.

Looking back on it this was really the end of our chances for the big time in the U.S. Beggar's started looking for a new outlet for us Stateside.

My new Hampstead Road home was becoming the focus for all things party-wise.

I bought an Opel Manta GTE which I perceived to be a sports car. It certainly behaved like one.

These were pretty good days despite the recent setbacks. The first time I'd ever had a bathroom and indoor toilet - luxury. The days flew by in a fug of booze, birds, drugs and the occasional gig to remind us what it was we were supposed to be doing for a living.

We would play almost anywhere and everywhere as we became an omnipresent live act and our following was building up all the time. We didn't trouble the charts much but word got around that the Icicle Works was an other-worldly force in the live arena.

The music scene was exciting and we were smitten with many of the new American acts who were invading our shores.

We would go and watch Green On Red, Robert Cray, the Long Ryders, Dream Syndicate and R.E.M. at the International in Manchester. It was fantastic. In the midst of all of this we decided to release a new single. A song I had written over the summer which we'd been playing live frequently to great reaction was chosen as our latest stab at the big time. 'When It All Comes Down' was very much in the vein of 'Hollow Horse', an air-punching anthem to freedom, adventure and romance (a style which was becoming my trademark).

The recording would be made at Ridge Farm residential studios near Horsham, and Pat Moran would be the producer. Pat had cut his teeth as an in-house engineer at Rockfield, had had success with Robert Plant amongst others, and seemed a fair choice.

Unfortunately he had a funny, high-pitched way of talking which would cause much unintentional giggling amongst us at very inappropriate moments during the making of the record.

The fact that we were bombed on Lebanese hash, speed and scrumpy only made it worse. We got the job done (just) and the single was issued in October backed with 'Let's Go Down To The River' and John Lennon's 'Cold Turkey'. We appeared on the long running British live music show *The Old Grey Whistle Test* to promote it.

Once again airplay was scarce and the bugger missed the charts by a mile. 1985 ended without any chart action for us, but in the space of a year we had established ourselves as a group with the potential to rise above their initial casting as a one hit wonder. We had much to offer yet, and a small but dedicated area of the populace continued to watch us with great interest God bless 'em.

Every few months the record company would force us to do a couple of weeks in Europe.

We were never popular in the places that you fancy going to, warm places like Spain or Italy or Portugal: we'd always groan when the international office would tell us we were picking up lots of play in Belgium or Ice-age Germany (ungrateful little shits that we were).

One time we had to hang around a TV studio in Stockholm all day when we just wanted to be on the town, drinking and smoking weed. We got so bored we all swapped instruments for the multiple camera run-throughs and the eventual miming to playback (me on drums, Chris S on bass and Chris L on guitar and vocal, fulfilling his dream as front-man. I still dream of this clip turning up on the Internet).

Before we did our bit, we had to stand, instruments ready, while the show's host grilled some old professor in Swedish for what seemed like a fucking full term. As he banged on endlessly, I just stared at the monitor and dreamed of all the nubile young Swedish crumpet I was missing by being here.

Chris S tapped me on the shoulder and whispered in my ear, yanking me back to reality.

"He's talking about the album."

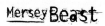

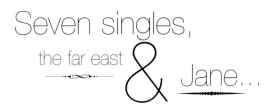

CHAPTER EIGHTEEN

Seven singles,
the far east & Jane...

We'd met Ian Broudie very briefly once before at the Columbia Hotel.

I bumped into him again in Macmillan's in January 1986. He was already a Liverpool legend.

Ian had originally been a member of Big In Japan, one of Liverpool's first punk/new wave acts.

A band comprised of a number of individuals who would all have a proper shot at fame much later on.

Bill Drummond would later become manager of the Teardrop Explodes and Echo And The Bunnymen, and would eventually score huge success with the KLF. Budgie would go on to be the drummer in Siouxsie And The Banshees. Holly Johnson would end up leading Frankie Goes To Hollywood.

Ian Broudie would later form the Original Mirrors, and then enter the production arena with Echo And The Bunnymen's classic second single 'Rescue'.

He formed a duo with Paul Simpson ex-of the Wild Swans (it didn't seem like there were a thousand bands in Liverpool in those days - there actually was) and they called themselves Care - having a near-miss with a great track called 'Flaming Sword'.

He then went on to have many hits with the Lightning Seeds.

Ian was a singular talent, was a great scholar of music even at this stage and I got into it with him about where he saw the Icicle Works going next.

Myself, the band and management were very excited about doing something with Ian - as were Beggar's.

I started writing with a new zest. A deal was struck for him to produce our next record, and time was booked at Amazon studios in Kirkby for the spring.

As a stop gap between a new album - which might not see the light of day for a good while - and our last release, Beggar's came up with a great idea.

They would release a deluxe package mini-album comprised of all of our singles up to that point for a knockdown, introductory price. The selection would also include 'Rapids' which had only been released as a promo at that point. Steve Hardstaff who had designed all of our sleeves thus far would come up with a great design that would be (hopefully) hard to resist for floating voters and confirmed fans alike.

This item was released with the title *Seven Singles Deep* to great acclaim and did a great deal of good for us, selling more than anything since the first album.

We were offered our first tour of Japan. We started recording the album and then called a brief halt as we headed east on Russian airline Aeroflot. The reason we chose this company to fly with was purely financial. They flew over Russian airspace therefore the journey was a few hours shorter, and therefore cheaper.

It was a fuckin' nightmare. The airplane had one aisle and was decorated with piss-yellow, peeling wallpaper. It stank of disinfectant-as-an-odour-mask, there was zero in-flight entertainment, all you could buy was cheap vodka (thank God), doorstep sandwiches with tough meat in them, and carved traditional dolls from the Motherland. All the stewardesses had moustaches. There was a two hour lay-over in Moscow airport where we were shunted around by armed soldiers.

I never got to see much of Moscow but I had a great shit there. It looked like Kirkby Industrial Estate from the air.

Thank you, comrades.

This hell eventually came to an end after what seemed like a month and we landed in Tokyo.

We all immediately fell in love with Japan as it seemed to house the most ancient world - and the future one - all in one place. If you've ever wanted to pretend you were in Ridley Scott's *Blade Runner*, get yourself over there as soon as you can.

There were little Japanese schoolgirls following us around everywhere we went who seemed intent on showering us with gifts.

We thought we'd suddenly made it and would be the next Beatles but quickly learnt that this was standard treatment for all visiting acts - which dispelled the fun only slightly.

We played great shows in Tokyo, Nagoya and Osaka, despite crippling jet-lag which hits you at showtime and takes about a week to get used to. We visited the old town of Kyoto. It was cherry blossom time and it was beautiful. I felt funny trying to pull any of the kids following us around and I ended up shacking up with our accommodating lady tour manager 'Daphne' for the duration. Daphne was not her real name, which had proven hard for previous western rockers to pronounce.

I had it made.

Doing gigs in Japan is very different to playing anywhere else. People come straight from work so stage time is usually around six-thirty.

If you're playing in a club you will find it's probably on the eighth floor of a shopping mall, squeezed between a clothes store and a restaurant. We played in a large theatre in Tokyo and all the sound crew wore white lab coats. Very odd. The audience will usually be utterly silent when you walk on, clap enthusiastically at the end of every song and then stop quickly,

but be wildly enthusiastic at the very end. The Beatles discovered this when they played there in 1966.

They were so used to audiences screaming throughout their show that they'd given up trying to play well as they couldn't hear themselves.

When they played at Budokan they sounded out of tune and sloppy and you could clearly hear every note. They freaked out.

It takes some getting used to. The only real problem in Japan was that we couldn't get any drugs.

Anywhere.

It's a little easier now but back in those days there was a zero-tolerance of any such things (look what they did to Paul McCartney). The day before we came home was a Sunday where they have a million tribute bands playing in the big park in Tokyo.

It's a weird sight to see to be sure - every band you can think of being impersonated by orientals - fantastic!

It was also our day off. Trouble ahead.

After much complaining on everyone's part (except Chris Layhe) we were able to get a hold of an illegal substance. There was no chance of any smoke, coke or speed, so we had to settle for some microdot acid.

You couldn't even see the bloody thing, and I was convinced it would probably get stuck in a cavity. We hit the streets in the afternoon sunshine and waited for the magic to happen. We walked around market stalls buying cool sixties-themed clobber, drinking Sapporo beer (which contained a magic ingredient - exclusive to Japan - some form of amphetamine which was removed when sold to the west, which gave you a little more than a beer-buzz), and watching Japanese versions of the Who, Doors, Jam, Beatles etc.

Just when we'd given up on a nice, trippy high to go with our drinks, the acid turned up with its mates. We were all out of our trees, and laughed at...well just about anything really.

Ringo in Japanese means apple, and everywhere we looked there were posters of him selling all kinds of stuff, including apples. He was everywhere, looking at us tripping. It killed us. It was like he was guiding us around and knew exactly what we were up to.

We ended up having a beer with some Hell's Angels guys who seemed incredibly friendly and amused by us. I even asked one of them for a go on his bike. Fortunately I was denied. One of them gave Mick Winder his hat (which he then wore for about two years). I was talking to one of the angels for about an hour - without either of us having a clue what each other was saying.

Tokyo is definitely one of the weirdest places on earth to take a trip and I recommend it heartily.

Just don't get fuckin' caught with any on you - you'll never come home again.

Pedestrians are very obedient in Japan and stop at every red light. When it's OK to cross the road there is a green light accompanied by the recorded sound of exotic birdsong which naturally suddenly seemed hilarious.

Mick Winder said he felt amazing and declared:

"Gimme a mountain to climb!"

We guffawed accordingly.

"Give us a fuckin' toilet first like..."

We ended up where every western visiting artist ends up in Tokyo, the Lexington Queen in Roppongi.

Full of models and rock/movie stars, good music and a five a.m. license to boot.

We tried to have our fill but it was difficult, the state we were in. Apart from the acid, we'd been drinking all day, and of course eating was out of the question.

We'd already been thrown out of one bar for acting too weird. I went to the toilet in the club and found a cubicle which had mirrors on the walls, ceiling and floor. I saw a thousand reflections of myself.

It took me half an hour to get out of there by which time I was the most confused I'd ever been.

There were loads of birds in there but chatting to any of them was nigh on impossible as I was having trouble passing myself off as human by this point. I don't know how I looked but I felt like a yeti. I had long hair and a thick beard at the time and was convinced my head had turned into a large ball of wool.

I was trying to drink more to come down off the spike but I kept missing my mouth and pouring the beer all over my shirt. We somehow managed to get through the evening without getting locked up and just about made it to the hotel, where we studied our respective ceilings all night. I watched the Argyle and Sutherland Highlanders playing babies instead of bagpipes on mine for about six hours.

We flew home the next day - after nearly missing the plane - still giggling as about fifty schoolgirls waved us off, showering us with yet more gifts and making us promise to return soon. It would unfortunately be the only time the Icicle Works would ever play in Japan.

As soon as we got back we continued recording the album which was going in a slightly different direction than anything we'd done before. We were desperate to get the hits rolling again which meant giving the tracks any help we thought they needed to sound chartbound, irrespective of whether the treatments fitted into anything we perceived to be an Icicle Works sound.

All bets were off. We wanted success and I, for one, was prepared to do almost anything in order to make it happen. We figured we'd probably get dropped if this didn't come off.

I was now properly in love with Karen and had actually at last decided to stop shagging around all the time just for the sake of it, such was my deep affection for her (I still fell off the wagon occasionally of course - but none of it ever meant anything your honour - sex without love is simply a physical release approximately ten notches above masturbation - sex - with love - is off the scale, but you knew that dear reader. It is, of course, very difficult to make your partner understand random infidelity, especially if they happen to be me). It was now common knowledge at Beggar's that we were an item and it caused a few problems.

Michelle, my - are we, aren't we? - L.A. girlfriend, chose this time to come and pay me a visit for a couple of weeks, having no idea that I was involved elsewhere.

This led to a few sticky moments but I came clean and told her the situation and managed not to cause a scene. This was pretty much the end for me and Michelle and she took it well. We were hardly boyfriend and girfriend over a distance of six thousand miles anyway.

No one got hurt.

Much.

I'd been hanging around with a lovely looking girl called Jane (platonically) who was a student at Liverpool University and used to work behind the bar at Macmillan's, when I realised she'd been getting intimate with a couple of my mates - and they'd been keeping it quiet. I found this more amusing than annoying and decided to pen a little ditty in order to expose them all without my having to say anything verbally. 'Understanding Jane' was the final song written for the forthcoming album and shocked us all by being the one that everybody thought should be a single.

I only wrote it because we needed a fast track for side two. A throwaway in my opinion - everybody loved it. Jeez. It came out backed with a comedy travelogue I'd written in a Tom Waits style - 'I Never Saw My Hometown 'Til I Went Around The World' - and got loads of airplay - Lemmy of Motorhead declared it 'Brilliant!' on Radio One's Roundtable. The video shot on Formby Beach got some exposure too!

But...

It entered the chart in July of that year and hung around for about three weeks, peaking at number fifty-two.

Ho hum.

Business as usual.

CHAPTER NINETEEN

We NEED a hit! ★

We had the album in the can.

It was now two years since we'd graced the charts.

As I write this, bands are being dropped if their first album doesn't sell a million. Our record company still believed in us enough to keep trying. It was easier in those days!

We sporadically made excursions to Europe where we did OK in certain areas, but nothing to write home about (we didn't like touring the continent as the rooms were really small and we couldn't afford to stay in hotels with swimming pools).

America had completely forsaken us it seemed, although there was still enough interest that we could probably have one more shot if we gave someone the right record. 'Understanding Jane' had been very well received but still the top forty eluded us.

We had a very healthy fanbase at home but one had to sell a lot more singles to chart in the eighties than you do now. Chins were stroked and heads were scratched.

Which was the best way to move forward?

Reluctant to release yet another album without a hit single to pave the way, Beggar's came up with an idea.

They would issue another single - 'Who Do You Want For Your Love?' A catchy, country-flavoured tune with the attendant McNabb big chorus, with a trick attached.

The plan was this - our last single stalled just outside the top fifty even with good airplay.

So, we would shrink wrap the new 7" single with a free bonus cassette containing rarities, and most enticingly of all, an individual lottery number which would be entered into a draw at a later date, and the winning ticket would secure a private Icicle Works concert in the living room of the lucky winner.

It was not the first time such a plan had been hatched, but it could be the factor that achieved more sales, and therefore, hopefully, propel us into that oh-so-near-yet-oh-so-far bastard singles chart, thus paving the way for a big album.

The single was issued in September '86 featuring live versions of 'Understanding Jane', and covers of the Doors' 'Roadhouse Blues' and The Clash's 'Should I Stay Or Should I Go' - from our recent sold-out Kentish Town And Country Club show as B sides, and sales were fast.

We did a short tour to promote it, and did the *Wide Awake Club* on ITV with Timmy Mallet (kids TV stalwart with a big audience) and waited like presidential candidates for the votes to roll in.

We were promised a chart placing by the record company and pluggers alike.

The fuckin' thing came in just outside the top fifty.

Arrrrrrrgh!!!

Apparently, it sold loads more than the last attempt, but the packaging which housed the free cassette obscured the bar code on many copies - which confused the shops who couldn't get the machines to read the sale.

We started to think we were jinxed.

We still had to go and play in someone's fuckin' living room though didn't we?!

We were asked to perform at an event called *Soap Aid* at St. Helens' rugby ground.

Marillion would headline and the rest of the day would feature soap stars from all the current favourite shows appearing throughout and entertaining the (hopefully large) crowd.

There was a weird vibe in the air all day.

The turnout was probably about sixty percent of what was hoped for. Everything was running hopelessly late and at one stage there were rumblings that the bill would be slashed somewhere for fear the event was going to run too late and get into heavy overtime charges from the ground.

Needless to say, it fell on us as being expendable and at some point it was intimated we would be playing for a lot shorter than our allotted time.

As the day dragged on (and it did drag - how many soap stars can you listen to cracking jokes about their respective programmes and singing a couple of numbers from their old night club routine?) things got quite tense and Tony Barwood had to argue our case for performing - at all - to the organisers.

We went on much later than planned and sped through a half hour set. After the show ended there was a private party at a nearby club for all the artists.

I turned up to find hard faced northern clipboard Nazis refusing to let anyone in due to an overstuffed bar.

On the door to said bash was a sign saying "Marillion, the Icicle Works and actors only."

I started arguing with one guy guarding the fort and he was having none of it.

There were about twenty people pushed up against this hallowed portal trying to gain entry as the bouncers let one or two people in at an agonisingly slow rate. I was becoming inflamed.

As a couple of people exited I made a push for it and ducked under the bouncer's arm and walked into the club.

The next thing I knew I was seeing stars. One guy grabbed me and threw me down a flight of stairs. I got quite badly beaten and made the front page of the Liverpool Echo sporting

139

a fabulous shiner (before the photographer arrived I got Karen to administer copious amounts of eye shadow to the bruise to make my injury appear worse).

There were pieces on the incident in all of the red-top dailies and it even got on the local TV news. It was the most press I ever had. I later pressed charges but was advised to drop them by the brass of St. Helen's police on the day of trial as the guy who had hit me was apparently mob connected, and stood a chance of losing his security business, and they were worried about my safety.

I was pissed off but didn't need that kind of threat over my shoulder. I couldn't afford to lose any fingers.

Chris S and Jo were well irked with me for a while as they had to finger the guy in an identity parade, which I was too lazy to travel up from London to help them with.

I needed a bloody holiday.

Me and Geoff Muir took off on a driving trip across the southern states of America.

We drove from Orlando, Florida, to Los Angeles over the space of about two weeks, staying in motels as we acted out our *On The Road* fantasy. We hit all points of interest (and quite a few of none). We drove along the Gulf Coast and I noted down all the names of the towns we passed through, or simply passed.

I later made up a poem, then a song, from the list:

> *'Ten Thousand Island, Cape Romano, Cape Sable,*
> *East Naples, up to Sanibel, Charlotte Harbor, Punta*
> *Gorda, up to Sarasota and Manatee,*
> *Tampa Bay, Clearwater, Dade City, Brookville, Crystal*
> *Bay...*
> *Waccasassa Bay, Dead Man Ray, up through Taylor,*
> *Appalachia Bay,*
> *Franklyn, Calhoun, Panama City, straight through*

Okaloosa,
into Santa Rosa, Pensecola, memories of Tampa Bay...
Gulfport, Harrison, New Orleans, Lake Pontchartrain,
Saint Charles, Thibodeaux,
Vermillion, Cameron, old Lake Charles where Levon's
gonna go! Galverston, Matagorda Bay, Rockport, Corpus
Christie, hey!'

It would eventually be titled 'Gulf Coast Rockin'' and see the light of day on *The Gentleman Adventurer* in 2002.

We met up with Geoff's friends John Leonard and Nick Barraclough in a town called Mamou in Louisiana. John and Nick both worked for the BBC and were doing a documentary on Cajun music.

We went to a small Cajun music festival where everybody ran around the site chasing a huge pig, killing it, then roasting it, and ultimately eating it, all to the sound of twanging banjoes.

We headed up to Nashville for a few days where we watched the great Bill Monroe (supreme bluegrass picker, author of 'Blue Moon Of Kentucky') play in a tacky theme-park type venue to a half-full room of tourists.

We also met the legendary John D. Loudermilk (songwriter - most notably of the classic 'Tobacco Road') who patted his thirty-eight in its shoulder holster and told me to get one if I planned on staying in Nashville for a few days.

"Gives ya a little edge." He told me.

Geoff and I visited the Grand Canyon which nearly proved a terminal event for this writer.

We set off down a path which we were told provided spectacular views. There were signs everywhere warning travellers to have enough water with them at all times. We had beer.

The path took us gently down the side of a canyon at a comfortable descent. We sipped merrily at our brews and took in the view. After about half an hour of this the booze ran out and we'd only shaved a fraction off the journey down. We decided to turn back, ever so slightly pissed. As soon as I turned around and started walking slowly back up the trail I knew I was in trouble. The heat was intense and every step I took devoured my energy and dried my throat. After twenty yards I had to rest. Geoff had realised we had a problem and barrelled ahead of me, realising one of us had to get to the top if only to alert the rescue team. I sat there sweating and started to panic. It was half an hour coming down.

At this rate of ascent it was going to take me hours to get back to the top. I took a breath of hot, dry air and stood up again. I must've looked a fuckin' fright in my comedy Hawaiian shirt, little shorts and trainers with white socks (I eventually, reluctantly, bought a pair of trainers. The boots just looked too ridiculous with shorts for even me to tolerate. I'd even gone through a period recently of wearing spurs. This latest addition to my wardrobe was short lived however after one incident where I couldn't hit the brake in my Manta and nearly went into the back of a bus at an intersection).

Geoff was now long gone - the bastard - and I sat down again after just ten yards now, wondering how I would be remembered. At least I had an album in the can.

This is what the bastards had been waiting for! Nothing like an untimely death to get the records flying over the counter. I put my head in my hands and considered sobbing, but realised I couldn't afford to lose any more fluid.

I was so dry that I was having trouble getting oxygen past my parched throat and into my lungs. I stood up and managed only five yards this time before I sat down again, completely drained of energy or will.

If I stay here I'm going to start hallucinating and then...

How far has Geoff got?

Will he make it to the top? What if he's in the same state as me further up? Shit. It was starting to go dark. I forced myself to my feet again. I turned into the grade and took one agonising step after another. What a fuckin' dickhead I was. I'd seen all the warning signs but naturally I thought they only applied to lesser mortals than me. I was superhuman.

Super-fuckin'-stupid more like.

Idiot!

I looked above me for vultures.

No sign yet. I must be good for a while.

I sat down again. I simply couldn't walk anymore.

After about five minutes I heard a noise above me. I looked up and saw an old Mexican geezer ambling down the path riding a weary donkey. He looked at me and started laughing. I tried to laugh too but it emerged as a cough.

"Are you alright amigo?" he said through pre-requisite missing teeth.

"No, not really," I replied.

"Here, take this."

He passed me a large bottle of water which I began draining feverishly.

"Don't drink it all amigo, save some for your journey!"

"Can I have it? I don't have any money on me."

"Take it! Take it! You need it more than I."

I thanked him as he passed me by.

"Thanks a lot! You've saved my life!"

And he had. I could hear him laughing as he rode out of view. It was like something from a movie. One which I didn't wish to be in.

The water enabled me to overcome the ale/heat-induced dehydration and I got to the top in about an hour. When I got there Geoff was standing sucking a cold beer at the nearby refreshment area with a shit-eating grin plastered across his face.

"Ah was gonna give it another twenty minutes then call

Thunderbirds." He chortled.

"Fuck off cunt... and get me a fuckin' beer!" I rendered as the sun dipped below the horizon.

This overseas activity seemed to give ground to a previously unreleased intense declaration of emotion from Karen - who somehow decided in my absence that she loved me beyond all reason, and when I returned she called me up at home.

"Come down here and live with me. I want to be with you all the time."

Wow. I loved her like no other and decided it was time to make the move. Chris Sharrock was living with Jo by this time and Chris Layhe was nearing the same point with Linda.

We were growing up,

Stage one was over. I was twenty-five and felt like an adult for the first time in my life (Karen was only just nineteen). I told my mum and she cried a little - but agreed I had to try this new path.

I was going to go and live in that London - two-hundred plus long miles away.

Karen started looking for places in the southwest London area. She wanted to be near the office in Wandsworth, and I didn't really care where it was as long as we were together. I was blissfully happy and a little scared at the same time. I was going to leave all of my mates and social circle, which was positively thriving at the time.

How would it be? My extra-curricular activities would have to cease.

I had a few friends down south but it still seemed like I was leaving the closest ones. It would be a big change for me.

We chose a winner for the play-in-your-living-room competition in Lytham-St-Annes, near Blackpool.

Not too far away, yet not too near - so as to make it look like they were chosen at random.

They weren't. Me and Chris S took a load of magic

Above: Poster outside gig in Tokyo - note early show times.

Left: Ian adopts a random local. Tokyo 1985.

JAPAN '85

Top: Hollywood Bowl.

Above: Just doin' my bit for charity with the then Liverpool team - we raised over five grand for Marie Curie.

Top: Fun on a day
off in Tokyo.

Above: I'm ready
for my massage.

Right: Me and
Michelle LAX 1984

On stage mid-eighties.

Above: Holidaying in New Orleans with Geoff Muir (far-left) John Leonard (left) and Nick Barraclough (far-right)

Left: First American trip.

Below: Lake Tahoe 1988

Bottom: Me and Karen - late eighties.

Above: Abortive
second Icicle Works
line-up 1990.

Left: Phoenix
festival 1993.

mushrooms and caused plenty of havoc. A great time was had by all and at the end of the night Mick Winder and I threw a messed up drummer into his bass drum flightcase, after he'd tried to pull the competition winner's girlfriend, and we headed home.

I don't know how he didn't suffocate.

We still didn't have a hit.

CHAPTER TWENTY

London
1987

Most people tend to head to the capital city as a career move.

I didn't need to do that.

There was talk of me being able to put my face around a little more in front of the powers that be and perhaps conjure up a little more interest, but ostensibly I headed south to be with the lady I loved.

We viewed several potential flats and eventually we both decided we liked a place in Tooting Bec Gardens, just off of Streatham High St.

This wasn't the most attractive setting in London - due to our modest budget, but the nearby common looked pretty, and there was a tube station situated conveniently at the end of Trinity Road (Tooting Bec Station as it happens, the one outside which actor Robert Lindsay - playing the part of seventies revolutionary 'Wolfie' Smith - would raise his arm and cry "Power to the people!" at the start of every episode of much-loved sitcom Citizen Smith).

Karen could drive to work in twenty minutes, and if she was happy, then I'd be happy too - in theory.

We paid fifty-seven thousand pounds for our two-bedroom place and moved in that March.

It was weird.

We danced around each other a little at first as we got the feel

of lovers co-habiting. When you first move in with your partner you tend to spend a lot of time in bed or in the bath together.

We were no different.

The move happened during a time of brief cessation in Icicle Works activity - much needed as we'd been incredibly busy.

A new E.P. - 'Up here In The North of England' - and single, 'Evangeline' - had preceded our new Ian Broudie-produced record *If You Want To Defeat Your Enemy Sing His Song*.

The E.P. and single had done their usual fifty-something chart position, but the album did really well, hitting number twenty-seven - our best placing for years.

We went on *The Tube* again to promote it, headlining this time.

The Tube was due to be axed and there was a feeling of impending doom on the set.

We were scheduled to perform 'Up Here...' and 'Evangeline' and we came in right on time at the camera run-through, but when the show went out Chris S decided to play the songs a lot faster.

This meant we finished our slot about two minutes early and the producers were faced with an empty stage and an audience unsure of what to do. We could've gone back on and destroyed them with 'Understanding Jane' but the stage manager was nowhere to be seen, such was the lethargy around the studio.

Channel Four filled the dead time with some footage of finger puppets.

We were properly pissed off.

We went to the States to do some promo shows for the album which would now be released on R.C.A. through Beggar's Banquet's new distribution deal in the U.S. - playing a couple of shows in Los Angeles, and a couple more further north in California - which I have almost no recollection of as the coke and pot situation was in full effect by this point.

The drugs were so strong that none of us (except Chris Layhe) knew where we were at any given time. I was loaded from the moment I got out of bed to the moment I collapsed. Drugs in America are loads stronger than the ones in Blighty.

The coke will freeze your face for half an hour and make you absolutely elated then twitchy and a bit paranoid as you start coming down.

Then you have another bump and you're off again. This carries on for as long as you want but the effect will last shorter every time.

The weed appears to do nothing for the first ten minutes and then you go to the Moon - establish base camp, and take up permanent residence there.

Quite why young men in bands behave like this with so much at stake is fairly easy to explain.

You are travelling the world in a pop group. You have money. You have girls.

You have fame.

You have respect.

You're high on life and want to get even higher on drugs just to make the experience completely orgasmic.

And you're rather bored between shows. Also, you can put your mind and body through all kinds of torture when you're in your twenties without really hurting yourself.

It's all free when you're young. The gigs were sloppy.

It was incredibly unprofessional of us to behave like this, and put the nail in the coffin for us for good in America (I should stress that we cannot completely shoulder the blame - we were unlucky with record companies, who never really invested in us as much as they could have, but... this kind of behaviour did not help at all).

We stumbled along the west coast for a bit and then flew east for a gig at CBGB's in New York City.

This was probably the worst show I've ever been involved with in my career.

Half an hour before showtime I needed to drop anchor and was told there was no dressing room or artists' toilets so I'd have to use the regular unisex 'john' with everybody else.

This wouldn't have been so bad had I not needed a crap and there were no doors on the cubicles.

And so it was that I had to evacuate myself in front of people who had just paid to see me play music and nothing more. I was fuming at this indignity and made sure I made the audience as miserable as I was during the shorter-than-usual drugged up set.

There were many media folk at this gig and most of them left whistling the death march.

I've only behaved like a real idiot at shows a few times, one of the worst which springs to mind was in Canada a couple of years previously when I smashed a cup into some loud mouthed jock's head backstage when he had the temerity to call me a one-hit wonder, on the occasion of my birthday.

I knocked him out - cold - and there was talk of an assault charge which mercifully hadn't appeared by the time we fled the country.

After the disastrous U.S. trip we embarked on the most successful U.K. tour of our career, selling out everywhere, making plenty of dough on the back of a popular album. This was the peak, although we didn't know it yet, and the slide had begun.

My time off was spent alone in London by day, as Karen got up and went to work each morning leaving me at home without anything to do (decorating the flat wasn't an option).

Getting smashed seemed like the only sensible course of action. I had a couple of friends who lived nearby in Balham (Howie Nicol - sound recordist and son of one time Beatle stand-in drummer Jimmy Nicol, and Geoff Horne - Icicle Works monitor engineer) and a couple of times a week I'd go around to their place in the afternoon and get fucked up beyond belief on white tequila slammers and Cocaine toots.

We actually did this a few times and then went swimming.

Madness.

One morning they woke me up and invited me round to the flat to do a Cocaine experiment.

There were six lines on top of the piano with a piece of card at the end of each one labelling them A,B,C,D,E and F. I had to tell them which was the best.

By the time I got to F, I couldn't tell them apart so the experiment would be repeated.

By lunchtime we'd be on our fourth pint, talking in Klingon.

Karen would leave me with instructions about what needed doing for the flat that day and I would usually ignore/forget them - never previously having to do anything for myself except write a catchy tune once in a while.

Chris Sharrock and Jo went to the Seychelles for a holiday.

When they came back he called me up and told me they'd got married. I was devastated.

Chris and I had grown up together and the idea that he'd do such a huge thing without me being involved in any capacity upset me beyond the telling.

This was clearly the work of his new wife - who, from my perspective, was taking him away from me a little bit at a time. It wouldn't be too long before she'd succeed in doing this permanently.

I saw a video of the wedding many years later when I was round at his mum's house with Pat (Glenys and Pat have stayed friends until this day) and Chris looked odd.

Scared even - or was that just my imagination?

I knew Chris as well as anyone and I reckon I read the situation well. He was sweating profusely throughout. Well, could've been the heat I guess.

Within months Jo would be pregnant with their first child, a boy, Jay.

After a while I became really bored and really homesick.

Karen and I would argue a lot, usually with regards to my failure to function as a house-husband.

I would trudge along Streatham High Street in a mild marijuana fug, hands in pockets, trying to stay out of trouble, usually eating too much to stave off boredom.

I put on weight. I hung around all the places I was supposed to in London and took loads of drugs with my alleged peers and media types.

It was horrible.

London is a very cold place if it doesn't love you.

Everybody scrambling over each other to make a buck. You don't live there, you exist.

New York has good energy, London has bad energy. It's a place for the young and ambitious or the very wealthy.

If you're neither - it's hard to fit in. I was young, but I wasn't particularly ambitious, I just wanted to be with my friends in the place I loved, which was Liverpool.

London is also far too susceptible to invasion by the Cybermen. Twice in the last two series' of *Doctor Who* to be precise! They even brought the Daleks the second time!

I will call Liverpool every bad name under the sun - but it's so much a part of me I can never seem to leave it for long.

I had a season ticket for home games and would drive up every other weekend to break up the monotony.

True love wasn't working out the way I planned.

As well as messing up my own mind with drugs I had now brought Karen down to my level (she was doing a lot of speed by her own accord it should be noted - offered to her on a regular basis by a lovable motormouth who worked in A&R.

Many evenings, after dinner, Karen and I would get the white powder out and have a toot or two and talk each other to death.

Eventually she would have to go to sleep due to work the next day and I'd sit there on my own for hours.

When I thought she was asleep I'd climb in next to her and try to do the same.

I loved her, but I knew it wouldn't last.

We were great at partying and fucking but the daily grind only seemed to emphasise our differences.

During one such shitty period I invited BBC Radio One DJ Mike Read around to the flat to discuss a project he wanted me to get involved with (Mike was a great champion of the band - even suffering from red top daily notoriety when a spurned lover told the press he could only perform sexually whilst listening to The Icicle Works - a major embarrassment for all).

The evening ended with Karen making Brandy Alexanders for everyone and then pouring the one she'd prepared for me over my head in the middle of a serious discussion.

I was so ripped that I carried on as if nothing had happened, cream dripping all over the carpet (for the record: the project Mike and I worked on was an album of Sir John Betjeman's poems put to music written by Mike. I offered a reading of 'Slough'.)

I'd first seen Neil Young play at the N.E.C. In Birmingham on the *Trans* tour in 1982.

It wasn't quite what I expected, he was running around the stage with Nils Lofgren, wearing a headmic and sunglasses singing through a vocoder, but it was still fantastic.

The first record I ever heard of his was his cover of Ian Tyson's 'Four Strong Winds'. It was like listening to a movie.

I fell in love with his music from that point on and owned everything he did.

We had the same agent by this point - I.T.B. - and we got tickets to the show he was doing, again at the N.E.C.

Afterwards we were escorted backstage to meet him and he was very friendly.

He was playing with his band Crazy Horse but they seemed aloof and kept out of the way.

We hung out for about twenty minutes and then split. I was thrilled.

I drove back to London in a daze and woke Karen up as soon as I got home to tell her the exciting news. She told me to be quiet and let her sleep.

The only NY she liked was 'Like A Hurricane' because the Mission had covered it.

It became clear to me that I'd better get back in gear. I started writing songs for a new Icicle Works record.

I hardly ever saw the guys now and I felt like I was working alone.

I wrote 'Little Girl Lost' (about Karen), 'Blind', 'Starry Blue Eyed Wonder', 'High Time', 'Stood Before Saint Peter', and many others in that little spare bedroom while Karen was at work.

I didn't consult the band about the recording process and told the record company to book studio time.

We decided we'd do it in London (convenient for me, a drag for everyone else), and time was arranged at Townhouse three in Battersea - just around the corner, formerly known as Ramport - which the Who owned, and recorded some of their latter day oeuvre there.

I would produce for the first time - I'd learnt plenty of tricks over the years.

The chaps came down and we rattled through the sessions with ease. I was eating lots of 'blues' (uppers) and was feverishly excited throughout.

It sounded like the most exciting stuff we'd done for years to my fizzing ears and everyone seemed more than happy.

Round about this time we did two shows at the Astoria on Charing Cross Road.

The band were all staying at the Columbia and after the second gig we had a day off before heading to Portsmouth.

We all got together and took some microdot acid (by now a

favourite) and went to Camden Palace.

During that afternoon the lads had got together with 'legendary' Mancunian band The Fall (we shared the same label) for a game of football.

The Fall were/are a unique band.

Their model was this: Form a band who can't play, can't sing, can't write songs, look pretty shit. Record them badly so as to make the end product unlistenable.

Keep doing this for thirty years without change.

Brilliant!

The cult band's cult band. Lead 'singer' and only remaining original member Mark E. Smith is now regarded as some form of skewed poet laureate in certain quarters.

I respect him hugely for maintaining a career without ever selling records - as long as I don't have to listen to him. As Buddy Rich once remarked to Keith Moon after sitting behind him onstage for the entire duration of a Who concert in the mid-seventies; "Man, they're paying you to play like that? Keep playing!"

The Fall weren't much cop at footy however, and my boys thrashed them five-two.

I didn't play as I needed a day in bed (also I couldn't imagine being much use on the field in Cuban-heeled winkle-picker boots - which were surgically attached).

Everyone was in great spirits after the game and a lot of silliness ensued. Karen wanted some speed but we couldn't get any so I gave her some acid and told her it was speed anyway.

How kind of me. She was having a wonderful time until she realised she didn't know what the fuck was going on in her head, and then she started to panic when she thought the carpet was on fire.

She started freaking out so we went home and argued for about twelve hours.

Note: never have an argument with someone who's tripping

when you're tripping yourself - it's endless. Sometimes I still feel as though we're still in that room - shouting at each other - endlessly...endlessly.

After these couple of gigs I resumed work on the album. I went to Eel Pie in Twickenham and mixed the record with Mark Wallis who'd recently done some U2 stuff.

Pete Townshend owned the studio and I'd bump into him nearly every day which was a gas.

One day Eric Clapton called and I answered the phone and had to transfer him to Pete's office upstairs - a buzz.

The album was delivered in the summer and everybody went about doing their own thing for a couple of months.

Karen and I stumbled along and at some point she got fed up with me and went home to her parents in Bromley.

Strangely enough this seemed to work and I carried on living in the flat on my own and having quite a nice time.

We still spoke everyday and she'd even stay with me some nights. I suggested we sell the flat at the end of the year and she agreed. I thought this would mean the end for us but it didn't.

We just couldn't live together - that didn't mean we didn't still love each other.

In August we were booked to play at the Reading Festival.

We were scheduled for the Saturday evening and drove over there on the Friday.

I had terrible neuralgia in one side of my face and spent the journey rubbing coke on my gums to numb the pain.

The paracetamol just didn't cut it.

When we got there we were told that Spear Of Destiny (who were third on the bill) had to pull out, so we were now higher up in the pecking order.

We were due onstage at seven o'clock.

Wow. A big deal.

We all got up at the regulation musician's rising time - i.e lunchtime, and started on the cocktails.

It had fallen on me to arrange the drugs for band and crew as I lived in London and knew the dudes, man.

We didn't eat anything as we were too excited and just basically drank all day.

One of our merchandise girls was to turn up at the hotel at some point and drop the coke off, about six hundred quids' worth all told. This was in the days before everybody had cellphones, so I would be off calling her friends from the lobby every ten minutes trying to find out where the fuck she was.

'No snow, no show' was the war cry of the times. Oh dear.

The traffic was gridlocked to and from the festival site and nobody was goin' nowhere.

About five-ish we all piled into the transport and began what should have been a ten minute journey by sitting in traffic just outside the hotel.

We were moving at about ten feet per minute and everybody was starting to panic.

We were worried we'd be late getting to the gig and I was concerned that we weren't going to score before we went on. After about an hour of this bullshit I spotted Vicky stuck in traffic on the other side of the central reservation under the flyover we were both sitting under.

I climbed out, jumped over the fence and got in the car with her. I gave her the cash and she gave me the goods. I got out again, headed back to our stationary vehicle - cops everywhere - with enough drugs in my hand to do a five-year stretch.

We got to the gig ten minutes before we were due to play. I lined up several fat ones, spilling loads of the stuff onto my black jeans in the process, and all took part (except Chris Layhe*).

Mick Winder came up to me and said:

"Ian, they're throwing bottles of piss at every band...the last lot just walked off."

I told him not to worry and pushed past him, buzzing on the coke.

Chris Sharrock suddenly looked a little green at the side of the stage as we were being announced.

I gave him a hug and he assured me he was OK - if a little wired. No shit.

We hit the stage and rocked. I told them not to throw bottles as we were from Liverpool and took no shit off southern poofs.

It worked would you believe, and we settled in for the gig of our career.

At the end of 'Who Do You Want For Your Love?' I turned around and looked at Chris S.

He was now the colour of death and he did a cut-throat gesture to indicate to me that he wouldn't be able to play any longer.

We had done three songs.

Never panic.

You can't kill a squadron!

Chris Layhe looked at me in horror.

Despite the fact that I was pissed and wired to the tits I knew I could handle this.

Somehow I started playing 'Wild Mountain Thyme' and encouraged the great unwashed to join in.

Fuck me if they didn't and before you knew it we were at the biggest folk gig in the world.

We did a couple more in this mode and then Mick signalled me that Chris was feeling slightly better and would give it another shot.

He came back on to rapturous applause and we launched into 'Roadhouse Blues' - the perennial boogie tune that gets even dead people nodding along.

"Let it roll, baby roll! All night long!"

And we did.

We got through the rest of the show, finishing on

'Understanding Jane' and brought the house down.

The reviews the following week said we saved the day and were the best band on.

Just lucky, I guess.

*Perhaps I should call this book 'Except For Chris Layhe.'

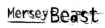

CHAPTER TWENTY ONE

Here comes Trouble

Karen and I put the flat up for sale.

It didn't take long before the offers started coming in.

We were still in the middle of the eighties property boom and it was a seller's market. The asking price was ninety grand. We'd only been in there ten months. For the first time since I'd been there I picked up a paintbrush and started to make the place look more attractive.

This was/is the only time I've ever been involved in any D.I.Y. activity.

In October Bob Dylan played at Wembley Arena and Chris S and Dave Green - our live keyboard player - came down for the show.

I also persuaded Karen to attend - I hadn't given up on her musical education yet. Karen drove us all up to Wembley and it was a great show. Bob was supported by Roger McGuinn of the Byrds who performed a solo set first, then joined Tom Petty and the Heartbreakers for a set of Byrds classics.

When that was over Tom Petty did a set, then there was an interval after which Bob took to the stage with Petty and his band.

Everybody was on stage again for the finale. Class. On the journey home the wind was picking up, and by the time we got back to Streatham a gale was blowing.

We started partying at the flat and outside the wind turned into a hurricane. The power went out and next morning when I opened the front door it looked like the apocalypse.

A genuine hurricane blew through the south-east that night, uprooting trees and flattening the landscape.

In November Beggar's released 'High Time' as a single.

Once again it got good airplay - and entered the lower regions of the chart.

We were all tired by now and nobody really cared anymore.

Chris S and L were happily on the nest with their respective women up north and I was once again up to my usual shenanigans.

Christmas came and went, we got shut of the flat and split the money. My reward for living in London for just shy of a year was fifteen grand clear profit.

As failed relationships go this was certainly one of my most lucrative.

So, once again we had a new album in the can with no hit single to preclude it.

I came home to Liverpool and we went in the studio ostensibly to record some B sides. We came up with a track called 'Kiss Off' which owed a great deal to the current favoured sound of Prince and INXS.

It was a sideways move which certain people in our orbit seemed to think might be the one to do it. We'd tried everything else - why not give it a shot? A dance mix was ordered (!) and the Icicle Works - now seemingly dying on the vine - would have yet another crack.

This time the disc came out - got zero airplay - was universally condemned (most notably by our fans) and bothered the chart little.

So I'm now back living at my mum's house from whence I started.

My London experiment had failed, although I had a few bob in my pocket. I had owned and sold two properties in two cities all within two years.

The band was now four long years down the road from a hit record, although we still had a large army of devotees built up from years of road work and good albums.

'Little Girl Lost' was earmarked as the next single and the new album, to be titled *Blind* was green-lit for a release soon after.

My friend Mark Jones - a DJ at Liverpool's Radio City - had introduced me to a proper superstar soccer player by the name of Craig Johnston.

Born in South Africa in 1960, Craig was brought up in Australia. He moved to the UK to play for Middlesbrough FC from 1975 to 1980, and then spent eight years as a midfielder at Liverpool, scoring a goal against Everton in the 1986 FA Cup final.

Craig turned out to be a big Icicle Works fan and we started hanging out together and having fun.

He even turned up on stage with us at a concert at Manchester Apollo. Top geezer.

Craig had become disaffected with his bit in life.

Seemingly growing bored with his job which he felt was growing stale, he started missing practice sessions and filled the gap by attending Icicle Works rehearsals instead.

He was keen to become a guitar player, and I went over to his house on the Wirral a couple of times and tried to show him how to write songs.

The local papers would be ruminating on where Craig had disappeared to, when usually he was crawling the bars of Liverpool with yours truly.

One Friday night Craig called me to enquire what he was doing at the weekend.

I told him I was unable to partake in the weekend's regulation debauchery as I had to fly to New York the following day for a week of promotional duties around the imminent release Stateside of *Blind* - the last Icicle Works LP to feature the original line-up, although we didn't know that then.

Craig suddenly becomes excited.

"Farkin' hell mate! I've got two first class tickets to New York that I can use anytime I want.

"They were given to me as a prize for being Player Of The Year last year! Why don't you fly over with me? I'm gonna call them in now!"

Craig couldn't get a seat until the Monday so I went over as planned on Saturday morning.

Fuck knows how the record company had me doing promo over a weekend - there were a few radio stations that wanted me to do some acoustic sessions live on-air on a number of shows that happened only on Saturdays and Sundays - and so it was.

There still was a spare ticket going courtesy of Craig so I persuaded him to give it to Mick Winder.

Mick was broke so I gave him five hundred quid spending money.

He flew first class with a legend and I went cattle alone.

On Monday afternoon I went over to meet Craig at the Chelsea Hotel (bereft of air conditioning in the sweltering Manhattan heat but pre-requisite to Craig's brief bohemian adventure).

I took my guitar over there with me as I was more than aware of the great art that this old, ghost-filled place located at 222 West 23rd Street had inspired (Thomas Wolfe wrote *Look Homeward Angel* here; William Burroughs wrote *Naked Lunch*; Arthur C. Clarke wrote *2001: A Space Odyssey*; Bob Dylan wrote 'Sad-Eyed Lady Of The Lowlands'; Leonard Cohen wrote 'Chelsea Hotel No. 2'. Andy Warhol filmed *Chelsea Girls*. Some of *9 1/2 Weeks* was shot here, as was the avant-porn movie *Stunt Girl*).

We walked the city for three days together in hothouse conditions.

Craig bought an expensive saxophone, presumably to wall-mount with a spotlight on it at his country pile back home, as he couldn't get a fuckin' note out of it to save his life.

This did not deter him however, as he spent every spare moment in his room walking around naked, producing horrendous honking sounds - which prevented me from producing a masterpiece for my generation.

George Michael was in town playing at Madison Square Garden and I knew some of the crew so we got the V.I.P. treatment for three nights. Everyone was in awe of Craig.

Benjy, George's sound technician, was our best mate for the duration and thrilled me with stories of his days doing Led Zeppelin's sound, which he used to do from the side of the stage!

Soon after we returned from NYC Craig hung up his Liverpool boots and returned to his native Australia.

I didn't hear from him again until April 1989, and it wasn't in the best of circumstances.

In fact it was in horrific circumstances.

Liverpool FC were involved in their seventeenth FA Cup semi-final, to be played against Nottingham Forest FC at Hills-borough, the home of Sheffield Wednesday FC. FA Cup semi-finals are traditionally played at neutral venues so as not to favour either club involved.

At the time, most stadiums had placed high steel fencing between the spectators and the pitch, in response to the hooliganism which had plagued the game for years. Hooliganism was not a factor at Hillsborough on the day of the disaster, but the fencing was later identified as one of the main factors leading to it.

The part of the stadium where the problem occurred was also a 'terrace' area. Terraces were frequently divided by further fencing into sections called pens to aid crowd control.

Hillsborough Stadium was segregated between the opposing fans as was customary at all large matches, the Liverpool supporters being assigned to the Leppings Lane End.

Kick-off was scheduled for 3pm but due to a variety of factors including traffic delays on the route to Sheffield from Liverpool many of the Liverpool supporters were later than usual arriving.

Between two and two forty-five pm there was a considerable build-up of fans in the small area outside the turnstiles at the Leppings Lane End, all eager to enter the stadium before the match started.

A bottleneck developed with more fans arriving than were able to enter the stadium.

With an estimated five thousand fans trying to get through the turnstiles and an increasingly dangerous situation, the police decided to open a set of exit gates which did not have turnstiles (Gate C). The resulting influx of hundreds, or possibly thousands, of fans through a narrow tunnel at the rear of the terrace and into the already overcrowded central two pens caused a crush at the front where people were pressed against the fencing. The people entering were unaware of the problems being experienced at the fence. Police or stewards would normally stand at the entrance to the tunnel if these central pens had reached capacity and would direct fans to the side pens, but on this occasion they didn't.

For some time the problem was not noticed by anybody other than those affected; it was not until six minutes after three that the referee, after being advised by the police, stopped the match, several minutes after fans had started climbing the fence.

By this time a small gate in the fencing had been opened and some fans escaped the crush by this route. Others climbed over the fencing, and further fans were pulled up by fellow fans into the West Stand above the Leppings Lane terrace.

Liverpool fans desperately tried to climb the fence onto the safety of the pitch. Even at this point there was still much confusion among the authorities at the match.

Senior police initially assumed that they were witnessing a pitch invasion and responded by sending in reinforcements to keep people off the pitch rather than helping the fans out of the crush.

Fans were packed so tightly in the pens that many died standing up. The pitch quickly started to fill with people sweating and gasping for breath, those with crush injuries, and with the bodies of the dead.

The police were slow to recognise the scale of the disaster and by the time that they had realised the size of the problem the police and ambulance services were overwhelmed.

Fans helped as best they could, many attempting CPR and some tearing down advertising hoardings to act as makeshift stretchers.

As these events happened some police officers were still being used to make a cordon on the halfway line of the pitch with the aim of preventing Liverpool supporters reaching the Nottingham Forest fans at the other end. Some fans attempted to break through the cordon to ferry injured supporters to ambulances.

The crush ultimately took the lives of ninety-six people, with seven hundred and sixty-six fans receiving injuries.

In the wake of this tragedy Craig returned from his home in Australia to comfort fans and help in any way he could.

In the week after the event he turned up unannounced at my mother's house on the Friday evening with two young female survivors. I was overcome with emotion as I sat there and listened to them talk about their experience. Craig had a request of me.

He wanted to return the following morning and write a song with me about the experiences of these two girls on that

dreadful day, and then drive straight to Anfield to perform the song at that afternoon's scheduled wake.

We drank tea until the early hours and then he took the girls home.

After he left I packed a bag, got into my car and headed to Wales for the weekend - leaving no contacting address - as I didn't know where I was going.

I couldn't handle it.

CHAPTER TWENTY TWO

The day the
Icicle Works
closed

Spring 1988.

A tour has been booked to promote the upcoming single and album. We're playing some serious venues this time around, Manchester Apollo, Hammersmith Odeon etc (seated theatres - which we are sceptical about, but once again the powers that be decree it's the way to go).

Mick Winder and I decide to head for California for a short break before the tour starts.

We go to L.A. where we meet up with a lot of our friends. The biggest surprise we have when we get there is that Echo And The Bunnymen are playing two shows at the Universal Amphitheatre.

I make a few calls and we're in.

The Bunnymen were at the arc of their success here, having released the pretty ropey but very visible 'Grey album' and buoyed up by their hit cover of 'People Are Strange' by The Doors which featured prominently in *The Lost Boys* - a cult hit about rock 'n' roll vampires featuring the young Kiefer Sutherland.

The shows were good if a little lacking in early Bunnymen magic - success - and other things - had taken something away from the earlier gigs I'd seen them do - but it was great to see fellow scousers wowing the yanks. Ray Manzarek of the Doors

joined them on stage for a couple of songs. Ian 'Mac' McCulloch was the greatest frontman/singer of his time and has been imitated many times over the years.

The Jim Morrison of the eighties, his star quality was unmatched in my opinion. I'd first met him in 1983, and his thick Norris Green accent belied his dark mystique. I would hang out with him many times over the years, and on this occasion, post-show he opted out of the usual L.A. limo routine to hop into my rental and hit the bars of West Hollywood.

We spent most of the evening trying to find a bar that served Bailey's - his favourite tipple at the time.

Ian was much quieter in those days than he became in later years, very shy, hiding under his fringe that night and muttering complaints about Bunnymen drummer Pete De Freites' huge beard.

I was hoping for a bit more excitement for those two nights we were on the town but Mac seemed reserved and insular.

There would be plenty of lunacy in the years to come however. Mac was/is a proper rock 'n' roll star and has always been able to party me into the ground.

He never slept. He'll never try and cancel the third world debt on you. We've been very close and sometimes very distant over the years, nearly coming to blows a couple of times.

When we were out on the lash I always thought of us as Frank and Dino.

I had to settle for Dino.

The Bunnymen would break up at the end of the year; only to return in 1997 with the best comeback hit ever - 'Nothing Lasts Forever'.

Mick and I headed up to San Francisco, turning right and heading to Petaluma to meet up with the Icicle Works U.S. guitar tech Scottie.

Scottie was the original architect of my deconstruction in America. A very handsome blond haired surfer type, he always had mind-blowing drugs about him.

This didn't prevent him from being a meticulous roadie however - certainly the only one I've employed who'd iron my guitar straps.

We got royally stoned as soon as we got to his house. When I could stay upright no longer, he showed me to my room which was painted black and housed a waterbed.

I spent a sleepless night sloshing around, paranoid, half-dreaming that some strange water beastie would soon rise from the depths and consume me.

The next day Scottie taught me how to ride a horse which I found terrifying. The fact that I was paranoid as fuck due to the fact that he gave me a line of super-charlie before I mounted up probably didn't help. I can't believe I was out in the country breathing God's good air and I was still bombed on drugs.

We came home (for a rest!) and then got into rehearsals for the tour. We were actually quite excited about the upcoming shows and it showed in our playing.

The set would run for two hours plus.

This would be the last time for this line-up of the band. The gigs were packed but not full. We had peaked it seemed.

Geoff Muir had persuaded me that Tony Barwood was no longer pulling his weight as manager and I had convinced the chaps that he was right. Or so I thought. Between them they harboured suspicions about Geoff's motives and it became an us and them situation.

Tony was victimised throughout this period. He'd done everything he could to keep the band on the right track - it wasn't his fault that we were stuck a notch below the level where everybody would be earning enough money to keep their girlfriends happy.

I was OK because I wrote the songs. The other two existed on a regular wage and occasional handouts from my publishing advances to show solidarity.

I could sense dissent and immediately handed them ten grand each out of my latest advance from Chappell Music to keep them sweet, which it did only briefly.

When women become involved in bands (or anything else for that matter) the dynamic changes dramatically. The guys onstage spend too much time worrying about the welfare of their ladies and the concentration wanders and the focus blurs. Bookings are arranged around other significant events in the couple calendar. I've been guilty of this myself a few times.

The difference between me and them was that the Icicle Works was my baby and I'd done a good job of making them feel like they were bit players in my story.

My move to London had widened the gap a lot. I've fallen in and out of love over the years but no female was ever as important to me as my career.

You are no longer an individual when you're in love, you're half of something instead of whole. Big decisions are made incorporating the opinion of your partner, who will usually have no experience of the music industry or the running of a rock band.

Chris Sharrock's wife used to work in a travel agency and now she was bending his ear about his job ("The Cult are looking for a drummer, why don't you play for them instead? They're much bigger!" was a comment that found its way back to me). I didn't like her very much and the feeling seemed mutual.

Partners of musicians I play with have a suspicion of me because I have the power to take their boys away from them for long periods of time.

My so-called 'hellraiser' reputation doesn't help.

Right after I sacked Tony (which was a heartbreaking thing for me to have to do after all we'd been through together), Geoff and I called a meeting to discuss the future.

Looking back on it now, I was a bully - I'd made up my mind (or had it made up for me) and that was it.

We sat down in the Everyman bistro on Hope Street in Liverpool and told the guys our strategy for the future.

Chris Layhe was guarded but willing to listen and still very enthusiastic about the band.

Chris Sharrock seemed edgy and nervous.

He listened, but I could tell what was coming. He'd been given his orders and was frightened to say what he had to say. The next day he called Geoff Muir and told him he was leaving the band.

When I eventually got some face time with him he showed me the blisters on his fingers, told me how hard he worked for me for little recompense, said he would have to stay at home and look after the baby while Jo went back to work, and how hard it all was now.

We were due to go to Australia soon to tour there for the first time, but he wasn't interested.

There was one more gig which we had to play which he would honour and then he would hang up his sticks.

Oh I cried (alone). The bastard was blowing me out. I wasn't important anymore. He didn't believe in me.

He didn't see the dream anymore. He was moving on. I went into a tailspin.

Everybody started taking sides. Mick Winder was devastated and would side with me for a while before HIS girlfriend made up his mind for him. I'd taken these cunts around the world with my talent for the past fuckin' four years and this was my thanks. The cash I'd just handed out from my own pocket in good faith was not returned.

We played our last show at a freshers ball in Oxford. We did it for the money. It was awful and I wouldn't speak to anyone or make eye contact. An embryonic Radiohead, then called 'On A Friday' opened for us.

And that was it.

Thoughts...

Why didn't the Icicle Works make it big? Not an easy question to answer. Bad timing, bad luck, some bad decisions. Bands who make it big tend to reflect the moment they're living in.

They have a style and a look of the people on the street. They illustrate the zeitgeist. We never did that.

We didn't look like part of the same band. We had no recognisable image. Three more different looking characters you'd be hard pressed to find in one group. No matter how we presented ourselves we never looked like one unified outfit.

Perhaps if I would've spent more time in the selection process this undoubted problem would've been avoided, but I wasn't a marketing man, I was a musician.

The most in tune with the times we ever got was on the first album, especially in America where we were seen as part of the new British invasion, the one time anyone thought they knew what we were.

I personally think we were more original than we got credit for, virtually up to the point where nobody knew where to file us.

We had our own sound. I don't think anyone else ever sounded like the 'Birds Fly' or 'Hollow Horse' forty-fives.

There are a lot of bands that sounded like R.E.M. or U2. How many sounded like us?

You've got to play and sing really well to pull that stuff off. It is, dare I say it - skilful.

It's complex in arrangement and performance. If you don't believe me, ask one of your favourite bands to try and play one of those tunes. We were closer to Rush than the Clash.

Whatever, the music is there to be heard forever, and that's really all that counts. When we're all gone you'll still be able to listen to the records or watch us on videotape in our prime.

That's a beautiful thing and - a kind of immortality.

There is also the possibility that we just weren't that good...

The decision is yours.

Bruce Springsteen released a record in 2007 called 'Girls In Their Summer Clothes', which sounded exactly like vintage Icicle Works '86/'87 - and it was his biggest hit in years.

I think that says something,

I'm just not fucking sure what.

"We'll be as we are, when all the fools who doubt us fade away..."

CHAPTER TWENTY THREE

Shit Creek

When a band breaks up it's like getting divorced from a dozen spouses.

There are band members, wives, girlfriends, managers, tour managers, roadies, drivers, merchandise people, additional musicians, publishers, record companies, drug dealers, fans, and also friends of the band who will all be forced into choosing a side.

Some will side with whoever is paying their next bill, others will look at the argument, try to intervene and cool things down a little.

I was very sad but quite passive. Well, at least until I found out that two weeks after Chris Sharrock had left the band due to fatigue, financial issues and diaper duty, he had joined the La's.

The La's had emerged from the Liverpool suburb of Huyton two years earlier. Effectively a retro act based on a hybrid of mid-period Beatles, Kinks, Stones etc, and fronted by scowling Georgie Fame lookalike Lee Mavers, they were the most curious of beasts. A revisionist group about eight years ahead of their time.

It wasn't until 'Britpop' came to the fore in the mid-nineties that they found their setting, consolidated by the timeless 'There She Goes'.

Mick Winder had introduced me to the band when I was living

in London. I loved them and immediately gave them a support slot on the Icicle Works' upcoming winter shows.

I dragged a stoned Chris S side stage to watch them at the Town And Country Club in Kentish Town. He liked them well enough I thought.

I didn't think he'd join them within a year.

This was treachery of the highest order in my book, and I became obsessive with rage for what lasted years.

I knew it wasn't a money issue as Chris was making about the same as he was working with me (probably less).

It felt exactly the same as being dumped by your bird for another.

I loved Chris and felt the deepest sense of betrayal I can ever remember feeling.

It didn't help that they were hot, were about to release 'There She Goes' - were loved by everyone and were all over the fuckin' radio and T.V. I was inconsolable.

My greatest ally in the Icicle Works break-up, Mick Winder, sided with me for about a year and then decided he was going to defect to the other side for reasons which were known to him alone.

I spent the long summer in a fug of alcohol/drug abuse (for a change) compounded by sleepless nights and a great deal of uncertainty/anxiety about the future. Beggar's released one more single, 'Here Comes Trouble' (oh the irony) which died an appropriate death. The *Blind* album when it was finally released, received glowing reviews and contented itself with a number forty chart position - for one week - by the skin of its teeth.

I didn't know what to do with myself. I had no direction. I felt like I'd failed in two of the most important areas - trying to make a success of my life through music, and finding a stable, lasting relationship with Karen in London.

Every night I would go out and come home drunk, usually dropping the bar staff home on the way. One night I got pulled by the cops, breathalised and arrested.

I spent a couple of hours in the can before my mother came and rescued me (they must've lost the paperwork - I was never prosecuted).

I took this as a sign and decided my drunk driving days were over. However my drinking days were not over and I carried on medicating myself into oblivion.

I was miserable and had no desire to be creative.

Geoff Muir was trying to manage me but he was working with a temporary burnout. I can't remember too much about this period, which is a blessing.

In September an old mate of mine, Dave C, who now ran the Royal Court theatre in Liverpool, called me up and asked if the Icicle Works would be doing a Christmas show this year (a tradition).

I told him that the band was no more. He suggested that I might want to do the show anyway as people expected it and there was money to be made.

We never made a formal announcement that we'd broken up - I became excited at the idea of doing some shows without the other two, and he assured me folk would still come as the band was all about me when it came down to it - I didn't really agree - a lot of the audience just watched Chris Sharrock but - I had a challenge.

What else was I going to do?

This was my life and I'd worked fucking hard to even get to this 'cult' stage. I knew it wouldn't sit well with Chris Layhe - which bothered me not (he'd just succeeded in freezing our bank account which caused me a lot of inconvenience. We all had to get together to unfreeze it - I sat in stony silence all afternoon while Geoff and our accountant sorted it all out - the poor sods even tried to make jolly small talk with me until I glared at them), and hell it might even piss Chris Sharrock off that he wasn't getting his Christmas bung-up this year - the

fuckin' La's wouldn't be playing to two thousand people in Liverpool this December.

I called Geoff and told him to tell my agent Bob Gold to book shows in London, Birmingham and Manchester to tie in with the home-coming.

I already knew who I was going to ask to replace the dead soldiers (I do have to say at this point that Chris Layhe didn't want to leave the band. He was shocked at Chris Sharrock's decision and I believe he may have even tried to talk him out of it.

People have asked me why we didn't just get another drummer and carry on - the fact is that I'd spoken to Chris S on a number of occasions about replacing Chris L with Roy Corkill who was currently playing with Black. Fronted by Colin Vearncombe, they were most famous for the classic 'Wonderful Life'.

Roy wasn't happy at the way he was being treated in that outfit. A great bass player and all-round musician who was a joy to hang out with, a great fan of the Icicle Works, he also looked great, and wouldn't whinge all the time about not getting any of his tunes on our albums, as he didn't write - or pretend to have the ability to.

Chris Layhe had worn me down.

We were opposites. I'd grown to dislike his playing live, whereby he would get so excited he would attack his strings with a heavy plectrum and the noise coming out would sound more like a low-strung banjo than a bass.

His backing vocals left much to be desired. His attempted scissor-leaps off the drum riser when I wasn't looking were an irritation too - Chris Sharrock didn't baulk at the idea of replacing our bass player, but he cowered from having any part in it.

Chris Layhe's strengths lay in his arrangement abilities in the studio - which were often excellent. Since leaving the band he has pursued a career outside of the music business as a teacher, although I'm told he recently put a new band together called Oyster).

Right after I got off the phone to Dave C and had my spirits lifted, it rang again.

It was a nurse at the Royal hospital. She wanted to speak to Pat.

My grandad had just dropped dead outside his local pub and they needed someone to go and identify the body.

That'll be me then.

CHAPTER TWENTY FOUR

Grandad

My grandad had died due to an aneurysm.

Pat and I drove to the Royal Hospital on Prescot Road and I was taken through to see him at rest.

Needless to say Pat was in a bit of a state.

I had to be a man and take control for a change. The doctor told me he may look a little different in death, he had some blood around his mouth, and I should be prepared. Tom Forsyth lay there, looking like he was simply asleep.

I loved my grandad.

He'd lived alone a long time, as my Nana, May, had passed away ten years ago.

He'd been a taxi driver for as long as I could remember, just as my dad had. They both drove cabs and it seemed like the most dignified job in the world to me.

They'd both fought in the war and they spoke down their radios like they were Spitfire pilots. My grandad told me he shot down the Red Baron - but he was actually a dispatch rider.

I edged up to the place where he rested which was in the corner of a big empty room. As soon as I layed eyes on him I knew he'd gone somewhere else.

It was just an empty vessel, spirit having departed. I don't know where he'd gone, but he wasn't in that room with me. I felt very sad but not deeply upset. It seemed like a good way

out to me. No lingering illness, no infirm, no loss of grace.

You gotta go sometime and dropping dead outside your local with a few beers in you was a good deal. We all should be so lucky.

He could've had more time but - couldn't they all. He was in his seventies He still had his jet black hair and his dark moustache. He always looked like a Mafia don to me (there's Mediterranean blood on my mum's side). He would often wear a cravat.

He loved to smoke a good cigar. He was dignified.

A gentleman.

Whenever somebody you know dies you always regret that you didn't spend more time with them. I didn't spend enough time with my grandad. I always seemed to be too busy.

Wrong. Him and Nana had raised two amazing people in my mum and my uncle Tom. What better legacy? My uncle Tom had served in the merchant navy and was now a very successful business executive. Strikingly handsome, he resembled Sean Connery. He has a wife, Pat, and three great kids, my cousins Sue, Mike and John.

This was my family. My dad was much older than my mum as stated earlier, and I never got to meet my grandparents from the McNabb family side.

What I did get was my dad's sister Kay, her husband Jim, their four children, Rob, Christine, Sue and Eva, who were all a lot older than me (my dad married my mum in his forties - I had to call my cousins aunties and uncles!), their multiple offspring (my second cousins), and all the love you could ever want from a family.

In the early seventies the lot of them relocated from Manchester and set up shop in North Wales (except Rob and his family who stayed in Ashton-Under-Lyne; sadly Rob was hit by a drunk driver one New Year's Eve and was left for dead. He recovered but soon after became riddled with cancer and passed away far too young). My cousin Eva had a guest house on the beach front at Prestatyn, and long hot summers and Christmas were spent there.

Everybody sang. It was wonderful. I couldn't believe I was the only person in the family who went into music - I was the least musical of the lot, I thought.

I was happy to identify my grandad's body for my mum - and my uncle Tom - who couldn't do the task as he was in Birmingham at that moment, where he now lived. Tom had done the same service for me when my dad died. So grandad was gone. Was he now with my dad somewhere plotting my future? I didn't know. I hoped so. I could use some help.

After the funeral there was a period of quiet reflection and a lot of time looking after my mum.

Eventually normality returned and I started thinking about who was going to be in the Icicle Works part two. Roy Corkill was a cert. Dave Green who'd played live keyboards with us since 1986 would survive the cull. He was a fun guy to have around as well as being a great player, and remained on my side during the 'cold war'.

I needed a drummer.

Replacing Chris Sharrock was not going to be easy.

He was/is a virtuoso.

There was only one person in my mind who I thought could fill his shoes.

CHAPTER TWENTY FIVE

Zak

Zak Starkey is one of three children.

The offspring of Richard Starkey (stage name Ringo Starr) and Maureen Starkey.

I'd first met Zak in 1986 when we ended up playing in a band together in Southampton for a live televised charity show called Action On Drugs.

Probably hypocritical on my part (and just about everybody else's) but artists are always ready to give their support to a worthy cause if it means hanging out in a nice hotel for a few days, picking up some expenses and getting to jam with others of their like. Zak was a drummer just as his father was, although he'd never aspired to be a Beatle - he loved the Who mostly - and when Zak was a wee lad, Who drummer Keith Moon had shown him how to play a few licks in his own style and became his mentor. Zak was pretty wild in those days.

He cropped up on the front page of a red-top or two around the time as being 'Out of control son of Ringo Starr' or something like that. I found him to be very affable, a great player, and a great fan of music. When he'd had a few drinks he got pretty loose and occasionally abusive, but no more than any of the other lunatics I hung around with. I was not one to pass judgement myself after all. We exchanged numbers and whenever the Icicle Works would play in London, Zak would

come and watch the show if he was around. He loved and admired Chris Sharrock's playing and Zak and I became lifelong mates. He introduced me to his younger sister Lee, and the youngest of the three children, Jason. He also introduced me to his mum Maureen who tragically died much too young a few years later of leukaemia, a crippling blow to all concerned.

I would meet Ringo later on and even get to play with him on a couple of occasions. I called Zak up and asked him if he'd like to play with the Icys on the upcoming shows.

He was more than willing. He came up to Liverpool for a week before the tour. Everyday we would rehearse until dinner time and then we would eat and go out on the lash. He mastered the parts with ease and seemed to like being in his spiritual home, even though he grew up in Surrey and London.

We had a great time. One night I dropped him off at Harry Graves' house in Woolton. Ringo's parents broke up when he was three and his mother Elsie married Harry soon after. Ringo loved Harry and he was the closest Ringo and Maureen's children had to a grandfather on the Starkey side of the family.

When I went to retrieve Zak after a few hours I had to carry him to the car and then to bed such was the depth of his revelry in reunion with the old boy.

The gigs were all sold out and the only voice of dissent publicly was that of Chris Layhe who attempted to piss on the picnic by telling the press this was not the real Icicle Works and people should boycott the shows. It must've been hard for him to see the franchise continue without him - with relative ease, and I did feel a little sorry for him, but the audience cheered and sang and danced just as they always had done.

When we played at the Astoria in London, Ringo and his current wife Barbara Bach came to the show and were first in the dressing room at the end.

Ringo was lovely - everything you think he's going to be and a lot more. Beatle wit intact.

Barbara was polite without being particularly friendly. This is the only time to my recollection that my dressing room was ever graced by a Beatle and a Bond girl.

Zak's sister Lee became a very close friend over the years, I'd actually come to spend more time with Lee than Zak as she lived in London (Zak was in Ascot most of the time with his wife Sarah and daughter Tatia) and everytime I was down there in later years I would more often than not stay with her.

I fell in love with her, as everyone else did who met her. She was luminous, beautiful, great fun to be around when she was in the mood, and man, she loved a party.

Muff Winwood, who was head of A&R at CBS, had always been a fan of the Icicle Works.

He'd shown great interest in us at the outset of our career, only to back down at the last minute when the bidding wars started. He came to see us at the Astoria with his head scout John Brice (later to become one of my longest lasting friends) as he heard our tenure with Beggar's Banquet may be coming to a close.

He was also excited that Zak now appeared to be in the band as he had tried to sign a couple of bands that Zak had been in previously.

It wouldn't do the band any harm in the U.S. market having such a famous offspring behind the kit, although when he hinted at this I baulked - I wasn't going to use Zak in that way - Zak wouldn't be used in that way - and it was all about the music in my mind, I didn't want a celebrity leg-up.

Zak was not a permanent member of the band anyway. He had his own furrow to plough, and being an accomplished guitar player in his own right, he had several irons in the fire at any time. We went into Amazon studios in Liverpool and did a couple of demos which never saw the light of day - I didn't really have many new songs at the time, being fairly worn out from the stress of the breakup of the band. I was also fried from my

ongoing relationship with Karen.

We were still an item despite us no longer living together, but we were inevitably drifting apart which made me very sad.

I thought she was THE one.

After a lot of wrangling, CBS bought my contract off Beggar's as part of a very lucrative deal for me with their sister company Epic.

Muff wanted Zak to be in the band, but such was his appreciation of my talent he was prepared to put his money on the line, even without hearing any new killer material or knowing who was going to be in the Icicle Works in future.

A bold step. He considered the Icicle Works unfinished business and was confident that we would go on to sell as many records as our promise showed.

Martin Mills' (Beggar's MD) comment at the time was something along the lines of "The Icicle Works on Epic will either be massive or do nothing."

Naturally we were all optimistic and I locked myself in my bedroom at my mum's house and wrote loads of new songs now that this belief had been invested in me.

I also started looking around for a new house.

I'd thought the band was over when the original line-up went their separate ways, but events had transpired to make me see things differently. We could still sell lots of tickets.

I wasn't completely convinced the name still had work to do, but Muff Winwood and a cheque for one hundred thousand pounds from Epic set aside my doubts for the time being.

Perhaps the bigwigs had more knowledge about such things than I? Time would tell. This would be a much needed new beginning.

Much needed.

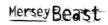

CHAPTER TWENTY SIX

Permanent
damage

Most of 1989 was spent writing songs and licking my wounds.

Muff Winwood was prepared to let me take my time.

Halfway through the year Zak told me he wouldn't be a part of the band in future, which I'd figured anyway but I lived in hope. It would've made things a lot easier later on.

We looked around for a suitable replacement and eventually a guy came forward by the name of Ged Lynch who was recommended by the engineer we were using at that time at Amazon, Mark Phythian.

I liked Ged's playing a lot more than Roy did (Ged would later go on to work with Black Grape and Peter Gabriel amongst others) but we pressed on.

We went into Amazon for a whole month to demo everything. A lot of these recordings would end up as masters.

We had money. We had a fridge in the control room that was stacked with a fresh slab of draught Guinness everyday and we ate a hearty meal at seven pm every evening.

It was great fun.

The new songs stacked up - 'What She Did To My Mind', 'I Still Want You', 'I Think I'm Gonna Be OK', 'Hope St. Rag', 'Baby Don't Burn' - all good, worthy pop songs with a streak of regret running through them.

The recordings were fast and loose and exciting.

We were moving at such a pace that we started to have some time on our hands which we proceeded to fritter away in a comedy style. One track - 'Love Gone Wrong' was a lovely bluesy piece in 3/4.

Roy had developed a habit of singing my songs in a pub singer voice at every available opportunity and this one seemed to be his favourite.

One night we were drunk and ahead of schedule when we decided to record a version of the song with Roy on lead vocals.

We got the original backing track, made it sound as low-fi as possible and gave Roy a hand held SM58 mic to work his magic.

The results were hilarious but there was still something missing. We decided there was no pub ambience on the track so we piled into two cars with some portable recording equipment and headed to the local country boozer.

We sat in silence around the mic for half an hour supping more ale, recording all around us in stereo.

We then headed back to the studio, put the ambience up on two tracks and mixed them into the existing master.

We lit a couple of doobs and sat their laughing our asses off until the morning light.

Too much time and money! I couldn't hear the original version of the song ever again without laughing so it remains unreleased to this day.

We delivered the tapes to Epic and the process of separating the wheat from the chaff began in order to make a coherent, commercial debut on a major label that would hopefully take us up to the level that the previous company had failed to do.

We were pretty sure we couldn't lose - we had real power behind us now - and confidence abounded.

We were asked to play a benefit show for the Hillsborough families (see 'Here Comes Trouble' chapter).

Two nights were booked at the tiny Picket venue on Hardman Street in Liverpool.

There was a heatwave on and both nights were oversold. On the first night the venue was so packed and hot and the audience so excited it looked as though we would be the first people in history to be part of a disaster taking place at a disaster benefit.

The crowd bounced up and down so much the venue's manager Phil Hayes feared the floor was going to give way and four hundred people would crash through the floor to the pub below, killing over a hundred people who couldn't get into the show upstairs. Fortunately the structure held, but so concerned was Phil that the following night's performance was moved across the street to the Polytechnic.

It was even hotter and fuller in here but at least we were playing on the ground floor. It was a very emotional occasion and we raised a lot of money for the cause.

It also alleviated my conscience for bailing out on Craig Johnston when he asked me to do something for the memorial the year before.

Muff, Geoff Muir and I went through a list of producers who we thought would be good for the upcoming album.

Money was no object and Michael Brauer - who had just mixed the Rolling Stones comeback album *Steel Wheels* was enlisted for the job. Time was booked at the old Air studios in Oxford Street, with mixing time to follow at Mayfair in Primrose Hill.

American producers, good ones - are fast workers due to the time constraints placed on them in hot U.S. studios - but work shitty hours for musicians. I don't know if it's because they have jet-lag but they seem to like to start work at nine-thirty in the morning and knock off around seven.

This must be very convenient for them but for us strummers it means having too much time on our hands in a place away from home with not a lot to do - so we usually drink.

This of course guarantees at least a mild hangover the next

day which is manageable at lunchtime but a motherfucker at eight the next morning when we are expected to perform.

Brauer did a good job but got on everyone's nerves by forcing us to play the songs over and over until you're just bashing away. He also spent a lot of time shouting down the phone to his manager and bragging about the nightlife he was enjoying in London (he never asked us out with him once). Anyway, eventually we got it all done and I assembled a running order which I hoped would please everyone.

I quickly came to realise I wasn't going to be enjoying the autonomy I'd had at Beggar's. Major labels like to feel that they're involved in the creative process even though they generally don't have a clue about music.

Advice to young bands: Give them a mix that is slightly wrong so they can comment on it and then you can go back into the studio and mix it including a suggestion they have made. They will then feel involved - greenlight the track - and you've got it the way you wanted it anyway.

Give them the running order you want but make a couple of deliberate mistakes - they will tell you you've not quite got it right - you fix it - and...bingo! You've got it your way.

This technique can be applied to every step of the journey leading up to your record's release.

Never let them put your record out the way that they see fit - as they will drop you as soon as it sells less than a million copies and your legacy will stand on work that wasn't your final vision.

OK? Good. Never compromise - it's your fuckin' record not theirs - even though they will own it for most of your natural life.

Muff had a lot to say about the mixes, the running order, everything really. But I stuck to my guns and the album would eventually be released the way I wanted it. If it was going to fail it would be my vision and ultimately my fault - which makes it easier to live with I promise.

The album was a two-headed beast. Half the tracks were

newly mixed poshed-up versions of the Amazon demos - the rest of the new recordings featuring ex-10cc drummer Paul Burgess in place of Ged Lynch.

I named it *Permanent Damage* after a track on the record - and it was scheduled for release in the spring of 1990. The first single would be 'Motorcycle Rider'.

At the end of the sessions Geoff Muir and I went to see Paul McCartney play at Wembley Arena.

We had seats in the very front row thanks to my agent Bob Gold, and guitarist Robbie Macintosh recognised me from the Pretenders tour in '84 (we'd hung out a lot).

He moved to the front of the stage and tried to have a quick exchange with me between songs, when Macca came over to ask him who he'd spotted.

Robbie shouted something in his ear and I lip-read him saying "Icicle Works".

Macca looked over at me, smiled, and gave the customary thumbs up. Everyone in the first three rows were looking over to see who I was. He he he.

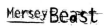

CHAPTER TWENTY SEVEN

Manchester,
so much to answer for

There was a storm brewing.

It was now 1990 and there was change afoot on the musical landscape.

A wave of new, often very good, exciting music was coming out of Manchester. They were calling it 'Baggy' and - God help us 'Madchester.' There had been a new drug on the scene for a few years now called Ecstasy. I actually remember going to score coke of my then dealer.

He was a scary dude.

He told me he was discontinuing the coke as there was only me and another high-profile Liverpool musician he was selling it to now, as everybody had moved on to the new thing.

I tried E and loved it like everybody else.

It blew my mind. It was around twenty-five quid for a pill when it first came out - but it was worth it.

People had grown tired of the inconvenience of having a sneaky smoke or doing a line.

You couldn't smoke weed in clubs, and bouncers patrolled toilets like the Gestapo looking for individuals in cubicles trying to snort a line or two. With E you went to a club with a few pills concealed about your person and popped them at will in dark corners.

It was ace.

A stunning high that gave you a tremendous feeling of well being - lasted a good couple of hours, and brought with it no paranoia or noticeable comedown - until the next day.

You could sleep on it - it felt so nice.

It was a revolution - the fast food of narcotics.

A quick, easy, convenient fix, moderately priced.

It was very easy to get girls when you were on it - you felt super-confident. If the chick you were trying to pull was on it you'd be snogging within thirty seconds. With a new drug comes a new wave of music - check the history books.

The Stone Roses, Happy Mondays, Inspiral Carpets etc., were everywhere. These guys were only a couple of years younger than me (in some cases older - hello Clint Boon! I later found out that the Stone Roses and the Inspiral Carpets used to come and watch us in Manchester when we played at the International in the mid-eighties - I'm still waiting for a name-check) but to the world it looked like my generation were their parents.

I sensed big trouble. I was about to relaunch a moderately successful brand name - very much perceived as the old guard - in a time of great change.

Nearly everyone I knew was cutting their hair short - buying baggy, brightly coloured clothes, and going out to all-night 'raves', listening to music they would've despised two years ago when they were drinking lager and snorting coke. I felt like I was in Gentle Giant when the first Slaughter And The Dogs single came out.

Not only that, but I came from Liverpool, which now appeared to be thirty miles west of the Centre Of The Universe.

Manchester and Liverpool were arch-rivals.

I would've had more chance if I'd have come from Croydon.

We couldn't pretend to be allied to this lot - we weren't. We would have to hope and pray that the fans would stick with us and help us ride out the storm. They would - for a while.

I needed a new keyboard player for the live show. Dave Green, who'd been playing with me for the past three years started out as a fine ally, but by the end was getting louder and louder, infringing on my space too often, and was getting as crazy as me.

Not good. I had to let him go.

Geoff found a great guy called Dave Baldwin who was very quiet offstage and did what he was asked on stage. I also needed a second guitar player (the new album had walls of them) and harmony singer, who came in the form of a very sweet lunatic by the name of Mark Revell.

He was one of Geoff's oldest friends whom I'd known for years and would be a great companion on the road - which was actually more important to me than his musical ability.

He looked - and acted - like a cross between Keith Richards and Harry Dean Stanton.

Geoff was succeeding in manipulating me to his way of thinking all the way here - but I listened - no-one else was talking. Mark, or 'Rev' as we called him - lived with a lead character in the legendary TV soap *Coronation Street*.

The actor was also a long term fan of the Icys. I would go up to Oldham to rehearse with Rev, and this guy would sit there listening, rolling us joints. When we got bored and stoned enough, we'd head out to the local nightclub at ten minutes to closing time, the actor, at the arc of his fame, would stand outside by the door while drunken lasses would recognise him and ask for autographs and kisses.

We'd pick a few out and invite them back to the flat. They'd immediately dump any blokes they were with.

We didn't even have to buy them drinks.

We shot a video for 'Motorcycle Rider' at the Royal Court in Liverpool. It was released in March and got - zero airplay!

One Saturday morning I was watching Philip Schofield presenting a kids TV show that I'd been told we had a chance of

getting on - as the producer was apparently a fan - when Philip went into a rap about how many new records the show got sent every week.

He tipped over a huge postbag, and as all the forty-fives spilled out onto the studio floor, there was my new single on the top of the pile in its little black sleeve with an old motorbike on the cover.

The single barely scraped into the chart despite being issued in multiple formats; knock down retail price, and begging letters to the Queen.

I was still only twenty-nine and I felt I was already being put out to pasture.

And the worst was yet to come.

CHAPTER TWENTY EIGHT

Beech House

We had a tour lined up that was the biggest I'd ever done in the U.K.

The gigs were booked on the understanding that we were about to have a hit single and album.

We certainly weren't about to have a hit single. Many fans complained that the single wasn't up to snuff and what the fuck was I doing singing about motorbikes?

I liked the record - I wouldn't have released it otherwise.

You can't sing about women ALL the time can you?

We had to circle the wagons now - have faith in the album and hope that it would register - somewhere.

I started seeing a delightful little blonde creature from the Wirral in her early twenties called Anne O' Neil.

She was quite posh and her dad was a doctor. This helped me through the pain of another dose of shitty news.

She had originally been seeing my friend Mokka, who had a band called Grown Up Strange but the fire had gone out apparently (I don't know if both sides saw it this way).

Mokka was from Ulverston in the Lake District, lived in Liverpool, and had been my drinking/drugging buddy for a good few years.

He would eventually join me onstage in a couple of future band incarnations as both keyboard and/or guitar player.

I bought a huge, beautiful place called Beech House - so

named due to the enormous Beech tree which sat to the left of the driveway - in Newsham Park for one hundred and five thousand pounds.

Despite the fact that my career appeared to be stalling I had plenty of cash thanks to the advance from the record company and my ongoing publishing deal with Chappell (now merged with Warners).

My songwriting has always made me money.

Beech House is a listed building, the best thing I ever did with my money, and I still live there to this day.

A proper rock star abode with sprawling rooms, a great cellar, gardens front and back, with its own driveway, garage and gates.

It became party central for everyone in my little world.

Music could be played at life-threatening volume at any hour of the day, and permanent darkness was guaranteed to twenty-four hour party people who enjoyed the sin and sanctuary of my cellar den which was decked out with sexy lighting, cushions, sofas and every CD/record I'd ever bought, stacked in essential alphabetical order, across one whole wall.

Over the years many have staggered from this establishment at every hour of the day.

Lithe young maidens (and a few other types) have hobbled in high heels to their cars parked in the driveway, or have been virtually carried to my car in order for me to return them to their flats, or their parents - usually on the Wirral (I think this is due to my love of girls who can speak nicely - and girls from the Wirral usually do.

This is not to say I would turn down anyone who took my fancy simply because they spoke with a scouse accent - I wouldn't - but when a lady starts talking to me - or I to her - who is lovely to look at but sounds like they're eating a packet of Golden Wonder whilst supping a Bacardi Breezer - I am less likely to be there at the conclusion of business).

The original idea of Beech House was that it would eventually house a studio (which it did for a while) and an office (which it never has).

I moved in bit-by-bit and rattled around the place for months. It seemed so big. I'd only ever lived in small places.

I couldn't decide which bedroom to sleep in so I tried them all. First the one with the en-suite bathroom (like staying in a hotel), then the south wing, and then eventually the north.

Two bathrooms upstairs and one down. It took me ages to get used to. I still pee in the garden most days. Old habits etc.

The tour sold well. The album didn't.

Once again venues were packed up and down the length and breadth of the country.

People clearly wanted to see the Icicle Works but we were already an oldies act and half a dozen years into a career.

We drank and drugged our way from John O'Groats (no, literally) to Portsmouth. We had a wonderful time but in my sober moments I realised my time with this band name was now clearly limited and I would have to think about my future - outside of the mothership - soon.

The other guys were doing it.

Over the course of the year Epic released two more singles in multi-pack formats - I have to say they did try.

'Melanie Still Hurts' (a tribute to all the girls I'd loved before - they were mounting up) slipped out quietly and was followed a couple of months later by 'I Still Want You' which actually did manage to pick up a few plays but once again barely scraped the charts.

We went to Europe to try our luck there. I knew it wasn't happening and consoled myself by getting wasted even more than usual.

I was by now pretty much sinking a bottle of Smirnoff every night, waking up feeling rough and having a little sharpener for breakfast to take the edge off.

One night we pulled into a services somewhere in Germany. I staggered out of the shop clutching a bratwurst; a pint glass full of screwdriver and a porno mag, slipped in some oil by the bus, and ended up under it - covered in booze. I lay there for a few minutes and the bus nearly drove over me.

Another night after some serious clubbing apres show in Paris, Rev and I pulled a couple of birds.

We were sharing a room to keep costs down. I made out with the unfortunate lady that was with me, and then, realising that Rev wasn't going to be able to perform (I heard him slide off the bed and hit the floor - unconscious), I climbed onto his date and did the deed for him.

Charming.

This may sound like rock'n'roll fun to the max to the uninitiated but I can assure you it wasn't - it was desperate.

I was deeply unhappy, seeking solace in bad boy behaviour.

Epic wanted us to do a showcase at a new retail store which had just opened in East Berlin.

The wall had just come down. The idea was that we would blow the East Germans away and be one of the first bands to start shifting records there. They put us and most of our equipment on a flight from Utrecht. When we arrived we were driven through the city to a huge shopping precinct. There was a stage set up outdoors with a vast area in front where the recently emancipated were expected to gather and hear our exciting western rock und roll.

When we went on, much later than planned, there was still no audience. There was a tramp standing about a hundred yards from the stage drinking from a brown paper bag.

About halfway through our brief set he fell over and went to sleep. Rev shouted down the mic to try and wake him up. A small dog went over to him and started licking his face.

There were about three other people watching us from even further back. We finished, signed a bunch of albums for the store, and flew back to Holland, eastern Europe safely conquered.

After the last show in Paris I decided the Icicle Works had had an extension on their time, and it was now officially over.

I would come home, get my shit together and become Ian McNabb. Solo Artist.

Now then, when lead singers go solo from previously successful bands they generally have a hard time getting attention. I was going to go solo after leaving a band that was clearly on the skids - I had a long hard road in front of me.

Back in London I told Muff Winwood that my next record would be released under my own name - the Icicle Works were through.

He told me he would consider my case and decide whether or not Epic would keep me on. It was now November.

A couple of days before Christmas we got the word that I was being dropped from the roster.

I cosied myself in my new mansion and wondered how I'd got there. I decided I had to write some serious songs that no-one could ignore next time.

Chris Sharrock had now left the La's and had joined one of my favourite bands, World Party, who were being celebrated and adored in the press, and worshipped by the public.

They had a brilliant album out called *Goodbye Jumbo* and were on the verge of a smash hit single.

Jealous? You bet.

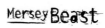

CHAPTER TWENTY NINE

Great dreams of heaven

January 1991.

There was a war about to begin. On August 2nd, 1990, Iraq had invaded Kuwait. Coalition forces had given Saddam Hussain until January to get out or face the consequences.

Operation 'Desert Storm' began on January 17, 1991. Twelve countries had sent naval forces, joining the local navies of Saudi Arabia and the Persian Gulf states, as well as the huge array of the U.S. Navy, with no fewer than six aircraft-carrier battle groups.

Eight countries had sent ground forces, joining the local troops of Bahrain, Kuwait, Oman, Qatar, Saudi Arabia, and the United Arab Emirates, as well as the seventeen heavy, six light, and nine marine brigades of the U.S. Army, with all their vast support and service forces - and four countries had sent combat aircraft, joining the local air forces of Kuwait, Qatar, and Saudi Arabia, as well as the U.S. Air Force, U.S. Navy, and U.S. Marine aviation.

It was the strangest time. Every night the TV would show the war unfolding, usually with night vision cameras.

The world was dark green. Presenters would be reporting the day's events when they would suddenly have to break off and don gas masks for fear that chemical weapons were being deployed.

They would often continue their report wearing this apparel.

It would've been hilarious were it not so scary. It was in this climate that I decided to start writing again. My current run of bad luck seemed rather trivial given this situation.

I'd cleaned my act up a bit and was fairly sober. I cut my hair, shaved my beard off, and started thinking clearly about what I had to do. Geoff Muir assembled an eight-track studio in my cellar, got it up and running, showed me how to work everything, and told me to "Write a fuckin' song."

Everyday we were bombarded with news from the front lines. Many were saying it was going to lead to the end of the world. It certainly felt that way.

Over the course of three days I began writing a song which dealt with the fact that we live our lives constantly challenging each other's borders and beliefs, kill and maim each other at every opportunity, and then expect some eternal reward from our respective gods. I married it with a very catchy tune that you couldn't get out of your head if you tried. I called it 'Great Dreams Of Heaven'.

It was a classic.

Easily the best piece of work I'd done for years, it gave me great confidence and the belief that I still had much to say. I made a little demo of it and listened to it all the time.

I didn't want to write any more of these self-pitying songs which made up the bulk of my output for the past year.

I felt a new lease of life and began to notice the good things around me and realised how lucky I was.

My happiness or - lack of it - for most of my adult life had been built around chart statistics and attendance figures.

What bullshit!

The fuckers had sucked me in. I'd been immersed in the music business to the point of total myopia towards everything else. All I cared about was fame and fucking.

The first Icicle Works album was wide-eyed, innocent, overtly optimistic and all the better for it - because they hadn't got to me yet.

Everything that came after it sounded world-weary because I'd become a pawn in their game. I wanted to feel child-like wonder again - but with the benefit of age.

I unplugged myself from the mainframe and began to appreciate the light around me. Another song - 'That's Why I Believe' - came quickly. I'd had an epiphany.

In February I went into Amazon with Roy to record a couple of tracks. There would be no band, just us and some basic technology.

Ken Nelson (later to become a Grammy award winning producer for his work with Coldplay) would engineer the sessions.

We recorded 'Great Dreams' and 'That's Why I Believe'. They sounded so fresh and full of life I actually cried with pride. I decided I wanted to release a four-track E.P. and get it out there right away.

I wanted to show the world I was not to be counted out yet.

We went back to Amazon (which was closing down and about to move from Kirkby to central Liverpool) and recorded two more tunes - 'Power Of Song' and 'Make Love To You', with my trusty, regular engineer Mark Pythian.

I was in charge of the whole shebang as I paid for the sessions myself which meant I owned the masters for the first time since the 'Nirvana' single.

I opened for one of my favourite American bands Green On Red at the Town and Country Club, performing solo - with my Telecaster - under my own name.

It was scary but liberating. I opened for the Stranglers at Brixton Academy and went down very well considering I finished on a new, ten-minute opus entitled 'Presence Of The One'.

It was fun to be playing this new music, alone and sober.

I felt ten years younger.

In July the E.P. was released on a small indie label called Way Cool who'd approached Geoff to see what I was up to. It got more airplay and attention than anything I'd released for years.

At first it was hard to understand this, and then I realised it was simply because the record was very good.

If it's good enough - it will find its place. These recordings last forever.

Someone, somewhere will find it eventually. It started selling well and my thoughts turned to a full length album.

I started seeing a girl called Bridget who was lovely (you keeping up?). Anne had gotten sick of my ways and legged it back to the Wirral.

Bridget was a school teacher - a breath of fresh air. I would go around to her flat in Aigburth a couple of times a week, we would drink a bottle of wine, watch a movie, and she would talk about her day and I would listen with a smile on my face.

I'd known her for a few years as she used to go out with Phil Wylie - Pete (The Mighty Wah!) Wylie's brother. I didn't even try to bed her. In fact I shied away from it for so long she began to think there was something wrong with me.

I was at peace with myself. This was a period of light after an extended period of darkness.

It was wonderful.

A new studio had opened in Oldham and Geoff knew the guy who ran it. They offered us a couple of days free time to see how the gear worked. We went over there and recorded two new songs, 'These Are The Days' and 'Trams In Amsterdam'.

Both had the vibe of the E.P. - new, optimistic Ian - and we recorded and mixed the pair of them in the time allotted. We were delighted with the results and struck a deal with the studio to record an album there.

The songs were flowing out of me now - 'Truth And Beauty', 'If Love Was Like Guitars', '(I Go) My Own Way', 'I'm Game',

'Trip With Me' - all invitations to the new dance.

'These Are The Days' was released on our own label which I called Fat Cat (after an unreleased track from the Permanent Damage sessions) in October and consolidated the ground we'd reclaimed with the E.P.

One night I was round at Bridget's tucking her up in bed for the night and about to go home when I heard a noise in the darkness behind me. The next thing I knew I could feel the barrel of a gun on the back of my neck.

"Don't turn around or I'll kill you." said the voice.

There was one guy in the room I figured. He told us both to get on the floor and crawl into the living room. I sneaked a look - he was wearing a balaclava and didn't want to be looked at. I couldn't see anyone else.

"Turn around! Turn around! I'm not messin'! I'll fuckin' kill ya!"

We crawled through to the living room in darkness. Bridget was practically naked. She didn't seem as scared as I was.

"Give me all your money - I mean it!" spoke the intruder.

"Go on . . . I'm sick of this! (She'd been burgled twice already) Get out! Get out of my house!" shouts Bridget.

The lady had balls.

"Tell her to shut up mate! Tell her to shut up or I'll shoot youse both!"

"Bridget..." I began.

Bridget stood up and ran at him. I was worried the guy had someone with him waiting outside - but we were committed now. I waited to hear gunfire but it never came. I jumped up and grabbed hold of the fucker. Bridget and I were all over him. He was tall but not weighty.

We pushed him out into the hall where it was light. We got him to the front door - there was skin and hair flying. I opened the front door, grabbed him by his collar and pushed him onto the step. Bridget was giving him a harder time than I was.

I felt something like metal pushed against my chest. I'm going

to die I thought. I'm going to die - here - now.

I pulled off the balaclava.

A young black lad. I made a fist, pulled it back and let it fly. He fell backwards into the street and we slammed the door. I don't know what his face looked like after I smacked him, but I couldn't use my hand for a week.

I'll never know if he had a gun or he was bluffing.

Fortunately.

I got home at about three in the morning after Bridget called the cops and they grilled us for about an hour. Pat was still up, watching the telly with a blanket over her.

"Fuckin' 'ell. You won't believe the ordeal I've just been through."

I tell her.

She looks at me and then whips back the blanket around her legs. She's bandaged from thigh to knee on her left leg and there's bloodstains all over. She had been walking down the stairs at the Balmoral to change a beer barrel when she fell through the rickety wooden stairs.

One of the stairs snapped into and made a gash in her leg so deep and long that she would eventually need forty stitches.

Quite an eventful night for the McNabbs. Bridget became depressed and quite morose after that night. She became paranoid that it could happen again. She began making plans to move.

In the meantime her doctors prescribed some strong anti-depressants which she didn't want to take, so she gave them to me. I wasn't depressed, although I was worried about my mum.

She contracted an infection in her leg and had to go into hospital. When they looked at it they were horrified and told her she may lose it.

She was in hospital for two weeks and things became very bleak. I had to look after the house and myself again and I figured this was enough of an excuse to start taking Bridget's pills. So I did. They were fantastic.

I'd go and visit my mum everyday, fairly out of it and feeling very cheerful for absolutely no reason.

I'd swoop round the ward and introduce myself to everyone, cracking jokes and generally trying to lighten the mood.

I'd ask my mum how she was, she'd say "Terrible, terrible..." I'd sing a few bars of 'Cheek To Cheek' and tell her she'd be fine.

She was, thank God.

Her leg healed and she got to keep it.

The pills ran out and normality was restored.

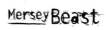

'Love Is A Wonderful Colour'
High on a hit.

Sanctuary

On tour with
David Gilmour 1984.

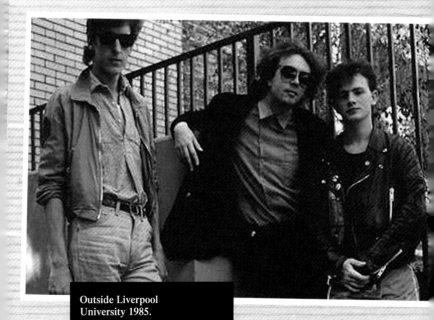

Outside Liverpool
University 1985.

Top & Above:
Recording second
album - Miraval,
south of France
January 1985.

Early promo shot - banks
of River Mersey 1981

Hollywood Bowl 1984.

Left: Me and an ice cream - Mojave desert 1994.

With Billy Talbot - Red Zone studios, San Fernando Valley 1993.

Left: On deck on the Barge - Twickenham 2000.

Top: Photo shoot for 'Head Like A Rock' Mojave desert 1994.

Above: Morden Street 1980.

Right: On stage mid-nineties.

Sanctuary

CHAPTER THIRTY

Joe 'f******' Walsh

It's a slow Sunday (is there any other kind?) in March '92.

I'm laying on the couch watching a black and white WW2 movie. It's set at sea and there are no dogs in it called 'Nigger'.

The phone rings. It's Zak.

"Boots!" He exclaims merrily.

(Zak is one of the small rank of folk who address me by my nickname instead of my Christian name. My Christian name is actually Robert, but for reasons still difficult to fathom, my parents elected to call me by my middle name - good move as it turns out, as there was an Arsenal player in the seventies called Bob McNabb - phew!).

For the record, my nickname is 'Boots' for two reasons:

1) There is a line in the Icicle Works tune 'Hollow Horse' ("...I'll keep my boots on..."), which one-time Icicle Works monitor engineer and good friend Geoff Horne (nickname: 'Chewbacca' - due to his resemblance - sans fur - to Hans Solo's faithful Wookie sidekick and co-pilot of the Millennium Falcon) used to sing at the top of his voice at every show he did with us.

2) He also found great amusement in my footwear around the time, which, for practically the duration of the 1980s, consisted solely of winklepicker boots (I even wore them with shorts -

there are pictures of me in Hawaii dressed as such - which you will never see).

Hence 'Boots.' So now you know.

"Zak!" I retort with equal gusto. "What's goin' on man? I can't wait to see the show tomorrow."

(Zak is playing in his dad's touring outfit - Ringo Starr And His All-Starr Band - at the Liverpool Empire. A pretty significant date in the Scouse music calendar, to be sure).

"Listen Boots, someone in my dad's band is stuck in a snooty London hotel this weekend, we've got a night off tonight, he's bored, and he wants to come up to Liverpool today instead of tomorrow.

"I've given him your number, but he probably won't call...I just wanted to warn you in case he does."

I digest this for a moment and concern sets in.

Firstly, I'm skint.

Secondly, it's Sunday.

I don't do anything on a Sunday, apart from loaf around with a hangover, try and avoid the Antiques Roadshow on BBC One, and ponder the sadness of my life, the love lost, and the missed opportunities.

Or I might go to the pictures.

"Er...OK." I muster with fake enthusiasm.

"Who is it by chance?"

"Er, (slight giggle) it's Joe Walsh."

Joe Walsh.

Joe Fuckin' Walsh as comedian turned serious actor Dennis Leary likes to call him.

Joe Walsh. Legendary American Guitar Hero. Founder member of ace power trio the James Gang.

Writer of 'Rocky Mountain Way', 'Life's Been Good'.

Member of squillion selling soft-rock outfit the Eagles.

Co-writer of 'Life In The Fast Lane!' What the fuck am I going to do with Joe Walsh on a shit Sunday night in Liverpool?

Oh well, he probably won't call. He does.

"Ian?!" That's Pat.

"What?"

She hands me the phone from the top of the stairs.

"Joe Walsh!" She mouths.

"Hey! Hi, Ian gerd buddy..." comes the twangy yank voice down the line from snooty, boring London.

"Ah gart ya number frahm my buddy Zak there an' he tole me te give ya a holler dude...ahm gittin on a train in a lil' while can ya come git me at the other end? Gits in eight-thirty your time!"

He probably thinks there's a time difference (one of Neil Young's band once asked me what season Britain was in when we were sitting in a hotel room in L.A. He also asked me if we had mountains).

Americans.

Sure thing Joe, I'll be there.

Right.

Think.

What am I gonna do? Try to round up some mates, get some weed, he'll smoke pot won't he?

I can't afford any charlie, plus that might offend him. Is he clean at the moment? These bastards can get all sanctimonious on your ass if they've stopped using.

Go to the offy and get a bottle of Jack (I'll have to borrow the money off me mam - I'm busted.

Paying for the recording of the new album and my vast mortgage repayments are eating into my party funds.

I had to sell the Opel Manta and I'm currently driving a red Ford Fiesta Estate, a right fanny-repellent, but all my gear fits in the back - Christ, I sound like a drummer in a cabaret band).

Can't get hold of any of my chums - it's Sunday remember. I left them all in pieces last night.

I call Bridget, she's a great talker, a looker, and might take the pressure off me having to make conversation with Mr. Hotel

California all night if I get stuck. She's not happy about it - it's a school night - literally, but she'll help me out.

Cool.

I get to Lime Street station just as the London train pulls in - on time (they did in those days).

I stand at the end of the platform and survey the disembarking throng. Just as I'm starting to thank my lucky stars that the bastard has changed his mind, some geezer dressed from head to toe in white - panama hat, open neck shirt, cotton summer suit, tennis shoes, carrying a solitary shoulder bag - slowly alights from the rear end of the train and walks - very slowly - the distance of the platform towards me.

There's sod-all going on in town tonight apart from a gig at the Royal Court Theatre where Scots radio-friendly rockers Del Amitri are plying their trade.

They are being supported by local-ish Wirral rockers Pele, fronted by my mate Ian Prowse.

It's hardly a night of Chateau Marmont-style debauchery we're looking at here but it's better than taking rockin' Joe back to my house to watch *Quiz Night* with a local TV star Stuart Hall on ITV.

I called earlier and got me, plus two on the guest list. My hands are sweaty.

"Hey Joe, where you goin' with that bag in your hand?"

It's not a bad ice-breaker. We shake hands and I ask him what he fancies doing?

"Oh y' know, whatever dude... jus' glad to be here."

This is gonna be hard work.

"Do you want me to take you to your hotel so you can freshen up and stuff?" I offer.

"Whaa? Do ah smell?"

He smiles at me with raised eyebrows.

"No, I just thought maybe you'd wanna check in before we do something."

"Er...well, y'know...ah don't know which hotel ahm s'posed to be stayin' in...they had me a room in London there..."

Bridget meets us in the gig and we immediately retreat to the bar. Joe isn't arsed about seeing Del Amitri... he's muttering something about "Don Amichi..." I can't tell if Joe is stoned or he's just like this. I think he's just like this. He has a rubber mouse in his pocket that he squeezes every time there is a gap in conversation.

Each squeeze produces a high pitched squeak which attracts the attention of everyone within a six feet radius. If he doesn't wish to be noticed he's failing badly.

"So Joe, have you been to Liverpool before then?"

"Huh? Wassat buddy?"

SQUEAK! He is starting to freak me out.

We set up camp in a brightly lit corner.

Bridget is valiantly trying to make conversation but she's struggling.

She's looking at me with the facial expression of one whose finger has just gone through the toilet paper.

Joe is now squeezing his rubber mouse at an alarming rate, which I am beginning to realise is his unique way of expressing boredom. He's beginning to attract the attention of a bunch of scallies standing behind my chair who are with the support band and are more interested in drinking than watching the headline act.

After a couple more awkward minutes one particularly refreshed young lad leans into my ear and talks to me in a broad scouse accent.

"Alright la'...oo's that fuckin' bloke youse are sittin' wid?"

I try to diffuse what could be viewed as a mounting tense situation.

"He's a friend of mine - from the States."

The lad looks closely at me and then surveys Joe in what can only be described as a 'Rocky Mountain Way'.

"Tell you what la, 'e doesn't 'alf look like that bloke from dee Eagles."

I take a hearty swig of my white wine and soda and consider moving our swinging party elsewhere.

I dunno where, but somewhere other than here would be a good idea. Soon.

The lad is now talking in an animated fashion with his mates and pointing to our corner excitedly.

There is a lot of laughing going on. Joe is squeezing his mouse. A different, larger chap now comes toward us. He leans over me, spilling some ale from his plastic glass onto my jeans.

"Eh mate!"

He is addressing the man in white.

"Are you dat bloke from dee Eagles?!"

Joe looks from under the brim of his hat.

"Ahh... yeah... that's me." SQUEAK!

"FUCK OFF??!!"

The lad seems to be doing something brilliant here. He is asking a question whilst making a suggestion.

"Fuckin' 'ell! Lads! It's fuckin' Joe Walsh from dee Eagles!!!"

Several large young men, a couple of older ladies, presumably mothers and relatives of the band Pele, flanked by a number of middle aged geezers who look like they don't go to gigs unless related by blood to the artist in question - but must now think major international rock stars flock to any concert on any given night off - rapidly move towards our corner with gleeful, barely contained excitement.

"Hey, man, I gotta git outta here..." whispers Joe to no-one in particular. He now appears more animated than I have seen him since we met twenty long minutes ago.

The mouse is silent.

I am ahead of him. I drag both him and Bridget towards the door just as a chorus of 'The Boys Of Summer' is getting under way.

We march briskly across Roe Street to my cabaret drummer-style red Ford Fiesta estate and clamber in and take a breath. Joe jumps in the front seat and breathes outward loudly, Bridget climbs in the back and I hear her laughing quietly to herself.

I think she's beginning to realise this is turning into a story she can regale fellow teachers with at Christmas parties for many years to come. She would've only been at home marking maths books tonight anyway.

Joe squeezes his mouse. I think quickly about what the rest of the night has in store for me and decide to take charge.

"Joe, don't you think you should at least try and find out which hotel you're going to be staying in tonight before it gets too late?"

I'm starting to think he won't find one and will have to spend the night at McNabb Towers.

My mother is working in the club tonight, and she won't be home until the early hours – but the idea of these two disparate cultures meeting in the hallway should laughin' Joe be wandering around in his boxers in the morning is just too weird to bear.

"Ahh, yeah... Ahh guess we could do that..."

Joe can't raise anyone on a payphone to find out which hotel he may or may not be booked into. Sunday right?

I end up driving him to half a dozen hotels before he decides which one he'll be happy in.

He settles for the Crest which is conveniently located around the corner from tomorrow's gig.

We head back to mine to chill out. I give him a warm glass of Liebfraumilch (this was still in the time before I got cultured) and he pulls his stash out.

Some bonkers grass.

Rock star grass.

Bridget goes home as she has to be up at seven a.m. I put the telly on. Stuart Hall is hosting *Quiz Night* as predicted. Gawd.

I've got all my guitars out and Joe is showing me how to play Eagles songs. He shows me how to play 'The Bomber' by the James Gang.

He insists I leave *Quiz Night* on and keeps shouting - clearly wrong - answers out.

I've got an electric fake fire in the living room. There is an orange bulb in it which, when hot, causes a piece of metal to rotate above it and give the appearance of flickering embers.

When I come back from the toilet, Joe is on his hands and knees in the middle of the room studying it. He does this for about two minutes.

"Oh! Hey! I got it now. That's really fuckin' clever dude!"

I get Joe a cab back to his hotel and promise to meet up with him the next day.

He wants to trade me a Fender Telecaster for my Gretsch White Falcon. No way.

Next day I turn up at the Empire just after soundcheck. It's great to see Zak again. Joe introduces me to Todd Rundgren, Nils Lofgren and Dave Edmunds.

I'm in my element. I worship these guys.

They want to go to a bar, a good way away from the gig. I take them to the Philharmonic pub on Hope Street, a beautiful old boozer with huge chandeliers hanging in every room.

Joe looks up and surveys the two above him as he's waiting for his drink.

'Hey! Look at that! Stevie Nicks' earrings!'

SQUEAK!

CHAPTER THIRTY ONE

The only way is this way up

Steve Webbon from Beggar's Banquet did a really nice job on the Icicle Works 'Best Of' package.

It was released in August in the U.K.

It got some nice reviews and even got to number sixty in the charts (for just a week). Bless.

My first solo album was finished and we started shopping it around.

I did a few promo gigs for the *Best Of*. One in particular I recall was a BBC radio outside broadcast from Derby where I was followed on stage by a bunch of very fruity looking young lads who called themselves Take That. They were the gayest thing ever and argued with each other constantly in the caravan which was used as a make-shift dressing room. One of their gang was louder and girlier than the rest, I later identified him as superstar redcoat Robbie Williams, whom Chris Sharrock would later hook up with (in his touring band), after his stalled first album was ignited by the 'Angels' single.

Funny old world.

The Icys' re-release gave out a lot of good feeling and people started talking about the band in a positive light - now that we no longer existed. Geoff and I did the rounds in London with the new record but we weren't getting too much of a bite. One particularly frustrating afternoon after yet another disappointing

meeting, we were sitting in the Zetland Arms in South Kensington just about to go and see another company, when I finished my pint and informed Geoff that I'd had enough and wanted to go home now.

He literally had to drag me around to the office of Andrew Lauder's newly formed This Way Up label. I nearly fucked off again when Dave Bedford - who we were supposed to be meeting with - wasn't present (he'd had to go home as his child was ill). A lady by the name of Judith Riley (who was Andrew's partner) looked at me - as I was about to stomp off - with sympathetic eyes, and asked me if I wanted a beer.

So I stuck around.

Good job I did. These three people were about to turn my life around.

Andrew Lauder walked in ten minutes later. He was a tall, handsome man, now hairless apart from those bits at the side, and his streamlined goatee. He had cowboy boots on, a bootlace tie, and was carrying a bag from Tower Records which appeared to be bursting under the strain. This would not be his last visit to a record store this day.

In 1970 at the age of twenty-three, Andrew became head of A&R at Liberty/United Artists Records Ltd. He signed and developed a multitude of eclectic and influential artists including:

The Groundhogs, Hawkwind, Brinsley Schwarz, Man, The Flamin' Groovies, Dr. Feelgood, The Stranglers and The Buzzcocks.

He was also instrumental in bringing Creedence Clearwater Revival and Can to the label. He went on to co-found Radar Records in 1978 (Elvis Costello, Nick Lowe, The Pop Group, The Yachts, The Soft Boys and Loudon Wainwright III), leaving in 1979 to set up Demon and Edsel Records along with the offshoot, F-Beat (Rockpile, Carlene Carter). He left Demon ten years later to launch the Silvertone label for Zomba and had considerable success with The Stone Roses, J.J. Cale and Buddy Guy, as well as reactivating the career of John Lee Hooker with the Grammy-winning album *The Healer*.

Andrew's next venture was This Way Up Records which was still wet behind the ears as Geoff and I sat there surrounded by cardboard boxes and picture frames of classic pop/rock artwork from the past forty years, still unhung.

Judith asked me if I was the guy whose CD Dave Bedford had been spinning on heavy rotation in the office with the "Funny telephone voice." She was referring to the vocal effect on 'Great Dreams Of Heaven'.

Well, at least they'd listened to it. We had an amicable meeting and I did my best to be charming despite being tired from meetings all day and a generally suspicious nature of record company types by now. These were different.

They called up the next day and requested a further meeting, this time with Mr. Bedford present, who was head of A&R. So we headed south again, stuck in a couple of other meetings just to be safe, and things moved on a pace. They asked us what we wanted and we told them.

One week later the lawyers were drawing up the papers. It was that easy. Another chance.

I signed with This Way Up on my thirty-second birthday and we all went to a posh Soho eaterie to celebrate.

They would release the album exactly the way I wanted it in the spring of '93. Wow. It was precluded with a single in February - 'If Love Was Like Guitars' - which got single of the week in indie bible the N.M.E. and started getting some serious airplay on BBC Radio One - which amazed us frankly. The beeb hammered the fuckin' thing until exactly one week before the release date - when they stopped playing it completely.

Well, I guess my rehabilitation couldn't all happen at once.

And so it was that the debut Ian McNabb album *Truth And Beauty* came out, got great reviews and sold steadily.

Not quite enough for us to deck the halls with bunting, but it meant I would at least get to do another one - all an artist could hope for from my point of view.

I put a new band together comprising Gordon Longworth (formerly a member of Black with Roy Corkill, and lead guitarist on a couple of tunes from the new album - I was trying to step back from playing as much lead and concentrating on singing), Dave Baldwin from the last Icys line-up, a new drummer I'd found called Steve Gibson, and my long-suffering guitar tech Nick Warren was promoted to second keys and samples (there was a lot of stuff on *Truth And Beauty* - probably the most ambitious album I ever made). Roy maintained his position as mediator and bassman.

We toured.

A lot.

We played at the Phoenix festival in Stratford-on-Avon, we travelled around Europe for about six weeks in a gold bus opening for Big Country and then Suzanne Vega.

Lead singer/guitarist Stuart Adamson never said two words to me, and when the long tour eventually ended somewhere in Germany he proceeded to thank everyone involved from the stage (including the caterers) except me and the band.

Suzanne Vega was rude and ignorant.

Quite what gives certain artists the right to behave like pricks just because a few people have paid a few bob to see them remains a mystery to me - I mean good manners don't cost nothin' do they? Anyway, judge the art not the artist.

Sometimes I used to love being on a tour bus. You climb into your bunk after a show, go to sleep, and when you wake up the next morning you throw the curtain back and you're parked next to Lake Geneva on a beautiful, sunny morning.

Not a bad way to get to work.

Stuart Adamson killed himself a few years later and I felt bad for him and his family, but he showed no endearing qualities to me in a time when we could've been chums - at least for the duration of a long and trying tour. He seemed grumpy and ill tempered throughout.

Another single was lifted from the album - 'I'm Game' - which we only put out to tie in with all of the shows.

We opened for Aztec Camera on a short UK tour (Roddy Frame was nice, shy).

We performed three tunes on a new BBC music show broadcast from a church(!) in Glasgow called *No Stillettos*, where I managed to scare Edwyn Collins and Eddie Reader to death with my big beard and deafening band.

Eddie Reader had a hit with a Boo Hewerdine number called 'The Patience Of Angels', where she appeared as an angel singing in heaven. She had the fake wings on and everything, but she also kept her glasses on.

I guess the message is good and bad - there is an afterlife, but bring your specs - you'll need 'em. No laser treatment in the everafter then?

There was a feeling that *Truth And Beauty* had been delivered to This Way Up as a fait accompli, and they would work it as hard as they could, but Andrew looked forward to what direction he could point me in for the second record.

We re-recorded '(I Go) My Own Way' with John Leckie at RAK studios. John was a hero of mine having done sterling work with Pink Floyd, John Lennon, The Stone Roses, Be Bop Deluxe and XTC's fun, psychedelic hobby band The Dukes Of Stratosphere.

He would also produce *The Bends* for Radiohead. We also cut 'Play The Hand They Deal You' a great new heavy waltz I'd come up with.

Mickie Most owned RAK and it was a buzz to meet him and talk about all the brilliant records he'd made. Count 'em.

We mixed at Livingston studios in Brook Road in North London, which was a horrible experience.

John mixed on the big speakers at gig volume and after an hour I couldn't hear anything at all.

I hated the results when I eventually listened at home at sensible levels, and after John tried to remix the mess he'd sent me and failed again, I had to go into newly opened Parr St. studios (formerly Amazon) in Liverpool and spend three days salvaging with Mark Pythian.

John had mixed everything at full blast and it all sounded like squashed mud to me.

I could never understand this. John was/is one of the most enduring/respected producers in the business and has made so many great records. I guess he was having an off period. Mark P did a great job and the results were quite stunning (amazingly). We decided to make it a four track E.P. and added 'If My Daddy Could See Me Now', and my experiment in dub - 'For You, Angel' - which remains one of my favourite McNabb songs of all time.

It sold OK but we were all looking towards the next marker by now. *Truth And Beauty* had done its job and got me a record deal again. Time to move on - we'd toured it into the ground and - it wasn't really a stage record anyway.

I'd written a new song, which was heavily autobiographical, called 'Fire Inside My Soul'.

I thrashed it out on my Telecaster with my amp cranked up and recorded it on my Dictaphone.

It sounded like Bruce Springsteen playing a Neil Young song to me.

When I turned the machine off and went to make a cup of tea, I was pleased with myself for writing another strong song.

If you'd have told me where it would lead me - I would never have believed you.

Mersey Beast

CHAPTER THIRTY TWO

You must be prepared to dream

Geoff Muir and This Way Up were not getting along.

Geoff had his own way of doing things and liked to shield me from anything that might get in the way of my creativity - in the way he saw fit.

He did know me very well by this point having worked with me for ten years.

Judith Riley and Andrew Lauder had taken a shine to me and the feeling was mutual.

We instantly hit it off and Geoff wasn't happy about the closeness of the relationship - he didn't think it was healthy.

He could feel himself being edged out of the party.

Dave Bedford had brought me to the company and I know he didn't feel happy about the way that Judith appeared to have a monopoly over my time. Judith fell for me in a big way and more or less took over my professional life from hereon in. Usually a record company communicates with the artist through management but this seemed silly when I was staying at Andrew and Judith's flat for days on end in South Kensington. Andrew was happy to let Judith run with her new project as he wanted her to be happy.

I was happy simply because I was getting a lot of attention and didn't really mind who was giving it.

Don't forget I'd just come out of a very unpleasant corporate

situation and now here I was with a record company who seemed determined to make me a star at any cost. Also Andrew and Judith were two of the kindest, nicest, most respectful music people I'd ever met. We loved the same things. We became very close.

A strange situation for an artist to have with the brass.

They loved my music and they had the means to do something about it. I was so lucky to meet these people - I was blessed.

It was intimated to me in a subtle, respectful way that perhaps Geoff was not the right person to guide me at this new point in my career. So I thought about it for a while and decided there would be problems with this mix of players and decided to tell Geoff I was moving on.

I felt shit about it as he'd stuck with me through tough bits as well as the good. I told him backstage at Manchester Apollo at a charity gig. It was horrible.

Steve Coogan was on the bill and I was sharing a dressing room with him. I fired Geoff while the future Alan Partridge sat there looking at the floor embarrassed.

You couldn't make it up.

I've hurt a lot of people throughout my career. What has to be made clear is that I'm on a mission and I don't - can't - care about the debris I leave behind me.

I have to get to the place I need to be and all other considerations are irrelevant. People are expendable - apart from family and very, very close friends. Sentimentality is weakness and wars are won by brute force.

I know this sounds callous but it's just the way - the way it HAS to be.

I'd love everybody to be happy with me who's been in my life/career but it just isn't the case. I had to learn to use my wits and associate with the right people in order to survive. John Lennon said "You've got to be a bastard to make it and the

Beatles were the biggest bastards in the world."

It really is kill or be killed (apologies to anyone who is reading this and thinking they were one of those people I trod on.

I hope in the fullness of time you realise that it's nothing personal - your consolation could be that at the end of my life I'll have a wonderfully rich legacy of great music around me and no-one to talk to).

When Geoff was out of the picture, This Way Up's vision for Ian McNabb could continue without incident.

After a short holiday in Israel with Andrew and Judith and John Brice, I sat down in the office and listened to the plan.

Andrew was great friends with the English producer John Porter and suggested he should produce my next album.

Born in Leeds in 1947, John eventually found himself attending Newcastle University where he met singer Bryan Ferry, and soon became part of his fledgling band The Gas Board.

Ferry's later band Roxy Music had achieved some success in the early seventies, but having had some troubles with bass players, Ferry invited John on board to record the 1973 album *For Your Pleasure*.

In 1976 he moved to Warsaw, Poland for a while and put a band together called the Porter Band. Locally known as Portfel Band - which translates to Wallet Band (this would make more sense to me later). They released a number of albums there. He then went on to serve as a record producer for many later albums for Roxy Music and Bryan Ferry.

He's since produced for The Smiths, Billy Bragg, B.B.King, Buddy Guy, John Lee Hooker, Ryan Adams, and numerous other bands. John lived and worked in Los Angeles and the idea was that I would go over there and work with local musicians.

Local musicians in Los Angeles are plentiful and considered the best in the world. I had a long phone conversation with John, and wasn't convinced.

I was a punk at heart and playing with 'cats' in California seemed out of kilter with my shtick.

Then I remembered the song I'd just written that sounded like Neil Young. For a laugh I told Judith that I'd only go to L.A. if they could get me Neil's band Crazy Horse to play with me.

As it happened, John Porter knew the guys (he knew everyone - English people make friends easily in the States - especially English music types). Contact was established and the word "No" wasn't used. Neil Young was working with Seattle grungers Pearl Jam at the time and 'The Horse' weren't happy about it.

The timing was perfect.

When I realised there might actually be a chance that this bizarre union may come to fruition, I wrote a few more tunes in the same vein, just to will the magic along. 'You Must Be Prepared To Dream' and 'Child Inside A Father' came fast.

Crazy Horse eventually said "yes" despite hearing nothing and not having a clue who I was - I guess they were curious and needed the money - I don't know - I never found out.

I do know the word Liverpool brings about a positive reaction from musicians throughout the world.

Bass player Billy Talbot called me up from San Francisco and we hit it off right away. Arrangements were made and time was booked at Red Zone studios in San Fernando Valley for October.

John Porter and I would co-produce the record.

I was going to California to make a rock 'n' roll album with one of the best rock 'n' roll bands on Earth.

Fucking cool or what?

"Be careful what you dream of, it may come up and surprise you."
No shit, Sherlock.

The day before I left Blighty I went into the studio with Ian Broudie to do backing vocals on the new Lightning Seeds album. Ian had also asked me to write the lyrics to a new tune he had.

It ended up being called 'Feelin' Lazy' and was a cute, suburban, Kinks-type effort. Very nice.

I did loads of backing vocals in a couple of hours without actually hearing a song all the way through.

Ian paid me five hundred quid and I was out the door. The album would be called *Jollification* and would go on to sell the best part of a million. I didn't realise I would be hearing myself on the radio on these tracks for the next twenty years!

I didn't even get a gold disc.

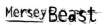

CHAPTER THIRTY THREE

Crazy Horse
in the Valley

October 1994.

I took Nick Warren, Roy, Judith, Andrew, and my live sound engineer Joe Campbell (who was coming along on his own dime for the jolly up) to L.A. with me.

We checked into the Beverly Garland hotel in the valley. The next day John Porter and I drove around L.A. buying strings and picking up bits and bobs for the session. To say I was nervous would be an understatement.

I'd worshipped this band since I was in my teens. Also they hadn't heard a note of my music (I refused to do demos).

What if they didn't like it? What if they couldn't play it? What if they were cunts? These guys had made music since the mid-sixties - I was just some upstart from Liverpool with high hopes.

I knew how the band worked however, and felt in no way was I about to attempt to punch above my weight. I had three or four songs that I knew they should be able to handle. Crazy Horse are basically the greatest bar band in the world and as long as I didn't try to get fancy, things should work out okay.

When I turned up at Red Zone there was a huge truck parked outside and their crew were unloading their gear. I walked in and saw Ralph Molina helping to set up his kit. I went and said hello - he was really nice but seemed very shy and... perhaps a little nervous?

Maybe he thought I was going to ask him to play in 7/4. Billy Talbot was already plugged in and was playing away contentedly on his white Fender Precision bass.

The guitar player who usually worked with them in Neil's band - Frank 'Poncho' Sampedro - would not be joining us for the session as he was not a full time member of Crazy-Horse-without-Neil (they had made many albums without him) as he had a full-time job outside of the band which he only took leave of for (very lucrative) sessions and tours with the great man.

Playing guitar with us today would be Mike 'Tone' Hamilton who had played with Billy and Ralph for some time and was a roadie for the Smithereens.

I had to trust Billy and Ralph on this one. Joe McGrath had worked with JP on lots of projects and would be our engineer.

John was walking around moving micstands nervously - keeping one eye on me to make sure I was okay. When the pleasantries had run their course the moment of truth arrived. As I stated before, nobody had heard anything yet so this was a big deal. I grabbed my acoustic guitar and looked around for a chair.

I couldn't find one so I sat on the floor. The three musicians stood in a semi-circle around me. Pressure. I took a deep breath and began to play 'Fire Inside My Soul'.

'Goin' where the sun is warmer, goin' where nobody knows my name, goin' where the trees are taller, goin' where there isn't any pain, goin' where the days are brighter, goin' where the load is lighter, goin' where they know a fighter, goin' down, down to delta, got a head like a rock, and a fire inside my soul...'

"Wow." That's Ralph.
"Great lyrics." Mike.
"Hey...G! My favourite key!" Says Billy.

They dig it. Thank Christ. I'm in.

"Let's cut! Come on!" Ralph again.

They're jazzed. Fuckin' 'ell.

We donned our instruments and started running the song down. This band records everything live so there'll be no overdubs or messing about. It's all about capturing the moment.

Mistakes are not to be concerned with. Feel is everything. We played the song all day until everybody felt they'd done their best. Eventually we nailed a version where the magic came together.

Billy decided we needed a break.

"Hey Ian, do you smoke pot?"

"Er... yeah!"

We "Pulled off the road" for a while and "Went to Brazil" (their phrases) for a spell. Needless to say the weed these hippies do is about twenty times more powerful than the shit I smoke back in the 'pool, and when I picked up my Les Paul to resume recording, I was in fucking orbit (Ralph didn't smoke - he claimed he'd taken so many drugs in the sixties/seventies he didn't need to anymore - he was still high).

We played the song a few more times but we already had it - you usually get the take within the first two or three goes if the band is right - it was.

The next day I showed them 'You Must Be Prepared To Dream' which they seemed to like even more than 'Fire' and it was nailed in half the time. 'Child Inside A Father' is up next.

After I show it to them, Billy decides we need to smoke a LOT of pot before we attempt to record this one. I am very stoned. This weed is off the scale. I am very, very stoned. Did I tell you I was stoned?

It seems I'm not alone. Billy starts hitting his bass behind the neck in a completely different key to which the song is in and starts pulling weird, grimacing faces at me.

He's in The Zone. I stand on every pedal I have in front of me and try to make my guitar sound like a terrorist attack. This unholy, beautiful racket goes on for about a minute and a half, with Ralph and Mike joining in the mayhem.

I'm in heaven.

This is the magic of the moment. It's hard to find - and when you do you never want it to end.

Perfect.

We begin the song proper and float somewhere above the valley into the cloudless night sky. Ralph Molina did the most beautiful harmony on this tune with me. He's incredibly underrated as a singer. (A couple of months later there will be a huge earthquake in Los Angeles which I'm sure had its genesis in the earth-moving volume and sonic rumble we unleashed at the beginning of this track.

The vintage Fender Deluxe amplifier I used for it was destroyed by the end of the song and has never been used since).

By the end of the week we'd done four tracks (including two very different versions of 'May You Always') and everyone hugged a big goodbye and said we hoped to see each other again.

Everyone was very excited about what we had in the can from Crazy Horse. After they left on the Friday we all went out to El Coyote, a Mexican cafe on Beverley Blvd and got hammered on Margaritas. My speciality at this time was running over cars.

This is literally what it sounds like. I would jump on the bonnet and then sprint over the roof and hopefully land on the other side in an upright position.

I perfected this talent over a number of years and became very good at it. I would encourage other drinkers to do the same but never had any takers.

I'd never done it on Sunset Blvd before so it was more exciting than usual. It was preferable if the vehicle was vacant although not essential. I stopped doing it after one particularly irate individual jumped out of his Datsun, pinned me against a wall and threatened to kill me.

Ah, the folly of youth (I was in my early thirties at the time). I also spent that Friday evening trying to put my hand down the jeans of producer Tom Lord-Algae's stunning blonde girfriend who put up with me for two hours and then legged it into the Hollywood night.

On Monday we were back in the studio with another set of musicians. John Porter was playing a blinder here. On drums: Joseph 'Zigaboo' Modeliste. Born in New Orleans, Louisiana, Ziggy is one of the most highly acclaimed drummers ever to hail from the Crescent City.

He remains a strong influence for drummers and a great many hip-hop samplers. He is best known as a founding member of The Meters and The Wild Tchopitoulas as well as his side work with artists like the Neville Brothers, Keith Richards, Robert Palmer, and Dr.John.

Zigaboo's style is unique - he is especially known for his syncopated rhythms and his unique second line funk styles, which have been sampled, imitated and copied many times over the years. On bass: James 'Hutch' Hutchinson from Cambridge, Massachusetts.

Hutch's portfolio of session work is vast: The Neville Brothers, Elton John, Brian Wilson, Al Green, B.B. King, Crosby, Stills, Nash And Young , Boz Scaggs, Jackson Browne, David Crosby, Ziggy Marley, Hank Williams Jr., Ringo Starr, Merle Haggard, Toots Hibbert, Delbert Mclinton, Kathy Mattea, Garth Brooks, Lyle Lovett, Tanya Tucker, Etta James, Willie Nelson, Pattie La Belle, Vince Gill, Bryan Adams, Ryan Adams, it goes on.

On keyboards: Tommy Eyre. Tommy was born in Sheffield, England. A very versatile and prolific keyboardist, he played with many great bands.

His name should be included in any hall of fame for

keyboardists, and although his musical contributions are very extensive he'll always be remembered by two of his most famous works: The playing on Joe Cocker's version of 'With A Little Help From My Friends' - Tommy's organ arrangements gave the song such classy style - and the playing on 'Baker Street' by Gerry Rafferty (Tommy would sadly succumb to cancer in May 2001 - miss you mate).

With this shit-hot band I would record the rest of the album - which was clearly going to have two very different styles to it. How would I hang it all together? I'd worry about that later. For now I had to show them some songs to play. First up was 'Still Got The Fever'.

Essentially a two-chord trick that rambled on in its own good time - it was all about the power of self-belief and wonderment at the world around us (a theme which I wanted throughout the album).

We played it exactly twice and the version you hear on the album is take one. 'Time You Were In Love', 'Potency', 'Go Into The Light', and 'This Time Is Forever' were all recorded very quickly one after the other. 'Sad, Strange, Solitary Catholic Mystic'- a wordless vocal instrumental consisting of track upon track of me harmonising with myself was a little harder to nail due to the shifting tempo - but was caught the next afternoon.

JP, Roy and I cut 'As A Life Goes By' as an acoustic three-piece that evening. Over the next few days I did all the vocals and a gospel choir was brought in to make even grander gestures on some of the tracks. Steel player Greg Liez (Wilco, Lucinda Williams, Matthew Sweet) came in and sweetened the dish even further. Tony Braunagel (Lightnin' Hopkins, John Lee Hooker, Charles Brown, B.B. King, Otis Rush, Etta James, Buddy Guy, Koko Taylor, Jimmie Reed) glued many of the tunes together with gorgeous, liquid percussion. And that was it. It just had to be mixed, which we would do in London.

I knew I had a monster on my hands. I didn't feel that the

songs were any better or worse than anything I'd written before ('Potency' was an afterthought), but the vibe on tape was like nothing I'd ever captured before. It was a peak.

True artists live for the fastest transit of the sound in their head to tape, and this was the most rewarding illustration of this process I'd encountered to this point.

The performance of the album would confirm my feelings.

CHAPTER THIRTY FOUR

Naomi in Mayfair

The plan was that everybody would reconvene in London at Mayfair studios in Primrose Hill in January '94.

John Porter felt that his work was done and delegated Joe McGrath to brave the English winter in order to mix the record.

However, Joe fucked up in immigration when he told them he was here to holiday but looked nervous. They went through his bag and found session notes and work related items and put him on a plane back home.

We had a couple of days to find someone else to mix and Pete Schwier was drafted in. I wasn't too happy with his mixing credentials (Pet Shop Boys - the opposite of music in my opinion, Marc Almond - what to say about Marc Almond? - loved him in Soft Cell. Yes, and a few others I didn't care for, but, he was available like, NOW).

He did a great job and we got on really well. While we were at Mayfair, supermodel Naomi Campbell was there recording what was to become one of the great turkeys of popular music, her *Babywoman* album.

Her ill-advised attempt to break out of her mere clothes horse status and be viewed as a true artist - the album would sell hundreds of copies when it was eventually released.

The album was being produced by current squeeze and luckiest-bass-player-in-the-world, Adam Clayton of popular

Christian rock group U2.

One evening during a long session I walked out into the recreational area to clear my head to find Ms. Campbell sprawled half asleep on a sofa in front of the TV She looked up, gave me a friendly smile, and asked me if I wanted the remote control as she wasn't really watching anything.

I said thanks and took it from her. She then appeared to fall asleep. I flicked around for a bit trying to find some news when she suddenly leapt up and faced me.

"Are you going to be doing that all fucking night?!"

She was yelling at me, full throttle - with a face that didn't look so beautiful anymore. I was shocked.

Shocked that an adult whom I'd never met before would suddenly talk to me like I was dirt on the ground. All I did was change the channel a few times. I threw the remote on the couch and walked back to the studio.

The next day the studio manager asked for a private word with me.

"Listen Ian, Naomi is very tired, she's just come back from a shoot in the Bahamas and she's shattered.

She's behind with her album and is very stressed. Could you not disturb her and could you please keep away from the lounge in future as she needs her space."

This was all I needed to hear. I bounced into the control room and got on the phone to Judith rapid style.

"Listen, I'm not being told what to do by some young bint with a superiority complex. I'm paying twelve hundred quid a day to be in this fuckin' place and I will not be told to keep out of the lounge."

(Naomi was in the much smaller, cheaper studio, and if anyone had dibs on the TV it would be me).

I demanded an apology from the studio - effective immediately - and threatened to walk if I didn't get one.

Sure enough I got one later that day. Ms. Campbell however,

asked if the TV could be moved into her studio so she could watch it alone. When she was told that the TV was for the use of all the clients at the studio, she complained that I had tried to hit on her and she was afraid I might try something.

What a silly woman.

Typical of women blessed with great beauty, NC had been given what she wanted all through her life and had not developed the simple skills of polite social interaction and good manners.

Spoiled since day one, fawned over by all and generally made to feel as though she was above all simply due to the virtue of her looks, she was completely bereft of charm.

I hear stories on the news about her to this day and conclude that she clearly has learnt nothing in the passing years.

Head Like A Rock - for that is what my new album would be called - was mixed and ready to go.

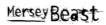

CHAPTER THIRTY FIVE

Fragile Souls

I was still seeing Bridget.

However, I was now becoming restless and knew it was time to move on again.

Bridget was very upset about this as we'd become very close. She'd seen me through some very lean times, was caring and compassionate, but as usual I only really cared about myself.

I loved Bridget but I wasn't in love with her.

That old chestnut.

We parted on good terms, I think. I started seeing a great girl (once again from the Wirral - a place called Little Sutton) called Lisa. An effervescent, sparkly, young (eighteen), blonde, intelligent, chatty being, I'd met her at the newly-opened Lomax club on Cumberland Street in Liverpool, where she was watching a gig which she would review for a local magazine.

After eyeballing her all night, I tapped Martyn Campbell of the Lightning Seeds on the shoulder and asked for an intro. She loved music, had catching enthusiasm, was rather lovely to look at, and never stopped giggling.

The age difference (I was thirty-three) seemed not to bother her - it certainly didn't bother me. Lisa would stay with me most weekends and we started having a lot of fun together.

The Lomax was great, basically three floors in a tall, slim building, it would showcase a staggering amount of emerging

bands for the short amount of time it would exist.

Owned by local businessman/builder Mick Hindley and spearheaded artistically initially by local musician Andy Redhead, it would breathe life into a local music scene which had begun to stagnate.

I remember seeing Radiohead, Stereophonics and Oasis there amongst others in the mid-nineties. Unfortunately the Lomax opened a bigger venue in Hotham Street off London Road a few years later and fell victim to expansion into a wider, more competitive market.

Both venues would close forever after a couple of years never to return. A great loss in my opinion, which still rankles to this day.

The new album was pressed up and ready to go. It would be released on July 4th 1994. We would shoot a video clip for the first single 'You Must Be Prepared to Dream' in Hollywood in early April with Crazy Horse. On the morning of the shoot the news broke that lead singer of grunge supergroup Nirvana - Kurt Cobain - had blown his face off with a shotgun. His suicide note quoted a Neil Young song - 'My My, Hey Hey (Into The Black)' - which Crazy Horse played on. "It's better to burn out than fade away..." It didn't dampen the mood of the visual performance completely - we had a job to do - but everybody felt sad all day.

We'd lost one of our own. How could such great success bring so much misery? A mystery wrapped in narcotics.

"Fragile souls..." Billy Talbot kept saying all day.

Crazy Horse had lost their guitar player Danny Whitten (writer of the timeless 'I Don't Want To Talk About It') to a heroin overdose twenty years previously when Neil Young had given him some money to get home from a rehearsal he was too strung out to take part in. He used the money to get high instead of travel - and he checked out for good.

"Fragile souls..."

Thank God I'm not one of them.

Somewhere along the line I'd gotten tough. Drugs and Alcohol were often in my blood but the downers that inevitably followed any ups didn't bring havoc to my nervous system the way it did with a lot of people I knew.

Firstly, I very rarely got muntered in order to kill pain - I just did it for fun.

To mask misery with stimulants is a foolhardy thing to do. When the stuff wears off you have the problem again except this time the hangover makes it even harder to bear.

So you do it again until the dosages are higher and subsequently the fallout is terminal. Being in showbiz has a strange effect on the human mind.

The ups and downs are frightening. When success eventually comes, it comes so fast and hard that you can barely hold onto the reins. You finish a prolonged period of live performance which is intoxicating and somewhere approaching a mental orgasm, and then you have a lengthy period of trying to adjust to normal everyday life like doing the dishes or paying your bills.

You also have to cope with failure as well as success (which in some cases is easier - failure has boundaries). You can't take the knocks and disappointments of this job and continue if you don't measure up.

It's sometimes soul destroying to see the effort you've made come to nothing, but you get used to it and climb on again. Many find this extremely difficult to do. Not me.

Lucky. Lucky. Lucky.

The director of the clip was Eric Zimmerman who did a great job of capturing a rockin' lip-sych performance and a surrealistic angle - featuring Reggie Trickpuss, the ventriloquist dummy which graced the cover of the album - and myself doing weird things in the Mojave Desert. Nick Warren gave me an ecstasy tablet while we were working and I found myself in the unenviable predicament of coming up fast on a pill in searing desert heat whilst wearing heavy denim which I couldn't

remove due to continuity. Should you get to see this clip someday bear this in mind and it will improve your viewing enjoyment vastly.

We hung out on the Strip for a few days after the shoot - visiting all the regular haunts and then headed home with great anticipation for the album's eventual release.

Would it get me back in the game? The wait was killing me.

We'd know soon enough.

CHAPTER THIRTY SIX

TheOx

Summer 1994.

It was decided that we would bring Crazy Horse over for some shows previous to the album's release in order to drum up publicity. We secured a slot at that year's Glastonbury Festival preceded by a date at Manchester University and two nights at King's College in London.

Crazy Horse would come to Liverpool to rehearse with me for a week prior to the shows.

Everything was coming together when it began to look like there may be problems getting them over here. There were a number of financial concerns (they had a big problem flying coach) and Neil Young was gearing up to do some more recording with them (they had already started work on what would become the *Sleeps With Angels* album - heavily inspired by Kurt Cobain's recent passing). While people were worrying about this I had to record a bunch of B sides to go along with the projected single releases from the album (I was assured there would be at least two).

I asked Zak Starkey to come to the Windings studio in North Wales with me and spend a couple of days knocking things out. He came up on the train and we drove over together.

Zak had stopped drinking and was in great mental and physical shape.

257

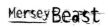

He'd lost his booze fat.

We recorded several things - 'Woo Yer', 'Rock', and 'That's Why The Darkness Exists' - being the only ones I can remember ever being released.

I told him that I may have a problem bringing Crazy Horse over for the gigs and he offered me a solution. He suggested that he'd play drums for me and he'd mention it to his best mate John Entwistle of the Who (nickname: 'The Ox') that I was looking for a bass player.

I laughed out loud as I dropped my bacon sarnie, but he assured me that this was a real possibility as the Who were currently on ice and John was bored to death in his stately home.

I passed this information on to the record company who thought it was a fabulous idea.

Zak called me a few days later and said that John dug the new album and would love to do the gigs.

We still didn't know if Crazy Horse were coming or not, so I asked Zak to organise a meeting with John so we could find out if this was a pipe dream or the real deal. Even if nothing came of it I knew we'd have a good night on the town - we've all heard those Who stories.

One chilly spring afternoon in London I was waiting for Zak to call me and tell me where we would be meeting. My mind was rife with possibilities - what a great band this would be - who else would I get on guitar? Which Who song could we cover?

Which fabulous rock star night spot would we be dining in this very eve? Zak called and told me that his siblings Lee and Jason would be coming. Great! A party! We would go and meet John and his girlfriend Lisa at Bailey's hotel in Knightsbridge, and then proceed to...The Hard Rock Cafe.

The Hard Rock Cafe?! A tourist joint that any fucker could hang out in. I was a bit deflated. I was hoping for The Ivy, Brown's or at least San Lorenzo. Oh well...

We went and got them from the hotel, jumped into Zak's Mercedes and headed for Mayfair.

Zak insisted on playing the Who at full volume on the journey and I had the surreal experience of listening to 'Pictures Of Lily' while John criticised his French horn playing in the song's instrumental break from the back seat.

We arrived at the Hard Rock where Lee, Jason and a couple of their friends were waiting for us. The waiter guided us to our table and we were seated. As I settled and got my bearings I looked up and around me to realise that we were sitting by the Who memorabilia section of the restaurant.

We were surrounded by wall-mounted smashed guitars in glass cases, Union Jacks and gold records. John was taking part in a display of which he was a living, breathing member. During dinner a few Americans stopped to marvel at the collection only to have near-heart-attacks when they saw the actual bass player of the Who sitting beneath one of his basses from the seventies sipping his brandy coffee.

John loved being a rock star and didn't shy away from it for one moment. He died eight years later - full of cocaine - in the company of a couple of hookers - in a hotel in Las Vegas with a guitar sticking out of the roof.

Now if I had a choice?

We got on great. He was well into the stuff and wanted to do the gigs. He was a raconteur of the highest order.

A witty bastard.

"What goes clip clop, bang bang, clip clop? An Amish drive-by."

He reminisced aloud about the days gone by with reverent pleasure.

"The Doors? We played the Singer Bowl in New York with them in 1969. Worst fackin' band I've ever seen in my life. Shockin.' They should be called the Bores."

"What was so bad about them?"

"Well they didn't 'ave a fackin' bass player for starters..."

After dinner we headed up to the West End for drinks and ended up in the Borderline off Charing Cross road.

We all got royally sloshed until the small hours and made our grand plans. John would sing 'My Wife' from *Who's Next* in our band.

As I staggered up the stairs behind a very refreshed legend, I grabbed his arm and shouted into his ear (he was practically deaf).

"Hey John! I bet Pete (Townshend) doesn't have this much fun any more!"

"What? He never fackin' did!"

Zak told me another story about John once. Just before he died, the band and hangers-on were ensconced in the bar of the Sunset Marquis hotel in West Hollywood. The Who were about to commence a tour that John would never play on.

Rolan Bolan - son of Marc - was in the bar and went up to John and introduced himself.

"So did you know my dad then?" asked Rolan, pleasantly.

"No, but I've driven past the tree a few times," said John.

(Marc Bolan died in a car which ploughed into a tree on Barnes Common, South London).

We never played together in the end - Crazy Horse came through for me and John went and played in Roger Daltrey's touring band.

When John Entwistle died we lost a musical genius.

The most original bass player of his generation, a rock 'n' roll gentleman, and an innovator.

Ladies and Gentleman...I give you...

The Ox.

CHAPTER THIRTY SEVEN

Crazy Horse in the UK

Crazy Horse finally arrived.

They came up to Liverpool straight from Heathrow Airport and set up camp in the Adelphi Hotel.

Terry Staunton from the N.M.E. would hang out with us for a couple of days, documenting the rehearsals and watching us (hopefully) morph together musically and personality-wise.

As well as Billy (bass), Ralph (drums) and Mike (guitar), we had Jerry Conforti their long-standing roadie with us for the duration. Rehearsals started in Crash studios and all was good. We sounded like a juggernaut.

In fact we sounded like a couple of juggernauts as everybody played slightly behind everybody else (the secret of the Crazy Horse sound).

Billy and Ralph spent a fair amount of time arguing with each other over tiny details which was very amusing. They went at each other like a couple of old Italian Restaurateurs.

It was like being in a band with the Mob - without killing - just shouting.

They loved being in Liverpool and told me they'd never been before (they had - they just couldn't remember).

There were many funny moments, my favourite being when Billy went for a big note on the chorus of 'Firepower' and his false teeth flew out of his mouth.

It was an amazing sight - it was obviously a regular occurrence, as he flew after them with his mouth open and managed to catch them again - incredible. It reminded me of how the alien's mouth worked in those movies.

I dropped the song from the set in fear of a repeat performance. We learnt a bunch of other songs from my past - four songs wouldn't make a show - and they nailed it all in four days.

We also learnt 'I Don't Want To Talk About It', which was a great thrill for me. One night we went out for dinner and my mum came along. Billy was enjoying the free-flowing booze and was getting a little loud.

"Hey Billy... shurrup will ya... I bet you don't behave like this around Neil?!" That's my mum.

Ralph nearly choked on his vegetable curry.

"Pat! You're right! He never says a fuckin' word around Neil!"

Much laughter.

One night we were all sitting in my kitchen and my mum chastised Billy for going in the fridge for a beer without asking.

Priceless moments.

The first gig in Manchester was sold out and went like a dream. People stood open-mouthed.

They couldn't believe they were seeing local shit-kicker McNabb playing with these guys. Neither could I.

I was in heaven.

The two London shows were even better although we struggled a little on attendance the first night as there was a problem on the Northern line underground.

We played in defiance.

We were ON.

Noel Gallagher of the newly-emerging group Oasis was due to get up and do the encore with us on the second night.

We'd become mates recently and he was a huge Neil Young/Crazy Horse fan. Listen to the guitars on an Oasis record.

Noel was quite shy in those days as opposed to the confident, slightly arrogant chap you see before you today.

A few weeks beforehand I'd spent an evening with him and my friend John Brice round at Noel's manager Marcus's flat and we'd got blasted and played our respective new music to each other.

I played him all of *Head Like A Rock* and he played me Oasis' demos. I told him I thought he'd do very well but I thought my stuff was a lot better.

The last thing Noel said to me as I fell into the street that night was: "Hey, I hope you're gonna talk your album up as much as I am - I'm gonna tell everyone how fuckin' great it is!"

I'm still waiting for this to happen.

Noel turned up about halfway through the show and met me side stage as we came off.

"I'm not fuckin' gettin' up with you ya cunt! Ya too fuckin' good!"

"Come on man! There's a guitar on stage for you. We're gonna do 'Pushin' Too Hard' by the Seeds. It's A minor to G for five minutes. Piece o' piss!"

"Is that all there is?"

"Yea...take a solo when I give you the nod."

"Fuck off!"

He was shitting himself. I introduced him to the guys and dragged him on by his sleeve.

"Ladies and Gentlemen...Noel Gallagher from Oasis!"

"Who?" Someone in the front row exclaimed.

The audience were nonplussed. Oasis had only had one single out thus far and my audience were a little old to read the N.M.E.

Backstage everybody was hugging and shouting a lot.

A triumph.

Someone offered Noel a joint and he declined - apparently being allergic to the weed. He offered me a line and I passed.

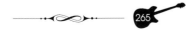

We were driving to Bath tonight in preparation for tomorrow's Glastonbury show and I had to get to sleep or I'd be croaking through the set.

We were scheduled to play the Pyramid Stage in the early afternoon.

Too early in my opinion - but you take what you're given at festivals unless you're headlining. I'd asked my friend Mike Scott of the Waterboys to join us for a couple of tunes during our hour-long stint (a grand gesture - Mike would be there playing solo on the acoustic stage).

We had dutifully learnt two of his songs - 'Glastonbury Song' (right?) and 'Preparing To Fly'. Both were tunes from his last album *Dream Harder*, which had been a great, positive influence on me whilst writing *Head Like A Rock*.

We arrived early afternoon at Glastonbury and played a blinding set to a vast crowd for the time of day we were on.

World Party were also playing that day and I got to hang out with Karl Wallinger and Chris Sharrock, which was fabulous. I was punching my weight again, up there with the dudes, where I thought I belonged.

The show was filmed by Channel Four and shown later in the day. Mike did us proud and - we'd done it. The album wasn't even out yet. People were stoked.

After the show I collapsed in my dressing room and tingled. We'd worked incredibly hard and now it was time to party. I wanted to get fucked up. I gave a gofor about two hundred pounds and told him to get me a bunch of drugs.

Pills, anything.

He arrived twenty minutes later with a huge bag of Coke. I tried to keep it quiet but Billy walked in as I was lining a couple up.

"Is that what I think it is?"

"Well, I dunno. What do you think it is?"

He was on it before I could tell him.

Soon enough we were jumping around the dressing room, talking each other into the ground.

Ralph walked in and observed Billy's newly found energy.

"Hey Bill...had a little tootskie have we?" he delivered as man who'd seen it all many, many times before.

We all fell about the place in laughter.

We decided to get amongst it and have a walk round the festival site (or as much of it as we could handle). The yanks loved it and told me they'd seen nothing like it anywhere else. After a couple of hours we left the site and headed back to London, exhausted.

The party kept going in the bus and the three guys sitting at the back - me, Billy and Mike - kept stoking plenty of coke on the fire. By the time we got back to the Embassy hotel in Bayswater we were very high. We decided we'd go for something to eat (no-one was going to sleep) although no-one had much of an appetite either by this point (for those who don't know, class A drugs generally destroy any thoughts of food - it's like eating straw).

We found an Indian restaurant on Ladbroke Grove and sat there looking at our food for a couple of hours. I was floundering by this point as was everybody else. Billy became very emotional and was depressed about having to go home early the next day. He'd loved every minute of it.

Next morning we all got up early and it was time to wave Crazy Horse off. The trip had been a great success and now it was time for the much-feared come-down.

We hugged and made promises, and then they were gone. I felt a bit like Neil Armstrong after the Moonshot.

What could follow that?

At least I had the album release to look forward to. I walked around the corner to Queensway, bought some cigarettes, a coffee, and the morning papers.

I crossed Bayswater Road and entered Hyde Park. I sat down,

lit up and breathed a sigh of relief. An early morning jogger passed and smiled at me and said hello. Unusual for London.

I pulled deeply on the Marlboro light. Job done. What an amazing experience. The past couple of weeks just seemed like a dream now.

I figured nothing like that would ever happen to me again, although who knows? I took a sip of coffee. I could feel my throat tighten and my eyes begin to sting slightly.

I read the paper and tried to return to normality for a while.

CHAPTER THIRTY EIGHT

Mercury

Things quietened down a little.

Q magazine ran a three page piece on the new album which David Cavanagh wrote after returning from interviewing us in L.A. Time Out ran a piece also (I had to go and do the interview again, this time in London - after Ross Fortune, the guy that we flew out to the States to do the job found out that his recording hadn't come out audibly enough for him to transcribe it - honestly).

Terry Staunton who'd spent a couple of days in Liverpool interviewing and observing us went on a bender for two weeks after his girlfriend dumped him and he 'forgot' to write up our promised article for the N.M.E.

You've got to laugh.

I also had the indignity of Q magazine running a news piece with the headline 'Noel And Crazy Horse' with a picture of Noel Gallagher's head superimposed where mine originally was on a publicity picture taken of me with the band in L.A.

It went on to describe in great detail how Noel had played with them in London a couple of weeks ago. I barely got a mention. I was not fucking amused, but I remained silent.

'You Must Be Prepared To Dream' did my regular just-outside-the-top fifty placing. Boo! (They just don't like playing me on the radio I guess).

The album came out (at last!) and made everyone happy by getting into the top twenty U.K chart in its first week of release. My highest ever placing.

Success!

Andrew and Judith from This Way Up - who'd guided me through everything to do with the record, and then some - went away on holiday to Venice to catch their breath.

I spent time in Liverpool with my mum, friends and Lisa, as I tried to relax and pondered my next move.

I feared the whole thing was going to grow cold very quickly if I didn't do something again soon - or if external forces didn't come into play to prolong my second bite of the apple.

Fortunately they did.

One night I was slumped on the sofa at home when the phone went. It was a producer from BBC Radio One who I'd met a couple of times.

He asked me if I would answer the phone again the next day at exactly one-thirty p.m. as there was some very exciting news coming my way.

I was buzzing, but clueless as to what this may be.

I slept fitfully and rose early next morning bristling with anticipation.

I put the radio on and wondered what this could possibly be about. Then a news item came on reporting that the nominations for this year's Mercury Music Prize would be announced shortly from Kensington's Rooftop Gardens.

I assumed - correctly - that my name must be on the list.

The station called me and broke the news to me on air at the designated time.

The MMP was in its third year, was a big deal by music biz standards, previous winners having been Primal Scream and Suede.

It was certainly a big deal by MY standards - having previously only being nominated for ejection from nightclubs.

I would go up against nine other acts:

M People – Elegant Slumming
Blur – Parklife
Shara Nelson – What Silence Knows
Michael Nyman – The Piano Concerto and MGV
The Prodigy – Music for the Jilted Generation
Pulp – His'n'Hers
Take That – Everything Changes
Therapy? – Troublegum
Paul Weller – Wild Wood

Blimey, all these people had sold loads of records. Even I looked at the line-up of names and went, 'Who?!' When I saw:

Ian McNabb – Head Like A Rock

But there it was.

Everyone started freaking out.

The record had only been serviced to the board a week before they announced the nominees. Dave Bedford from This Way Up had attended the ceremony - expecting his personal project the Tindersticks to be on the list - and was amazed when my name came out of the hat.

I was interviewed live on air a few times that afternoon, and I tried to sound as nonchalant as I could - when asked if I was surprised to be among the great and the good I replied "Of course not, no."

I was amazed, of course.

A great album at the right time, with a great story attached.

That's the trick, Dufus!

The awards ceremony would be held at the Savoy hotel in September and would be televised live by the BBC. The publicity generated would be huge.

A compilation tie-in album would be put together and priority-

racked in all the High St. record stores.

You couldn't ask for more.

In the meantime we would put out a new single to hopefully keep my name around during the summer.

'Go Into The Light' was chosen as the new single. A lesser track from HLAR, but it was short, funky and poppy with the gospel choir used to full effect, and my plugger Scott Peiring reckoned we had a shot with it. Jah Wobble (P. I.L.) was drafted in to do a remix.

He did a good job I thought, but nothing special. I went into the small studio at Parr St. and did a couple more B-sides.

The single came out in September and did the usual.

The last time I had any significant radio play had been with 'If Love Was Like Guitars'. I'd resigned myself to the fact that I just wasn't a singles artist and my mark would be made by albums.

Sometimes you have to put a single out just so as you can go round all the stations and talk yourself up.

People always need something to hang an interview on.

It's not a bad idea if you decide to have an affair with someone more famous than you - they'll definitely play your record or do an interview with you then.

The awards ceremony at the Savoy was strange. I decided I should take someone with me (along with my mum and her friend Karen), so I decided to ask Karen.

I was still seeing Lisa but she was so young and I didn't know how she'd fit into the situation. She was very bubbly and could get loud quickly when nervous.

Karen and I had maintained contact after our quiet parting and she seemed like the right choice - ladylike, demure and very easy on the eye.

Essential rock star ornamentation.

We sat on a huge table with all of the Island brass (This Way Up's parent company) who behaved like they were up for an Oscar even though none of their own acts had been nominated.

They wanted their night out on brandy and cigars and Christ knows they'd paid for it.

I was their ticket.

They hardly looked at me all night. I was determined not to get pissed and make a show of myself - I had to get up and say a few words when they gave me my statue - I hate it when musicians jump up at these things with a bottle in one hand, a fag in the other and mumble some incoherent in-joke or swear a lot to attract attention.

I was incredibly nervous. Drugs were an absolute no-no too - I wasn't going to get kettled with my mother sitting next to me. I couldn't eat my two hundred quid's worth plate of salmon, fidgeted nervously and puffed away on Marlboro lights throughout the ceremony.

Mick Winder was there with Therapy? And once again I got to stick it to the deserters. This was turning out to be a great year.

I had to get up and say a few words when they called me. I didn't have a clue what to say so I asked Andrew. He suggested I bend the classic Bill Shankly maxim of yore to my advantage.

'Thanks for this, it's a great honour. Music isn't life or death, it's much, much more important than that.'

I got a huge round of applause and sat down happy in the knowledge it was nearly over. I wasn't used to this sort of thing.

M People won.

I wasn't even remotely disappointed.

Getting this far had been fantastic.

The party afterwards was a blast. The actor Phil Daniels (*Quadrophenia*, later *Eastenders*) was there celebrating with his mates Blur.

He was sitting at a grand piano trying to get a Cockney knees-up together. When he ran out of steam I sat down next to him on the piano stool and started playing 'Love Reign O'er Me' from *Quadrophenia*.

"Go on Scouse!" he cried.

We sang it together until I forgot the rest of the words (I was well hammered by now). I got talking to Damon Albarn from Blur.

"Don't do it Damon! Don't do it!" "Do fackin' what?!"

"Make a double concept album about a deaf, dumb and blind tennis player from Highgate!"

He looked at me like I was cracked and shuffled away muttering "Scousers"- shaking his (big) head.

He's a clever bastard that Damon Albarn.

There had been live coverage of the event on BBC2 and a few people called me to tell me I'd been trashed by the panel of hacks assembled to critique the selected albums.

All the other acts up to that point had been praised and I guess I was chosen as the one to present the negative balance (I couldn't possibly entertain the fact that that they didn't like my little masterpiece).

Tony Parsons - that odious little jumped up, key-tapping cockney wanker - made the most offensive comment.

"I find it quite funny that someone who comes from Liverpool could say they had a 'Fire inside their soul'."

Strike another one up for north-south relations.

Typical of the myopic, self-opinionated, never-been-north-of-Watford dunces who've only ever succeeded in writing about IT as opposed to doing IT.

Oh, well. I've never seen a statue of a critic.

Have you?

I fell into bed - alone (well at least I was being faithful to Lisa) and fell into a deep sleep with a huge smile on my face.

I like it up here, where the air is rare and fine.

Later on in the month the Liverpool Echo gave me the 'Artiste Of The Year' award which was presented to me at a swish ceremony at the Adelphi hotel. I was extra thrilled as Dean Sullivan, who played vagrant drug addict/general louse Jimmy Corkhill in *Brookside* gave me my prize.

When I was thirty-three, it was a very good year.

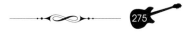

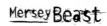

CHAPTER THIRTY NINE

A Merseybeast is born

March 1995.

I spent the winter writing songs. There wasn't much else to do. I was still seeing Lisa and everything had settled into a comfortable little groove.

I was going out and getting pissed fairly frequently to keep myself occupied. The Lomax club was usually my port of call.

I always had a lump of hash by the side of my chair which I would flake into a joint to be smoked with my first cuppa of the day. I would then spend the afternoon jumping with fright everytime the phone rang.

But I wrote a lot of great songs.

'Merseybeast' - a rock 'n' roll limerick about imagined misfortunes from a Liverpool perspective.

After the American flavour of my last album I was eager to remind people how English, nay Liverpudlian - I was.

'Camaraderie' - a little ditty about pretending to be someone's friend when really you are desperately in love with them. A popular theme (I believe).

'You Stone My Soul' - more anthemic love declaration.

'I'm A Genius' - listen love, I may be crap at this, crap at that - but I know how to get you to the place that counts.

And about a dozen others. I was cookin', anxious to build on the success of HLAR.

I wasn't going to let my reclaimed ground slip from under me again in a hurry. During this fertile period, Richey Edwards, the guitar player from the Welsh band Manic Street Preachers, disappeared - never to be seen again. I compounded his story and that of Kurt Cobain's into a short acoustic lament titled 'Too Close To The Sun.'

"Fragile souls."

I went into Parr St. and banged them all down in demo form in about four days, playing everything myself.

I'd been flirting outrageously with the girlfriend of a big fan for a couple of years. Ursula Neinhuis was a beautiful twenty-three year old Dutch girl who reminded me a bit of Claudia Schiffer. She was living with the guy who'd introduced us and I never crossed the line, as the guy was very cool, came to loads of gigs and bought all my records. Being such a twat, though, I knew it wouldn't be too long before we exchanged more than glances.

We spoke to each other on the phone when she could speak to me without fear of being heard, and things started getting interesting. One Sunday afternoon after I'd taken Lisa back to Little Sutton after one of our usual debauched weekends, I came home and found a message on my answerphone from Ursula. I called her back right away.

"Listen..." she purred in her very sexy, deep, Dutch accent (there is such a thing believe me).

"Peter is away for the weekend, why don't you come over?"

I was in the car and on my way to their flat in Crosby within minutes. I picked up a couple of bottles of wine on the way and we were having fun within moments of me arriving.

This arrangement carried on for months. I was now juggling again and had to plan things carefully. Ursula was very cool with all of this (northern Europeans seem to take all of this stuff in their stride - they're very liberal in their way of thinking with regards to sex. Southern Europeans, well that's different. Dan

Stuart of U.S. rockers Green On Red once told me this: "If you don't fuck a Mediterranean chick four times a day, she'll either think you're gay, or you're fuckin' someone else. Man, you better be gay!")

So we carried on. Lisa of course had no idea what I was up to and her fiery temperament would guarantee a severe beating from her, and soon after - her hardcase extended family - should I ever have the misfortune to be caught out. For now though, I was enjoying myself.

Naturally the danger only made it more fun.

It was time to record a new album. The new demos had gone over very well with the powers that be and we were greenlit to start work. We held auditions for new musicians in London as I wanted to put a new band together who could tour at will. We couldn't tour HLAR due to Crazy Horse being:

1) American residents
2) Expensive
3) Unavailable most of the time

Eventually I settled on a wonderfully eccentric Swiss drummer called Daniel Strittmatter. He was born in the town where L.S.D. was invented (Sandoz, in Basel) - which I thought fitted the bill. On bass I plumped for a great guy from London by the name of Russell Milton. I would produce the album with Pete Schweir, as he'd made HLAR such a success.

We went to Rockfield in South Wales. I hadn't been there since making the first Icicle Works album and it was great to meet up with all the good folk there again.

We struggled. England was in the middle of a prolonged, sweltering heatwave, and trust me the last place you want to be when it's hot is in a recording studio - even if it is in acres of rolling hills and greenery.

The air-conditioning system was in overdrive but we had to

turn it off much of the time as it was so loud it was finding it's way onto tape, also we couldn't hear the playbacks properly as the constant hissing noise was deadening the top frequencies.

Apart from that it was all a bit of a comedown from recording in L.A. and it just felt like proper work again. Crazy Horse had been a dream and I was back where I started - all be it with more money and a lot more attention.

Also, I'd shot my wad on the new demos which contained a great vibe and performances but in no way could be considered a finished record - there were no drums on there for a start.

I just couldn't get in gear. Being in a residential studio for a prolonged period of time is a bit like being in prison. You eat at the same time everyday with the same people. Nothing different happens so you talk about the past and what's on the news.

You don't get a shag (even that happens in prison as long as you're happy to be Bubba's girl).

A couple of times a week you go to the Slaughtered Lamb where the country locals look at you the way farmers usually look at musicians.

It's fucking boring.

I was staying in the same room Noel Gallagher had stayed in when Oasis were recording their second album just a few weeks before. He'd left a target sticker on the bathroom door so I carefully peeled it off and put it on my Telecaster, hoping it would bring me some of his luck.

Oasis had become huge since his little stint on stage with me a year ago.

One day I was trying to put a vocal on 'You Stone My Soul' and I just couldn't nail it. I kept listening to the demo and wondering why I couldn't recreate the vocal.

I got fed up, went to the pub which was overlooking a riverbank, and sang the song to the hills. It sounded brilliant. Something was wrong with the vibe in the studio and it wasn't going to happen the way we needed it to.

When you find yourself in this situation you need to stop trying.

It will get harder and harder, you will begin to hate the songs and start dumping them.

This happens a lot with many artists but never with me. We decided to take a break and I came home for a while.

Eventually we got stuck back in and got most of the album finished. Time was booked at Eden studios in Chiswick and I headed south in the torturous heat to begin mixing. It was hell.

Pete wasn't delivering in my opinion and I was freaking out so much I thought I was gonna have a nervous breakdown.

Andrew Lauder called a halt to the proceedings. We had a meeting and I told everyone I thought Pete had had his shot and now we needed to look elsewhere for help finishing the record. Needless to say this information was not received well but Pete agreed to walk away as long as he got his full fee - which he did.

Everyone blamed everyone else. I listened to those mixes recently which I still have on Digital Audio Tape and they do indeed suck (I'm sure if Pete Schweir ever writes his own book - most people do - and my little slice of his story crops up you'll hear a different tale - so it goes).

American producer/engineer Bruce Lampcov's name was bandied about as someone who could come in and fix things (he had a vast track record which included Dire Straits, Bruce Springsteen and Echo And The Bunnymen amongst others) and he signed on to do the job.

First of all we went into Swanyard studios in Islington and re-recorded at least half the tracks.

They sounded great this time. The energy of the city got my juices flowing again and I sang and played real good, real quick. Next we went over to Air Lyndhurst studios in Hampstead to mix.

We banged out a track a day and it all sounded fantastic.

George Martin owns Air and he popped in to have a listen and say hello. We spoke for a while and he mainly chatted about the work he'd done on the Broadway production of the Who's *Tommy*.

It's always nice to meet a legend - when they're in a friendly mood. It was decided that we would include some of the live stuff I had recorded with Crazy Horse at King's College the previous year as part of the package on a bonus disc.

We mixed 'What She Did To My Mind', 'Evangeline', 'I Don't Want To Talk about It', 'When It All Comes Down', and 'Pushin' Too Hard' - which Noel Gallagher had played on.

We had to get permission to use Noel's name on the recording so a CD was dispatched for his approval. Three weeks later we got a message back asking if he could re-record his guitar part as he thought his playing was not good.

I sent a message back saying it was a live recording and I wasn't going to mess about with it. He told me that I would have to take his name off the record in that case.

It came out - with Noel playing on it - uncredited. A little while later I read an interview with him saying he was fed up of people using his name to sell records.

Oh well, at least I had his target sticker.

Merseybeast was ready to go.

I went to see the Who perform *Quadrophenia* at Hyde Park.

Zak was now a full-time member of the band and we had a fantastic day out despite the shit weather.

We were in the V.I.P. seating area and I was sitting directly behind Ringo and Barbara.

Ringo was shouting and cheering Zak on all the way through. When Pete Townshend sat at the piano and sang "Why should I care if I have to cut my hair?" Ringo burst out laughing at the sight of Pete's bald pate on the huge video screens.

A friend in America called me and told me they had been to see a movie called *Scream* recently.

As they were leaving the theatre they recognised the music playing over the credits.

It was 'Birds Fly (Whisper To A Scream)' - my sole U.S. hit - being covered by a band called SoHo. I called Warner Chappell and asked them about it. After much to-ing and fro-ing I got through to the relevant person. It turns out that their American office in L.A. had been approached some time ago about the song being included in the movie, and my publisher had forgotten to ask my permission.

They agreed a flat sync fee with the movie studio and didn't consult me about it.

And so it was that I was paid four thousand dollars and nothing more for my song being included in its entirety in the highest-grossing horror movie (re-booting the genre) of the nineties.

It was also included on the soundtrack album from which I've never received a penny.

Wes Craven owes me.

CHAPTER FORTY

You're dropped
(again) sonny!

Where to go next?

This Way Up/Island/Universal (how many record companies was I now with? Everyone was merging and breaking away on a daily basis) were very excited about *Merseybeast*.

It was after all, the follow up to a top forty Mercury-nominated album which had sold well, and they believed this one had strong enough songs to take it further than HLAR.

The problem with HLAR was that the songs were all very long, and when edited for airplay they lost much of their power.

The new record was (deliberately on my part) stuffed with short, concise pop songs. We had a meeting with my plugger Scott Piering and his people and we played Hunt The Hit. From my point of view I felt the obvious singles were 'You Stone My Soul', 'Camaraderie', and 'I'm A Genius'.

Everyone at Scott's office however was leaning towards 'Don't Put Your Spell On Me' - which I thought was a good rocker, but never a single. They insisted - and I bowed down to their expertise.

A (very expensive) video was commissioned, the track sent to radio, and a very elaborate (and expensive) package for both single and album was put together by Cally Calloman, Island's celebrated art director. The single got one play on Radio One, on a review programme.

Steve Lamacq, a rising star on national radio and one in the running for the title of The New John Peel (as if there ever could be another) said he "would rather sleep in a ditch than listen to that again..."

That was the end of DPYSOM on radio.

The video fared slightly better, picking up plays on VH1. The record peaked at number seventy-two when it was released in April.

The album came out soon after and did well, peaking at number thirty. It was basically a re-run of HLAR without all the publicity. We were treading water. There was one more shot at a hit single with the title track of the album being released in June and hitting number seventy-four.

My cries to release one of my original choices of single fell on deaf ears as all the money had now been spent.

Merseybeast had had its shot and would now be left to fend for itself (it has – becoming easily my most popular album, many of it's songs still in my live set to this day).

We went on tour around England and Europe and had a very nice, tiring time.

We played Rock Am Ring and Rock Im Park, two of Germany's biggest outdoor festivals, and tore it up as best we could. In July we were scheduled to play at the Phoenix Festival again with Neil Young and Crazy Horse headlining this time around.

We did an instore at Tower Records in Piccadilly the night before and Billy and Ralph were in town and came along.

The next night I watched them play from the side of the stage alongside Paul McCartney, Jason Pierce from Spiritualized and a host of other luminaries.

It was elating and depressing at the same time. I was still a million miles away from that kind of success, the kind I'd always strived for.

However I was also a million miles away from the pies and peas circuit where many of my old muckers were still bashing

away. You can't have everything.

After Stratford I sank into a funk. A promised slot on *Later... with Jools Holland* failed to materialise. The album had done all it was going to do, there was nothing else in the calendar, so my old friend the bottle called me. I accepted and splashed around in a glass for the rest of the summer. Eventually I got bored of that and started writing lots of new songs with a view to doing killer demos in the autumn.

In August we did a short Irish tour. We played with the Band at the Olympia in Dublin.

They were in a bad way. Levon Helm had a box of Kleenex on his floor-tom and he blew his nose between every song, sometimes during a song.

Rick Danko walked offstage after four numbers, too fucked-up to play. It was very sad to see.

The next day my mum bumped into Rick in the gift shop at the hotel. She told him her son had supported them the previous night and was very disappointed at the performance as he was a huge fan.

True! I'd looked in their dressing room after the gig and all the rider was untouched.

Booze, food, the lot. These guys were deep into their darkness. An angry mob tried to beat Levon up as he left the stage door.

It was ugly. Mum got Rick to sign something for me, which I still have. He told her he was a diabetic and his insulin hadn't turned up. He died not long after. Tragic.

I'd just signed a new publishing deal with Chris Blackwell's Blue Mountain, and decided I had to blow them away.

I figured it would be fifty/fifty that I'd be doing a new album for This Way Up/Island/Universal as there's no way they'd be happy with the relatively modest sales of the album considering the amount they'd spent on it - I had to make new friends fast.

I was going to make up-and-coming whizz kid Alistair Norbury

GLASGOW
THURSDAY 19 OCTOBER
ABC Club

BIRMINGHAM
FRIDAY 20 OCTOBER
Birmingham Carling Academy 2

MANCHESTER
SATURDAY 21 OCTOBER
Manchester Academy 2

SHEFFIELD
THURSDAY 26 OCTOBER
Sheffield Leadmill

LONDON
FRIDAY 27 OCTOBER
Shepherds Bush Empire

LIVERPOOL
SATURDAY 28 OCTOBER
Liverpool Carling Academy

NO FUN ON TOUR!

8106

plast-u

25ᵗᴴ ANNIVERSARY

THE ICICLE WORKS

IAN MCNABB
THE CHIEF OF POLICE

Top: Me snapped by. . . Who?!.

Icicle Works 25th Anniversary tour pass - Note instructions from McNabb senior.

JAMAICA `98

Top: At Noel Coward's house with songwriter Barry Reynolds.

Above: Backstage with Mike Scott, Glastonbury 1994.

IAN McNABB FEATURING RALPH MOLINA AND BILLY TALBOT OF **CRAZY HORSE** WITH MIKE TONE HAMILTON - RHYTHM GUITAR

Promo shot with
Crazy Horse.

In studio recording 'The Gentleman
Adventurer' - September 2001.
The planes had just hit the towers.

Above: Phoenix
festival 1993.

Right: Recording
vocals - Rockfield
1995.

IAN M^{C}NABB

FEATURING RALPH MOLINA AND BILLY TALBOT OF
CRAZY HORSE
WITH MIKE 'TONE' HAMILTON - RHYTHM GUITAR

Another promo shot
with Crazy Horse.
Crash rehearsal
rooms - Summer
1994

Above: Jazz Cafe Camden 1998.

Left: Me and Lisa Southern - Lomax 1994.

Top: Merseybeast promo shot 1996.

Left: Warehouse approx 1983.

IAN M^CNABB

TEL: 071 584 9944

(who had signed me to Blue Mountain) realise he had the next Great British Songwriter. I set myself a goal of twenty new songs which I reached with ease. In October I went into Parr St. again and recorded and mixed all twenty tunes in four days (again). I'd start by setting up a click track, putting a couple of rhythm guitars on, then I'd overdub the drums, then the bass, a vocal, then perhaps a bit of keyboards and percussion. Whatever the track required. I did it all very quickly without much thought for precision. I just wanted it all down on tape very quickly.

I was happy with the results and so was Alistair at Blue Mountain. The recordings were dispatched to the record company, who were still deciding whether or not to pick up the option for a new McNabb album. A few weeks went by and then I got my answer.

This Way Up were being dropped from the Island/Universal imprint due to cutbacks (Island had had a bad year in the U.K. Despite the fact that *Merseybeast* was their bestselling record of 1996, it just hadn't paid for itself and I was being 'let go' along with my label).

I wasn't suprised, nor was I upset. My contract decreed that they would have to give me a golden handshake if they no longer required my services.

And so it was that they paid me the grand sum of seventy thousand pounds to not make an album and leave the building quietly. Not bad for absolutely no work whatsoever.

My only regret was that I'd forged such a great relationship with Andrew Lauder and Judith Riley it would be terribly sad to see it fade away, which it inevitably would at some point.

I had a load of songs, money in the bank, lead in my pencil, and piss and vinegar running through my veins.

I decided to kick back for the rest of the year and plan my next move.

And then, In January '97, I got a phone call out of the blue.

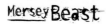

CHAPTER FORTY ONE
The Waterboy, Sly and Robbie & Jamaica

As you will know by now, I'd known Mike Scott for a few years.

I'd always been a fan (how could you not bow down to the man who wrote 'The Whole Of The Moon'?). Mike had hung up the Waterboys moniker and was now operating under his given name.

He'd had some reasonable success with his debut solo acoustic album *Bring 'Em All In* - and was now set to make a full blown electric opus with a view to a hit. He asked me down to Olympic studios in Barnes to contribute some backing vocals and perhaps some guitar to his new record, which would eventually emerge as *Still Burning*.

We had a great time working together and Mike looked after me very well. When it was all put together and ready for release, Mike was still short of a bass player and asked me if I'd mime the part in the video to the album's first single 'Love Anyway'. I had nothing else to do so I agreed.

We had such a good time jamming during the shoot that I suggested he should have me as a member of the touring band when he went on the road with the album. He didn't seem too sure for whatever reasons, so I forgot about it.

My friend John Brice was now working in A&R for Warners. He was put in charge of organising a collaboration between Mick Hucknall of Simply Red and legendary Jamaican rhythm section Sly Dunbar and Robbie Shakespeare.

John told me he had to go to Jamaica to meet with the guys and I told him I would come with him. I hadn't had a holiday in years and it would be great to meet these people. I was also eager to splash my recent redundancy pay around a bit.

We flew over and were driven into Kingston. It's a pretty rough place and I was a bit taken aback at how third world it felt. I felt nervous from the moment I got there to the moment I came back. This wasn't helped much by the fact that we were smoking superstrength skunk from the instant we landed which increased my paranoia to previously untouched heights.

Sly and Robbie were lovely, charming people, but every time Robbie Shakespeare saw me he went into fits of giggles as I was usually horizontal, ripped to the tits, could hardly speak - and generally came across as the poster boy for the lobster-coloured Englishman abroad.

One night John and I were taken to a dancehall in the seedier part of Kingston.

There were around two thousand people there and we were the only white faces.

I was shitting myself. I'd layed off the smoke a bit as I thought it might be wise, but I was still paranoid.

At one point John wandered off and I was left to fend for myself. It was fine at first but then I noticed a couple of scary types giving me the evil eye. I wasn't stoned so I wasn't imagining this.

I moved to another part of the venue just to make sure I wasn't being daft but about three of them followed me and continued with the staring. I was starting to sweat. I couldn't find John anywhere and began to panic.

I moved very quickly into the car park and didn't turn around to see if I was being followed. I eventually found our car, but John had the keys. Our phones didn't work out here so I truly was alone. I was so scared I got under the car and hid for about half an hour until John came out to find me.

He told me I was being very silly but I was convinced I was going to get a hiding or worse. We went back to the hotel and I locked myself in my room and tried to calm down. This was a holiday?

After about a week we flew to Miami for a change of scenery and to check out a couple of bands. We hung out for a couple of days and then John had to get back to London. I wasn't in a hurry so I stayed on for a couple of days. We had to get out of the place we were staying so I got my travel agent to find me another hotel. It was fourth of July weekend so I struggled.

The only decent place I could get was a golf hotel about half an hour away from the coast. It was horrible. Then we got a hurricane warning. I stayed in my room and watched movies all day. I was too paranoid to travel round alone. I got so lonely I thought about calling an escort agency but that's not really my style (I pay for company in other ways).

I counted the minutes until my flight took off. I've been to Florida a couple of times. It's not a rock 'n' roll town (unless you're Tom Petty or the Allman Bros.) and I wouldn't recommend it - although the kids will love Orlando. I won't be going back there soon.

Not much happened for a while and then I started getting a few probing calls from Mike. He was starting to dig the idea of me being in his band but I think he was a little worried about there being two band leaders on the same stage - eventually through a lot of consideration on his part (and I hear a little badgering from his band - James Halliwell on keys, Jeremy Stacey on drums and Gavin Ralston on guitar) he relented and eventually he asked me if I fancied the job. It was something I'd never done before, being a member of somebody else's band. It would be a challenge of discipline, abstinence, and, as I would later learn, tolerance.

Mike was a highly spiritual, intoxicant-free individual - probably

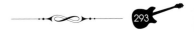

the direct opposite of myself at that point. This would be fun, hard work, and also quite lucrative.

We started rehearsing in London soon after, Mike was a taskmaster. Every note was arranged, pinned-down and presented with consummate professionalism. My style was much more knockabout and I learnt a lot from all of this. I was living high on the hog as Mike always treats his bandmates with the same respect he would like to be shown himself. I was booked into the finest hotels, paid good per diems (daily expenses) and lived in the big city like a proper rock star.

I went and bought a white Mexican Fender Precision bass on Denmark Street and practiced and practiced. My favourite bass players are McCartney, John Entwistle and Bill Wyman, and I synthesized the three into a nice cocktail - I'd like to think. There are two strings less than a conventional guitar on a bass and they are a lot thicker, it's a different art. You have your own frequency in the overall sonic picture and if you play a bum note everybody notices it. You play all the time in every song and you have to listen very closely to the drummer at all times. You can get away with murder on guitar and keyboards. Not so down in the engine room.

It was a fantastic new experience for me. I learnt a lot more about the groove. It's hard to concentrate on what's going on behind you when you're a frontman.

Your attention is focused on engaging the audience, singing in tune, remembering all the words and trying not to look a tit. You'll probably notice if it's not swinging, or if it speeds up or slows down, but that's about it.

We rehearsed throughout the scorching summer and eventually debuted the band in August with three nights at the Garage in Highbury. Everybody went home happy. Lisa was working in London by now and we spent a fair bit of time together.

She was struggling with accommodation and basically stayed

at my hotel with me a lot of the time.

We toured throughout the winter and largely had a blast. I locked horns with Mike on a number of occasions, largely due to the fact that Mike is a controller and I had a very hard time being controlled - but disagreements were laid to rest pretty much as quickly as they occurred. It was, after all, his band - and I had to do as I was told. It was fantastic to play 'Medicine Bow', 'Be My Enemy', 'Don't Bang The Drum' and so many other of my favourite Mike tunes as the weeks and months passed. I celebrated my thirty-seventh birthday in Nagoya, Japan, and the lads bought me a Doors box set and got me pissed. Jeremy Stacey unfortunately had left the tour at the end of August to go and play with Echo And The Bunnymen, and the drummer who had replaced him, Geoff Dugmore, couldn't stay with us indefinitely, so I called Zak Starkey up and he came to Europe with us for a few shows.

I got to be a rhythm section with him which was unbelievable fun. Unfortunately he defected to the Lightning Seeds after a very short time which left me cursing Ian Broudie as we had to audition a load more fucking drummers.

Mike Scott was/is one of my heroes. I learnt a lot from him. One of my favourites being: If you are touring with a band, and you are prepared to stand in the lobby of a hotel for about ten minutes complaining about your designated room, it's more than likely you will end up in a suite just so as they can get you out of their face. They won't ask you to leave as there is a whole party of you staying at the hotel. Try it sometime.

We played up to the end of the year and it really was good fun. It was nice not having to worry about ticket sales or go through the tedium of interviews. One particular highlight for me was when we opened for Sheryl Crow at Wembley Arena. I'm always chuffed to tell people that yes, I have indeed played at Wembley - I wasn't playing my own songs - I wasn't even playing playing my own guitar - but I've played at Wembley -

OK? The album we toured didn't perform as well as everybody would have hoped - more of a timing/marketing problem than a quality issue in my opinion.

But we know that one don't we?

We finished up in the mighty city of Dublin in December with a great show at the Olympia and I went home to let the fingers on my left hand return to their normal size. I was also suffering from repetitive strain injury in my right wrist. Playing the bass is not like playing the guitar!

CHAPTER FORTY TWO

The Emotional party

1998.

Mike's album has done just about all it's going to do and we're told there'll be no more work for us. Bummer. I don't know what to do with myself. I embark on an ill-advised dalliance with a young girl called Sabrina, who wants to save the world, whom I met in Glasgow on the Mike Scott tour the previous year.

She's a flighty, flirty, sexy thing who seems to be playing me. I'm throwing money and kindness her way and don't appear to be getting much back in return.

I seem to enjoy this as it's never boring, and every day brings a fresh kick. She keeps disappearing into the ladies bog with the coke for long periods of time and coming back with hardly anything left.

I suspect she's giving it to a lad she fancies. One time I catch her snogging another girl in a dimly lit booth in a club where we are supposed to be spending time together. I then - in true sugar-daddy style - foolishly make the decision to take this little charmer to Southern Ireland for the occasion of her birthday, where we will hang out with Gavin Ralston (from Mike's band) and his girfriend, and drive around the coast like happy couples.

She then turns out to be a moody cow who doesn't really fancy me that much – but is impressed with my credentials, status, and love of room service.

It all becomes a drag very quickly.

I realise I'm being played just a little more than I like to be and a lot of arguing ensues.

I pay for her to have her bellybutton pierced in Galway, and hold her trembling hand as it's done. She then won't let me near her for four days as she's too sore. Eventually I can stand no more and I kick her into touch.

Much crying.

Sort yourself out, love. Sort yourself out, Ian!

I'm sinking.

I quite enjoy letting myself spiral into the abyss occasionally, as I tend to write better songs as I pull myself up again. I've never actually walked through the valley of darkness, but I've sprinted through a couple of times and nicked a few postcards.

I write a bunch of songs to ease my suffering: 'You Only Get What You Deserve', 'The Man Who Can Make A Woman Laugh', 'Absolutely Wrong', 'Girls Are Birds', 'Little Princess'.

Really good songs. I don't know what I'm going to do with them, I haven't got a recording contract.

I drink and smoke and take drugs. I tell Ursula there is no longer a relationship going on with us.

More crying. Lisa has also moved on by this point and shacks up with a guy in London. I continue to fuck anything that moves.

Around this time my publisher Alistair invited me to a writing workshop at Chris Blackwell's luxury retreat Goldeneye in Jamaica. Goldeneye was once owned by Ian Fleming who wrote many of the Bond novels there, and has to be experienced to be believed.

Situated on the coast in Oracabessa, it is the quintessential paradise with an ocean view. At two grand-plus per night it is as exclusive as they come. Yoko Ono, Willie Nelson and Pierce Brosnan were all recent guests.

A writing workshop is where a bunch of songwriters from extremely varied backgrounds get together for a week and try to write songs together. Every morning straws are drawn and you get a different partner. You'll write all day and after dinner there is a small concert and everybody plays what they've done. It's not my idea of a good time but I wasn't going to turn down a trip to such a place as this. There were lots of writers there, mostly from the U.S. and Jamaica, the only two that I had heard of were Julia Fordham ('A woman of the eighties') and Barry Reynolds who was most notable for his work with Marianne Faithful.

It was a wonderful experience - much better/posher than my previous visit. I didn't apply myself to the writing much, preferring to bathe, smoke weed, drink wine and jet-ski most of the time.

I wrote a couple of things with Julia Fordham - whom I managed to annoy by giving her the nickname Laura Ashley - which caught on widely. They don't give you a room in this place, they give you a house with a fully stocked bar and every other amenity you could wish for.

Local servants (there can be no other word) would rush to light your cigarette the moment you pulled one out - which made me feel colonial and a little uncomfortable - but I learned to live with it. On our last night in Jamaica we went up to Firefly - Noel Coward's 'upper' home as he called it until his death in 1973. We did a little gig up there on a makeshift stage. I got to meet the brilliant Jamaican guitar player Ernest Ranglin and hear some of his war stories. The tales that all of these great people I've met have told me could fill another book - and maybe they will.

The days and weeks and months pass in something of a blur. There's money in the bank so I don't have to work. I buy myself an expensive car. No pressure. You need pressure.

Eventually Chas Cole from C.M.P. agency hassles me into performing a week of solo shows at Ronnie Scott's club in Birmingham. A grand per night. Six grand for a week's work. I'm

not fussed but I can't turn that kind of cash down. It turns out to be a revelation. Two sets a night, it re-awakens my muse. I start to get excited about my music again. I decide to make an all-acoustic album, something I've never done before.

When the dates are over I book time at Monnow Valley studios (next to Rockfield) and start picking songs. I take a few of the tunes I'd demo'd back in October '96 which haven't seen the light of day yet and strip them down and match them up to the newer ones. I'm going to call it A Party Political Broadcast On Behalf Of The Emotional Party.

It's going to be very personal and intense. I'm going to play everything myself originally, but I tell Mike Scott what I'm up to, and he and Anto Thistlethwaite from the Waterboys will eventually end up playing and singing a bunch of stuff on it. I also get in touch with upright bass player Danny Thompson (Pentangle, John Martyn, Nick Drake, amongst many others) and ask him to come along to the sessions. I tell Danny that most of the songs are about affairs of the heart - he laughs out loud and asks me if I'm still bothered by those kind of things - I reply in the affirmative.

It all worked out fine and the album was scheduled for release on my own new label Fairfield in the autumn with a lengthy tour, once again put together by CMP. I also put together a book, a collection of lyrics and comments fashioned to sit alongside the new album in your CD rack.

I went to Madrid for a few days with Andrew and Judith who were still helping me out, despite the fact that we were no longer bound together by any contract.

They organised a distribution deal for me with nothing in it for them except the joy of seeing me do good again. Bless 'em. The album and tour both did great business, culminating in a sold out show at the Jazz Cafe in Camden.

It felt great to be treading the boards under my own steam again.

CHAPTER FORTY THREE

Spaced
1999

In early 1999 I was offered the use of Pete Thomas's home studio in Twickenham.

Pete was the drummer in Elvis Costello's band the Attractions. I'd met Pete and the guys through Andrew and Judith.

About this time A & J were starting up a new label together with John Porter. They were very keen to sign me to the new label but John Porter wasn't very happy about it.

Word got back to me that John didn't like *Merseybeast*.

I didn't give a fuck whether he liked it or not, but if there was a deal in the air and he had the casting vote it'd hurt me. I thought I'd put some killer demos down to vibe everyone up a bit.

I called up Geoff Dugmore who I'd worked with in Mike's band and asked him to bring his drum kit around.

We cut six tracks in Pete's tiny studio - 'Whatever It Takes', 'What You Wanted', 'Rollin' On (The Things We Gave Away)', 'Hollywood Tears', 'Why Are The Beautiful So Sad?' and 'Nobody Say Nothin' To No one'. I was pleased with the results and CDs were serviced to all concerned. Nobody came back to me sounding particularly excited.

I twiddled my thumbs and waited. And waited. And waited.

This line of work is a strange one to be sure. Periods of great

activity where there is never enough time in the day to fit it all in, and then times of grinding inertia which send you mental with boredom.

I've always struggled with it - I don't have kids to look after, and the daily stuff has always been taken care of by other people around me.

Usually my long-suffering mother - who appears to have dedicated her life to removing mundane shit from my life in order for me to concentrate on my quest for greatness.

What a lucky boy. I naturally take a lot of this for granted having never really had to fend for myself.

A lot of musicians/artists are like this - usually it falls on the wife/husband/partner to hold the reins while golden boy/girl stands in the spotlight.

I always promise myself I must be more grateful/thankful for this opportunity - but often I forget, which I regret deeply. I will try harder I promise.

Andrew and Judith's new label is financed by an IT millionaire and it's all looking very exciting.

Judith reassures me that I will be involved but it's taking a long time to get any answers. I know I haven't got John Porter's vote and I'm fairly concerned. I can do nothing about it.

I could press on myself but I'm reluctant to spend a lot of my own money making a full-blown 'comeback' album - if you put stuff out on your own label you have to pay for recording, musicians, artwork, pressing, distribution, and eventually press and promotion - it adds up to a small fortune and if the record tanks you're in a lot of trouble.

I decide to get my face around so they can't ignore me.

I follow Andrew, Judith and John Porter to New Orleans where they are looking at acts and taking in the New Orleans Jazz Festival. I eat a lot of great food, drink a lot of nice booze and hear a lot of funky music - but don't feel much in the way of progress.

One night we were invited to Ernie K-Doe's house. Ernie was a proper 'Nawlins' legend with a side-order of colourful eccentricity.

He was famous for his 1961 number one Billboard hit 'Mother-In-Law.' When he was astride the charts all those years ago he predicted that in a thousand years the only tunes anybody would remember would be his sole number one and 'The Star Spangled Banner.'

The party was a hoot. His house was effectively a nightclub which he called 'The Mother-In-Law Lounge.'

It was little more than a corrugated metal shack in the poor part of town. He fussed over his guests constantly, bringing us food and booze, entertaining us with stories, and bursting into song at every opportunity whilst wearing the most ridiculous Little Richard-type rug.

He died a couple of years later. I got a real buzz recently when Boots the chemist used his 1970 tune 'Here Come The Girls' in a major advertising campaign and it was a hit all over again.

I moved on to L.A. for a week, following the gang once again - where I started to feel like a spare part. I hook up with an old mate Jason Falkner (ex-Jellyfish - seminal powerpop band - big Icicle Works fan) and get silly on margaritas.

I watch Eric Burden of the Animals get wrecked in the bar of the Hyatt on Sunset. Plenty of shopping, lunch and dinner, but John Porter barely makes eye contact with me. I note how his regard of me is vastly different now that he's not being paid to like me.

I try to rationalise this as paranoia on my part but it's just too obvious and I sink into a funk. I came home quite depressed and dealt with it my usual way.

The Lomax had held an exchange night with another club in Downtown Manhattan, called the Knitting Factory.

The idea is a simple one. Three or four New York acts come and play in Liverpool, and vice versa.

Funding is from the local council. A cultural exchange if you will.

What it actually is is a free holiday.

The Lomax asked me to host the Liverpool one, guaranteeing I'd be making the New York trip. Everything was so disorganised that my mum ended up organising the flights and hotel. There were about twenty people in our party.

Musicians, sound engineers, lecturers, and a couple of council representatives, plus Mick Hindley, owner of the Lomax. Virtually everybody got sozzled on the plane, but miraculously we got through immigration stinking of ale.

When we eventually got to the Mayflower on Central Park West everyone was nodding off. We couldn't have any rooms until somebody produced a credit card and everybody stood with their hands in their pockets, yawning.

Guess who was the only person who had a credit card? Bingo.

Mick Hindley was full of apologies.

He was meant to be in charge. Then there was an argument amongst the tribal elders as to who actually was in charge.

This went on for a bit until everybody realised that, given our current predicament, the only person who was really in charge was the sucker with the cash. That meant me.

Mick explained that he was so sleepy when he crawled out of his pit that morning that he had forgotten to pick up the sock on his wife Joyce's wardrobe which contained the thirty-five hundred dollars we needed to pay for the hotel.

He was very sorry.

So I'd only been in N.Y.C. for ninety minutes and was already in to my AMEX for three large.

It put a crimp in my day. (Out of respect and friendship I shall not name certain other individuals who were part of this sorry episode. But suffice to say they still occupy their positions at the helm of Liverpool learning).

The gig was fine by the way, and Liverpool/New York relations remain as strong as ever.

In October John Brice and I flew to San Francisco to attend Neil Young's annual Bridge School concert.

That year the line-up featured Neil, Pearl Jam, the Who, Sheryl Crow, Green Day, Smashing Pumpkins, Tom Waits, Emmylou Harris, Lucinda Williams and Brian Wilson.

An incredible concert over two evenings - the like of which you just know could never happen in England.

Ian Broudie had had great success with the Lightning Seeds since we'd last hung out properly.

Always a staple on radio, they'd gone through the roof when Ian wrote a song with questionable British comedians Frank Skinner and David Baddiel for the Euro '96 football tournament which took place in England that year.

The song's irresistible 'It's coming home, it's coming home, football's coming home...' refrain became the national anthem that year (and beyond) - and basically made Ian a very wealthy man. Ian now lived in Twickenham in true pop star style - with all the trimmings.

We started talking every couple of weeks, after a spell in the cold. I felt slightly aggrieved with him due to my being paid such a lowly fee for contributing distinctive backing vocals on an album which became massive.

And I had to listen to these vocals on the radio half a dozen times a day. There'd also been another incident, thereby he'd asked Judith if I could contribute vocals to a new album for the same payment.

He'd nicked Zak from Mike's band as well.

You get the picture.

Anyway, here he was now offering me a great deal to record on a barge he was renting off Pete Townshend, which was moored next to Pete's studio Eel Pie. It was a great idea and I'd waited around long enough for something else to happen.

I had a stack of songs - I wanted to make a big pop album stuffed with tunes - short, catchy songs with a lot of radio appeal. I needed to get out of singer-songwriter acoustic troubadour mode and get back on it.

I could see myself playing to fat, bearded blokes in chunky sweaters in the Outer Hebrides for the rest of my life if I didn't get back in the charts soon.

I don't mind playing to fat, bearded blokes in chunky sweaters in the Outer Hebrides - their money is as good as anybody's - but I'd much rather be playing to slim, sexy birds in, well, anywhere (I realise the shallowness of my ways and promise to punish myself accordingly at every juncture).

Once again I asked Geoff Dugmore to be involved. As well as being a superb drummer, he had a great ear and a great sense of humour. We put our diaries together and made plans to start work on the record early in the new year.

I tried to write the catchiest ditties possible over Christmas. This was going to be a FUN album.

In December I recorded two acoustic shows at the Life Cafe in Bold Street, Liverpool. I was invited to play there by a very suave and handsome young chap by the name of Steve Walter, who would become one of my closest friends from that point on.

He also had women throwing themselves at him and I figured I'd be around to pick up the slack.

CHAPTER FORTY FOUR

Here comes
the Noughties

Spring 2000.

The barge didn't have much in the way of recording space, basically just a vocal/overdub booth, so we went into Blackwing studios in Southeast London for a week to put all the drums down.

This completed, we went up river. Twickenham is a lovely part of the world and a fantastic environment to create music. Roy Corkill was back on board for this project, and we stayed at a B&B just the other side of the Thames.

Every day we would rise around noon, fetch a quick breakfast at a nearby cafe and then stroll along the embankment to the barge to make music. Fantastic. The engineer was a lovely Scottish guy by the name of Kenny Paterson, who years earlier had been in a band called Slide.

We were knockin' them out fast. 'Livin' Proof (Miracles Can Happen)', 'Liverpool Girl' (re-recorded from *The Emotional Party* in electric style), 'Alright With Me', 'Friend Of My Enemy.' The latter sounded like ZZ Top with Crosby, Stills and Nash harmonies. I met ZZ Top a couple of years later and gave a copy of the track to Billy Gibbons.

It's weird talking to a bloke with a tea-cosy on his head and a beard down to his belt. They did a great show at the Summer Pops in Liverpool. The stage set-up was: Frank Beard's huge

drum-kit on a riser, and two microphones.

That was it. I knew that Billy Gibbons had one of the biggest collections of vintage amplifiers in the world, so was a little miffed not to see any of them. I asked him about it.

"Where are all the amps then?"

"What's that son?"

"The amps. Where are they? Where do you keep them? Are they under the stage?"

He grinned then shot me a look over the top of his (cheap) sunglasses.

"Listen son, that stuff doesn't matter. This is what's important."

And with that he grabbed hold of his vast, grey beard an waved it under my face.

I was giddy with excitement. The new album was going to be full of life, short on torch songs, and its prime directive was to R-O-C-K. I've always had a love affair with power pop (a fairly derided genre by the record buying public at large for some reason - perhaps it's the name) and this was going to be my attempt at the form.

There was barely an acoustic guitar near the record.

It took ages to finish it as we were being meticulous in our work. Five months off and on. An age by my standards. Geoff in particular wasn't going to let anything shoddy get by. There isn't a fuckin' note out of place - or time - on that album.

The downside was that I was spending a small fortune on it and it would have to be a proper success for me to see anything come back. It was completed in July and I started shopping it around.

It took a while.

I was managing myself, with only Alistair from Blue Mountain as a real ally. He was into me for plenty now and needed to see a return soon or we'd both be in trouble. Sanctuary was a label that previously dealt with back catalogue only, but they were branching out and were keen to put the album out. They didn't want to cough up too much money though as they'd just taken a bloodbath with Pete Wylie's last album *Songs Of Strength And Heartbreak*.

Another great record which failed to crossover into the public consciousness.

A deal was struck - my album had cost about twenty grand to make and they agreed to pay for it - if I threw in the two other albums of mine that I owned - *The Emotional Party* and *Live At Life*. Fair enough.

A good result - I was back in black. They would own all three albums for five years until such time they would revert to me. A release date was set for April 2001.

Mike Scott called me up again early in '01. After the disappointing sales of his *Still Burning* record he decided to start using the Waterboys brand again.

This time he wanted me to play keyboards in the band. I'd never been more than a functional pianist but accepted the challenge and improved my limited skill a great deal I felt. My teacher became Mike's current keyboardist Richard Naiff, who I would work with in a later incarnation of my band.

We did a brief U.K tour supporting Mike's *A Rock In the Weary Land* record, ending at the Scala in King's Cross and saying farewell till the next time.

I was pushing for Sanctuary to trail the new album with a single but I sensed they'd already spent as much money on me as they intended and were going to depend on my loyal fanbase to do all the work.

I had a bad feeling. I wanted this to be a very visible release and not just a quick turn around. We had a lunchtime launch party at the trendy Cobden Club on Kensal Road in West London, the only money Sanctuary spent promoting the record.

Ian McCulloch turned up, as did Zak, along with Broudie, and a smattering of fans.

Unfortunately the media stayed away in droves as Giles Green from Sanctuary had booked the show the same week as a publishing convention, also taking place in the capital. Brilliant. I was beginning to notice how much I was suffering from lack of a manager.

I consoled myself by getting hammered all day with the two Ians. Broudie eventually bailed and I ended up back at Lee Starkey's place, wrecked with McCulloch.

He had a show the next night at U.L.U. and fell out the door around five with me not far behind him.

I went to the gig the next night and he showed no signs of fatigue.

Amazing.

The first show of our tour was at Dingwall's in Camden. It was very sold out and we sweated our way through more than two hours. Geoff Dugmore wasn't available for the gigs so I asked yet another Waterboys ex-drummer, Tom Windriff to fill in.

My old mate Mokka played keys and Roy handled the bottom end once again.

The night of the show BBC 2 showed the Icicle Works doing 'Love Is A Wonderful Colour' on *Top Of The Pops* from 1984, plugging the show and the upcoming album.

The album came out - simply titled *Ian McNabb*. The front cover was a shot of me as a wee boy dressed in a Batman outfit (taken by my dad's mate 'Uncle' Bill Mealey).

It got rotten reviews ("Bad Oasis" - Uncut), and disappeared quickly.

Sanctuary didn't take out one single advert - and that was the end of it.

I was crushed.

I thought it was the best record I could've made at that moment in time. Sometimes that's how the cards fall and you just have to lick your wounds and hope for a better result next time.

It's not easy. If it was easy we'd all be stars wouldn't we?

That summer Neil Young came over with Crazy Horse for a European tour. I went to a few shows but the most fun I had with them was in Dublin.

After the gig Neil was wandering around the dressing room with a ludicrous pair of big baggy shorts on and an even sillier hat.

I asked him if he was going somewhere hot (it was rather chilly in Dublin) and he told me he was off to Miami to pick up his new bus (I'd only meant it as a joke).

His dad Scott was there, a famous Canuck sports writer as well as a famous dad. Neil introduced him to me, then quietly slipped next door to smoke a little weed.

Billy Talbot pulled me into the corner and shoved a Coke can with a lump of hash burning on top off it into my mouth. It made me laugh to think that Neil Young was trying to hide the fact that he was having a puff from his dad.

Doesn't everyone in the world suspect that Neil Young likes pot?

Scott Young was very charming and spoke to me about real estate for about twenty minutes.

Neil came back in looking happy. I was also introduced to Jim Jarmusch who was making a film about the tour (*Year Of The Horse*). The shows were immense. They were still the greatest. J.J. filmed me for a bit - he was fascinated by my boots.

I never made the final cut. Sadly.

I trudged through the rest of the year with a less than sunny outlook it has to be said. I was seeing a couple of ladies here and there but no-one was setting me on fire.

This is my default setting.

I wrote many songs however, and planned to record another bunch of demos in the autumn. My publishing deal was going to die soon if I didn't start earning more and I wanted to show I still had much to offer.

In the interim I put together a collection of unreleased stuff in order to keep the cash rolling in and called it *Waifs And Strays*.

It came out towards the end of the year on Andrew Lauder's new label Evangeline (nice title!) and sold more than the Sanctuary album. Go figure.

We played at Dingwalls - again - to promote it. Lee came to the show. She looked healthy, beautiful, and tanned. Better than I'd ever seen her actually. She'd discovered the joys of the sunbed apparently. I'd always been slightly giddy around Lee and this was no different.

I'd also harboured a gentle, long-term fantasy about getting closer to her, but wisely assumed we'd never be more than mates. I didn't want to fuck that up.

I'd known her for nearly ten years already. Her brother's one of my best mates etc. Anyway, turns out she's recently finished with her live-in partner, Paul.

I'd met him a few times and he seemed pretty cool. He organised parties. I'd have to admit I envied him. Doesn't matter now. She's kicked him out.

Mmm.

We partied into the small hours (leaving me knackered/hung over for the next night's gig in Milton Keynes Stables) and I was entranced by her all over again. I started texting her and calling her a bit too often. She never ignored me. She was giggly and seemingly interested.

I made her laugh. I fancied I'd be good for her one day. Maybe sooner than later.

I went into Parr Street in September with twenty new songs to record. My original intention was to just use the demo studio, but the upstairs bar was being refurbished (and would later be the base for many an adventure) so they put me in the main studio downstairs.

I wasn't going to let this stroke of luck go unused so I quickly determined to make an album instead of another bunch of demos. A new engineer was brought to my attention, a very friendly chap called Mike Cave. He was excellent. 'All Things To Everyone', 'Lady By Degrees', 'Ain't No Way to Behave', 'The Human Heart And How It Works', 'Hurricane Elaine', I was writing well and often.

After some time-wasting technical problems we hit our stride. One afternoon we were recording 'Other People' when someone called me into reception to see what was happening in New York. We watched the planes fly into the towers over and over again and reacted the same as everyone else around the world that day.

The rest of the day was rather muted - we knew this meant war - and everyone went home early to watch it all again.

'Those things happen to other people, those things never happen to me...'

We mixed all the tracks - just me and a drum machine, Roy on a couple. I put fourteen of the tracks into a running order and I had another album for next to nothing.

I kept thinking about Lee.

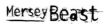

CHAPTER FORTY FIVE

Costa Rica
2002

I was going to the jungle.

One of my longest serving fans (I hate that term but what other word works better?), Chris Lee, brother of one of my other longest serving fans James Lee (now a high ranking police officer), had a fantastic job working for Reebok in Boston, Mass. U.S.A. He was the head designer of training shoes.

No mean feet.

He'd started off working for Wade Smith in Liverpool, and had proved so adept at predicting what kind of footwear His Majesty The Punter would want to wear next month, he'd become a wealthy man very quickly.

Chris and his brother James had grown up just down the road from where I lived, in a place called Portelet Road, off Green Lane, the other side of Newsham Park, about five miles from town.

Anyway, Reebok were to have one of their bi-annual off-site trips. The object of these trips apparently was to take the design floor to an exotic locale and have them design stuff not related to their work - to freshen them up and stretch their minds in other areas, presumably so as they could then go back to drawing shoes with limitless enthusiasm.

Occasionally they would invite other creative people, usually from areas far removed from aerodynamic sports footwear

design, to talk at these events to add further stimulation to their cause. Chris asked me if I'd like to participate in one of these events. Apart from getting a week in the sun, I would be paid a large sum of money for my efforts, and seeing as I was freezing my nuts off in the north of England in savage February I had no hesitation in replying in the affirmative.

I packed my bags, grabbed my Martin D28 acoustic guitar, put my career on hold (I think it had gone to sleep anyway), drove to Manchester Airport and jumped on a BA flight with Chris, firstly to Boston (security crazed after 9/11) where he had set up a beautiful home with his wife Gill.

We would spend the night there, then rendezvous with the twenty or so designers in order to fly to San Jose the following day, and then, upon landing, take a six hour bus ride through the jungle to our final destination, a swish looking holiday compound by the side of an enormous body of inland seawater connected to the ocean by a series of vast canals.

I was a little intimidated at the prospect of meeting so many new faces, and wondered what they would think of this wayward minstrel, whom most of them would not have heard of - as he moved amongst them like an alien body infiltrating a smoothly functioning, healthy cell.

I needn't have worried of course as I ingratiated myself into the mass with aplomb, being an experienced performer to small crowds as well as large ones, and spent the long flight south chatting to as many of them as I could, but mainly weighing up which of the yank totty I could nail when we reached our equatorial destination.

San Jose airport was hotter than hell, even with air conditioning, although I had been in hotter places, namely onstage with Mike Scott at the Garage in Highbury, London, during the fierce heatwave of August '97 when I was sure I could see my skin dripping onto my guitar through my stinging, sweat-soaked eyes.

The second, less expected discovery our merry band had in store upon passing successfully through immigration was that our cellphones would not work here.

We were to truly be alone together in the jungle, with no help, advice or counsel from friends or loved ones. I didn't have a current girlfriend to report in to, so I wasn't too perturbed, and, necessity being the mother of invention, I knew this harrowing fact of non-external communication would bring people closer together, faster.

Of course we could always use a payphone if any of us could be bothered to go through the lengthy rigmarole of such an act in this alien, inhospitable, non-technological, far away place.

The bus journey wasn't as bad or as long as expected, and we arrived at our destination knackered, but in high spirits, and ready to eat, drink and all the rest.

When I awoke the next morning I realised the place wasn't quite as posh as it had looked on the website, but fuckin' hell it was hot.

Great!

It became apparent fairly early on that I was going to have a lot of spare time on my hands as the designers had virtually every day mapped out for them. My shtick wasn't going to come into play for a while according to Chris, and I was still fairly clueless as to what my role was here exactly, so I just decided to try to relax, eat well, get some sun, maybe write a couple of songs and read a book.

Certain days were mapped out for 'Adventure Activities' which sounded ominous if not a little worrying, yours truly not being the typical outdoor type.

I began to socialise with more and more of the group and got on pretty good terms with a few of the guys. I began to relax, something which I find harder to do the older I get - perhaps the accumulation of knowledge - much of it unnecessary - bringing with it greater anxiety.

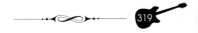

Anyway there wasn't much to stress about here, where the blue sky meets meets the water. A couple of days went by where I did nothing but laze around, eat, drink, get to know the folks, flirt with the girls, and play my guitar.

Just as I was beginning to chill to the point of sloth, I was told that on the next morning, we would be boarding a bus which would take us on a long drive to a mountain, where we would take part in an activity previously unknown to me, called 'Canopy.' I inquired what this actually entailed, to which my friend Chris intoned that I shouldn't worry, and it would be "Sound."

When pressed for more details he briskly informed me that it was something to do with being on a harness and sliding down a steel rope at a slight angle whilst surveying the beauty of the local surroundings. We'd be back in time for tea.

I wasn't convinced I was getting all of the facts here, but everyone else was going and I didn't particularly want to be a party pooper so early in the game, also, Chris was paying me a lot of money to come on a free holiday and I got the impression that my presence on the bus was not a request but an order. The next day I found myself on a rickety old bus with all the other campers, sat next to a pretty foxy brunette in cut-off jeans by the name of Pam.

I guessed that she was in her late twenties/early thirties and she was good company for the long ride. She told me that she was divorced, had a five-year-old son who was simply 'Darling' and really liked the songs she had heard me playing as I walked around the compound yesterday. After a couple of hours punctuated by a piss-stop we arrived at the foot of a large mountain which rose majestically from the jungle, still covered with huge trees all the way to the top.

Clouds covered the peak. I was a little apprehensive as to the nature of this 'Canopy' activity to be sure, but there were girls here and none of them seemed unduly worried at this point so how bad could it be? It didn't occur to me that none of them had a clue what 'Canopy' meant either, let's face it, they were Yanks and probably thought we were going to a cocktail party.

As we trucked up a fairly steep incline under tree cover over the course of forty-five minutes give or take, I found myself wishing we were going to a cocktail party. It was hot, humid and hard work. I remain reasonably fit into my forties due to a fairly stringent exercise regime, but this was taxing on the calf muscles to the point of genuine fatigue. Only another ten minutes or so, we are informed by our pigeon-English speaking guides. When we finally reach our destination it is impossible to tell how far we have climbed due to the abundance of huge trees in every direction. My spider-sense informed me that we are very high above sea-level.

One of our guides takes us to a large hut to the left of the trail where we are kitted out in very elaborate harness get-ups which feel very heavy and are difficult to walk around in, but - we are assured - will make a lot of sense when they show us what we are about to do. We are then led even further up the mountain - I am now starting to fantasise about a cold, large beer in a frosted glass - it is lunchtime by now - when we come to a clearing where there is a large wooden platform with a taught steel rope suspended above it. The rope snakes into the trees below and beyond. I'm now working hard to make sure I'm at the back of our group of twenty - I want to see how this shit works before I commit - it's still not too late to pull out is it?

A few of the gathering are beginning to look uncomfortable, questions are being asked as to where this fucking rope leads exactly. We are informed that the activity is completely safe, although people who have a big problem with heights should probably think twice before they saddle up. Erm... I have a problem with heights. I'm thinking it but I'm not saying it.

The only person who pipes up and says they're not going to go through with it however, is a fat lass with glasses on. This means if I shit out now I will be walking down the mountain back to the bus with her for an hour. I realise I am trapped in what can now be described as a rock and a hard place. The journey down the rope takes about twenty minutes with stops, and I am told there is a canteen/bar at the end of the show. A reward. Our shamed, bespectacled coward is now being led back to the harness hut in shame. I have the urge to run after her but I have to pretend I'm hard in front of this lot, there are another few days to go, and I don't want anyone to think I'm a pansy - Christ, I haven't even pulled yet.

A guide beckons a strapping lad forward from our group to demonstrate the art of riding the canopy. It's simple enough. They hook your harness onto the rope, and suddenly you are sitting in mid-air.

You grab hold of the thick strap holding you to the rope with your left hand, you then grab a hold of the rope itself with your right hand, which is now encased in a thick, heavy-duty glove, just behind your head. Squeezing on the rope slows your rate of descent, while gravity and the angle of the rope takes care of your speed. We are told not to slow down too much as there is a possibility you can then stop altogether, whereby someone will have to come down after you and get you started again by giving you a hearty push. Mmm...

Several of our group have now disappeared down the rope and into the trees. It looks easy enough. All that seems to be happening from where I stand is that you glide through the jungle about four feet off the ground. An old lady could do it. I'm pretty much the last guy to hook onto the rope and I'm up for it now. I'm pushed off with some gusto and off I go. The first twenty five yards or so I glide effortlessly, about three or four feet up. This is cool! I then start picking up speed and I'm starting to enjoy myself. Faster and faster I course through the jungle...and then...'FUCKING HELL! WHARRGHH!' The leafy trail I have just negotiated turns into a three-hundred and sixty degree panoramic view of the world as seen from the top of a mountain. I must be between one hundred to one hundred and fifty feet above the ground. I feel like I'm in an invisible aircraft about to crash in to the jungle.

Vertigo kicks in with huge levels of adrenelin - I am going to shit myself. Literally. I'm picking up speed at an alarming rate.

Slow yourself down! I think to myself. Loudly. I use my gloved right hand to clamp down on the rope and reduce my rate of descent. It works, but the pressure required is muscle-shredding.

I rocket down through the trees utterly alone above the world. This goes on for about two minutes when into view beneath me come a couple of guides standing on a wooden platform which is built into the biggest tree I have ever seen. I am cannonballing towards them.

"Slow down! Slow down!" They cry. I'm trying to. Drenched with sweat I squeeze on the rope with all my might and manage to kill some velocity. I slam into them as they try to catch me and I all but embed myself into the tree. I pick myself up and they unhook me from the rope. I'm shaking uncontrollably.

They grab hold of me and walk me around the perimeter of the tree. I realise I am standing on a small wooden platform attached to a tree which looks approximately two hundred feet down on the jungle floor. Standing here is worse than being on the rope.

"Don't look down just keep walking sir." I am informed by a guide.

Damn Fucking Right.

As I get to the other side of the tree I bump into the brave souls who came before me. All are huddled together, most are whiter than sheets, a few (like me) cannot seem to stop their legs from shaking almost comically. One lady is crying.

"Jesus Christ!" I exclaim to anyone who's listening.

Several of the group are now telling the guides that they do

not like this activity as it seems overly dangerous and they would now like to terminate the activity. Not possible.

Once on the ride you cannot get off. There are no ladders leading down to the jungle from the treetops and it's not that safe a place to be anyway, down there.

"How many more of these do we have to do before we get to the bottom?" I ask, sweat dripping from the end of my nose.

"Ten more stops."

Shit.

The next leg is as scary as the last one but I have now developed a method to ease my passage.

Don't look down. This works, and as terrified as I am I realise I'm just going to have to deal with it. It gets easier and dare I say it - it's becoming scary, heart-stopping fun. There is more adrenalin being released than I can remember. It feels like being chased home from school by a gang of yobs who will tear you apart if they reach you - but only if they reach you. What a rush!

By the time I get to the bottom, twenty minutes later, I feel like I'm on some amazing drug and the high is transcendant. I feel like I've cheated death.

Ian McNabb, adrenalin junkie.

Fuck me.

Later that night we're all pretty sozzled after a big, pissy dinner celebrating our daring-do.

Pam, my companion from the the bus ride (she sat next to me on the journey back as well), is very merry and is flirting with me with gusto. She's not exactly my type, but she's making it hard for me to avert her gaze. We walk back to her room and once inside she wastes no time whatsoever in seducing me. What a professional. She performs everything in the manual - and a couple of things that aren't.

Still reeling from my brilliance on the mountain, I feel like Sir Edmund Hilary being diddled by Pamela De Barres. She's bouncing up and down on top of me shouting expletives at the top of her voice. Jesus, they must be able to hear this at the airport.

"FUCK ME! FUCK ME BABY! YEAH YEAH YEAAAAAAHHHHHHHHHHHH!!!!"

I'm laying back with my hands behind my head thinking what a great life I have when something unexpected happens.

"I'M COMING! I'M COMING!" She cries.

Excellent. Another satisfied customer.

What? What's this? She becomes suddenly silent and throws her head back, mouth open and eyes wide. She throws her arms out horizontally. She's starting to resemble Linda Blair in *The Exorcist*. All of a sudden she secretes a glutinous, hot liquid from her tush all over me. Fuckin' hell! A gusher! I've heard about this, but never experienced it before. I'm freaked out, but intrigued. Within seconds the bed is wet through and I'm thanking the lord we're in her room and not mine. After a minute of this I'm thinking I've had enough. I feel like she's just given birth to me. I push her off as affectionately as I can - I think she's in a trance (damn I'm good) - and I jump up so quickly that I smack my cheekbone into the wall-mounted TV at the end of the bed. She's now writhing around on the bed oblivious to all. I'm suddenly in great pain. I grab my stuff and creep out into the night. I feel as though I have a football attached to the side of my face.

The next morning I wake up with the third black eye I've had in my life. I feel like I've been mugged. The phone rings. It's my mum. Zak's been trying to find me. He wants me to play bass in his dad's band at the Red Cross Ball in Monaco next month. It's a thousand quid and we have to play but five songs.

Beatles songs!

CHAPTER FORTY SIX

Ritchie

Richard Starkey was the drummer in the Beatles.

He has often had to endure many uncomplimentary words about his drumming (and singing), occasionally even from the Beatles themselves. When he appeared on a national chatshow but one week after being the main attraction at Liverpool's opening 2008 Capital of Culture celebrations, and appeared to have the temerity to laugh out loud when asked if there was anything he missed about Liverpool in forty-plus years of absence, he even had to endure media-saturated raw disgust from a vast number of the city's inhabitants.

He wisely did not respond.

He knows better than that. His presence alone that weekend guaranteed lengthy coverage across the globe and the message was: Come To Liverpool.

Ringo has a deeper connection than the other three with the beating working class heart of that great city. They lived in the suburbs. He lived in the toughest part of town.

He remembers that: "It was damp and I had T.B."

As soon as he could, he left.

And why shouldn't he?

Why should he return if he has no need or doesn't want to? Let's face it. Ringo's already done more for Liverpool than Liverpool did for Ringo. His and the other Beatles' background

has been discussed endlessly everywhere since 1963 so I need not repeat any more of it here.

Suffice to say the lad comes from Toxteth, Liverpool, and he is one of my kind. The only true working class Beatle. Regardless of what you may think of his talent, manner or attitude.

He is exactly one quarter of a phenomenon. As famous as J.F.K. and...whisper it, maybe even bigger than Jesus.

Certainly more prolific, and better preserved in the digital age.

"John Lennon? Working class hero? Middle class snob more like!"

John's guardian, Aunt Mimi, said that.

Ritchie's singing is not ripe for discussion - but as a drummer he has influenced more musicians than Buddy Rich. You'll hear a Ringo lick on almost every guitar pop record made in the last forty years.

As documented earlier, I've met him before. Well, meeting a Beatle is one thing - but performing with one of them in front of an audience - well let me tell you about it.

Ringo lives in Monte Carlo in the Principality of Monaco, among other places. Every year they badger him to perform at the Red Cross Ball attended by Albert II, Prince of Monaco.

Most of the time he gives them the slip, but this year he couldn't get away with it.

In order to facilitate such a happening with minimum fuss for the scouse legend, he had instructed Zak to put a little band together, rehearse a short set in England, bring said merry minstrels over, look after them on the Friday evening when they would arrive, bring them to the rehearsal on Saturday afternoon where they could run the tunes down with their singer, do the gig on the Saturday night, and send 'em home on the Sunday evening. A simple enough task to someone in the know - Zak's 'know' was to assemble his best mates so we could all have a good old laugh as well as do the job at hand.

That band in full:

Zak Starkey: Drums
Peter Gordeno: Keys/Vocals
Bernie Marsden: Guitar/Vocals
Gary Nuttall: Guitar/Vocals
Me: Bass/vocals

Bernie and Gary were two of Zak's best mates, both guitar players. He wanted me as well so figured I'd play bass.

Hell, I didn't mind. I would've played drums if it meant I got to do the gig.

Peter Gordeno was the son of the seventies dancer/actor of the same name (most famously playing the submarine commander in Gerry Anderson's U.F.O.), and played with Depeche Mode. Bernie Marsden was a founder member of seventies hard rock outfit Whitesnake, and wrote many of their biggest tunes. Gary Nuttall was a neighbour of Zak's and played guitar in pop-scamp Robbie Williams' touring band. We all met at Zak's on the Thursday to rehearse.

The songs we would play were 'Photograph', 'I Wanna Be Your Man', 'Yellow Submarine' and 'With A Little Help From My Friends'. During the rehearsal I sang all the leads.

Everyone sang well so the harmonies sounded glorious. The next day we flew to Nice and were driven to Monte Carlo. Lee and Zak's brother Jason met us at the hotel.

On the Saturday we went to the gig to rehearse and soundcheck. It was in a vast, enclosed circular arena by the beach. Ringo turned up and was all smiles in a cool leather jacket.

I asked Zak what I should call him - I could never get past 'Mr Starkey.' Zak told me to call him Ritchie, Ringo, it didn't matter. He was cool.

It all sounded good. Mr. Starkey had a few comments but

basically we'd nailed it. Marianne Faithful was on the bill too and came over to introduce herself.

When she got to me she dropped her cigarette lighter on the floor and bent down to pick it up. For about five seconds I had a sixties sex-goddess inches from my crotch. I had a little chortle about that one.

After a nice dinner we went back to the hotel and got ready for the show. It was incredibly exciting.

Every time I stopped moving around I noticed I was next to Lee. I couldn't work out who was following whom. She seemed as jazzed as I was with all the fun. The gig was a blast. We were all wearing black suits so Ritchie christened us 'The Ravens.' He looked cool as fuck in a purple suit and much younger than his sixty-plus years. There were mirrors all around the back of the venue and we could see ourselves clearly from the stage. I was playing my Hofner Violin bass (of course) and it looked left-handed in the mirror (when I pulled it out at rehearsal, Ritchie went "Oh no!" I went to take it off and he laughed and said it was cool. He must've known how important this was to a kid like me). To be onstage playing this music with a real Beatle is beyond description. I'm a Beatle nut. Bernie Marsden and myself would sing "Do you need anybody?" and Ritchie would retort "I need somebody to love!" It was amazing and I'll never forget it.

The next day Ritchie took us for lunch with his wife Barbara. He doesn't smoke or drink anymore and neither did anyone else that day except for me and Lee, so we were pushed together at the far end of the table. We all walked out into the street after the meal to take photos and within a few minutes Ritchie was attracting a small crowd.

He tried to shake them off but they kept following him. Eventually he turned around and shouted "Look, I don't know you - go away!"

I was taken aback with this - it seemed harsh. He turned

around to us - "You have to say that or they won't leave you alone." Imagine being that famous for that long. Nobody looks at anyone in Monte Carlo. Unless you're a Beatle. Wow.

We said our goodbyes and headed to the airport. This wouldn't be the last time though.

Ritchie was headlining a benefit in England later on in the year and would request our services once again.

It was an incredible moment in my life as both a musician, and a fan.

Ritchie: "So what did you guys get up to last night after the show?"

Zak: "We went back to the hotel and had a party in Lee's room."

Ritchie: "What? And pat yourselves on the back all night tellin' each other how great you played?"

Zak: "Er, yeah."

Ritchie: "Ha ha ha ha ha ha..."

I started hanging out with Lee a bit when we came home. Zak had been the one who told me that she'd finished with her fella and I took that as a cue. I got the impression that certain parties thought I'd be good for her. To all intents and purposes the relationship she'd just been through had been quite a destructive one. I didn't know.

I didn't ask. If any information was offered to me I listened in silence.

It wasn't my business.

Whenever I was in London I'd go and stay with her and we'd get suitably silly and feel rather ill and shameful the next day.

Sometimes I just went and stayed with her without any other excuse for being in London.

After a couple of days I'd come home and sit on the train wondering if I was getting anywhere.

Unfortunately, we only seemed to click when we were partying. It made me miserable.

If she would've jumped on me and told me this was it - I probably would've run a mile.

Probably.

Probably not.

I'll never know.

"I love you but... I'm not in love with you."

When anyone tells you that, it basically means you're in a glass case only to be smashed in case of emergency. I was so smitten that this almost seemed like a good deal. I knew it wasn't going anywhere but I hung on anyway.

In May I went on tour with the Waterboys again, playing bass this time. I knew the Waterboys songs on nearly every instrument by this point. This time we played in Spain and Portugal for about a week and a half, taking in Salamanca, Valencia, Barcelona, Madrid, Braganca, Covilha, Braga, and Lisbon (where we ran over time and the police stopped the show).

We had a great time needless to say, who couldn't in that part of the world? All despite the fact that it pissed with rain from the minute we got there, whilst Blighty basked.

I played with the Ringo and the Ravens band once more, in June at a charity concert at Cowdray House, Midhurst, West Sussex. Mike Rutherford of Genesis organised the event. The pitch was simple - loads of different artists performing three Beatle songs each. Ringo would headline. David Gilmour, Donovan, Lulu, Roger Taylor from Queen, Sir Bob Geldof, Paul Carrack and many more. Kenny Jones from the Small Faces and the Who was there.

Robbie Macintosh of the Pretenders too. It was a gas. I had a nice chat with Roger Taylor.

Dave Gilmour didn't appear to remember who I was "Ah yes! The Bicyle Works!"

Nice one, la.

Ian Broudie turned up with his son Riley and couldn't speak to me because Ritchie was standing next to me (I'd got a bit used to it by now). Ian's a Beatle nut too. I was made up because Gilmour's roadie had to move his effects pedal board to make way for my mic stand.

Headline act! (For the record: Gilmour's effects rack was the size of a small car).

We did the same set as Monaco with 'Boys' now thrown in. Gary Nuttall was busy with Robbie Williams and was replaced with Dave Caitlin-Birch, formerly of the Bootleg Beatles and World Party.

I put my latest collection of songs out quietly in September and called it *The Gentleman Adventurer*.

It was a similar album to *Truth And Beauty* in many ways. Reflective and homespun.

It was received fairly well and had a gentle charm, but there was a feeling of treading water once again.

CHAPTER FORTY SEVEN

Once more into the Bleach

March 2003.

The dark is beginning to lift. January and February have had their way with us.

Most of us have survived. We didn't think we would, but we did. Lee fluctuates from telling me she wants a child with me (!) to casually moving my stuff into the spare room when I nip out for fags. I'm confused. I've written lots of new songs and I'm thinking about recording them soon. Mostly they are torch songs.

If you want a big record, write songs about not being wanted by the object of your affection.

You can write the odd song about a German helmet or a JCB that many will find favour with, but if you want to get the ear of EVERYONE, write the unrequited love ballad.

One of the most wonderful things about being an artist is being able to emasculate your pain through creative expression. Better out than in. Show your shit to the world. They will like it, maybe even buy it, because it makes them cry - because they've been there.

I have saved thousands of pounds in therapy bills from writing songs. I have made money from singing about my misery. What a release! This is a strange irony. When I get my ass kicked by a member of the opposite sex I take great comfort in knowing

that I'll be able to turn it into a profit at some point.

The flipside of this however, is that I have became fearless about entering into any (unwritten) contract pertaining to a new relationship, due to my experience discovering that the spoils of war do not necessarily belong to the winner. 'There Oughta Be A Law', 'Before All Of This', 'Finally Getting Over You', 'Rider (The Heartless Mare)', 'The Nicest Kind Of Lie' - you get the gist. These were all new songs based in truth and experience.

I decide that I need a feminine touch on some of these pieces - so I don't sound like a complete woman-hater - and put the word out that I'm looking for a girl singer with a sweet voice, not a warbler or wailer, someone who sounds like the girl next door. Sympathetic. It doesn't take too long for me to find one.

"I know a girl singer."

This is some guy I've known for a short time. I met him at a party on a tour bus outside Cream that Lee had hired for a birthday party, one of her rare trips to Liverpool.

Cream was a trendy dance phenomenon epicentre located in Wolstenholme Square.

He sells me the odd bit of weed. Manages a band or two. Nice fella.

"What's she like?"

"Dunno, never heard her. She seems very confident though. She hosts a radio show out of Salford University. I met her when one of my bands did an interview for the station. She's dead fit too."

"How old is she?"

"Twenty-one."

"Is she cool?"

"Yeah...she's bonkers."

What's new.

"What's her name?"

"Livia"

"Olivia?"

"No, just Livia."

"Cool. Set it up."

Livia. That's the name of Tony Soprano's scary mother in the fab telly programme The Sopranos. Also the name of a Roman empress isn't it?

Mmm...

We meet a short time later at Barfly in Seel Street. She's really cute. Perhaps a bit too cute.

In fact she's dangerously cute. She's actually...beautiful. Blonde, big brown eyes, about 5' 6".

Kind of a hybrid of a young Michelle Phillips with a twist of prime-era Britney Spears, a bit of Billie Piper.

Crikey. There's a wildness in her eyes and an urgency in her manner that suggests she's in a hurry. Not to leave, to rise. I'm not sizing her up - for now - I'm still thinking about someone else.

Anyway, I'm not looking for a party, I'm looking for a singer. I'm also old enough to be her father.

Keep your mind on the job McNabb.

We talk a while and she's nice. Very chatty. She's up for the gig. Before I can ask her for a number she's shoved a piece of paper (prepared earlier) into my hand with her cellphone, home, and Salford flat numbers written on. She's put her email address on there as well.

I think she might've put the number of a payphone she might be passing later on down there too. Just in case. She wants this. I think I've been Google'd.

I call her the following week and arrange for her to come over to the house so I can hear her. She turns up wide-eyed and excited on Friday evening. She's got her own car. She's got it all together.

I think she's really nervous but hiding it reasonably well. We've gotten together early tonight because I'm producing Tom Dyson's band the Aeroplanes tomorrow at the Motor Museum

Studios off Lark Lane and I need to go and watch them rehearse later on at Vulcan Studios on the Dock Road. Livia's going to drive me down there and hang out for a bit. I dig this chick.

I make some tea and take her downstairs to the den. She's all wow at the size of my CD collection.

I play her some of my tunes and she seems to be blown away, Everything is all wow.

I can't decide if she means it or this is an act. It doesn't matter. I need to hear if she can sing. I pick up my guitar and strum around a bit, I show her a few things and ask her to try and sing some of them. She's shitting herself. She's making shapes with her mouth but there's nowt coming out. She's starting to panic. I put the guitar down.

"Chill Livia, it's cool! Don't worry, relax."

"Oh my God! Oh my God! I can't believe this...my voice is gone. I've had a really bad cold you see...and...oh my God!"

She's acting like she's auditioning for the X Factor. I tell her it's fine. I ask her if she wants some wine. She does. I roll a spliff. She's puffing away like an expert.

This is turning into a party. Focus. We try again. Same deal. I'm looking at the time. I have to get into town.

I'll have to hear her sing another time. She hasn't failed the audition, she just hasn't done one.

We jump into her car and head to the Aero's rehearsal space. The guys seem happy to see me - and Livia, who they've met before. We routine the numbers we're going to be recording tomorrow. I look over at Livia who is sitting on the floor texting away - that peculiar method of communication that has overtaken our lives. Neither a conversation nor a letter. More of a probe or a post-it note. Dangerous when used in conjunction with stimulants. She looks bored.

I'm starting to think I'll have to find someone who can sing as well as hang out with me and turn heads.

We wrap it up and say our fond farewells. I ask Livia if she wants to go for a drink in town.

She does. We're driving around the docks with Avril Lavigne on eleven. Livia is singing along to 'Complicated' at the top of her voice which seems to have returned thanks to the funkiness of the situation, but the tape is so loud I can't hear if she's singing or shouting.

I opt for the former and allow myself to begin enjoying the company of this kooky young lass.

We hit 3345 - our funky little new members club - recently refurbished - above Parr Street Studios - where the cool, arty types now choose to mingle. I get a bottle of wine and we sit in the corner soaking up the Friday night vibe. The place is starting to groove.

I'm enjoying myself.

Livia doesn't stop talking but I'm digging it. I'm fed up of the sound of my own whingeing voice anyway. I'm not really listening to her but she's young and thinks the world is amazing. She doesn't know the truth yet. I'm kind of jealous of her. I wouldn't mind being twenty-one and looking at the world like her (my mother always tells me she wanted a girl and sometimes thinks that she might've got one anyway). She's got an open road in front of her.

A long road. People are looking over who know me and wondering who this girl is.

I love being in the company of attractive young women. It's my job. I'm a fuckin' rock star aren't I?

It's getting late. I'm a bit pissed but conscious of the fact that I have to be in the studio with my producer's hat on and a clear head early tomorrow. There's nothing worse than trying to get a drum sound with a fuckin' hangover.

"Right then, I'm gonna head home," I offer.

I stand up and pull my jeans up a bit.

"So what are you doing then?" asks Livia.

"Do you want a lift home?"

"Well that's kind of you but you're going the other way."

(She's staying at her parents' house in Bebington. Across the water. Through the Mersey tunnel. The other way.)

"Oh I don't mind... can we just chill out at yours for a bit and listen to some music?"

She wants to come home with me. What's the deal here? I usually have to try harder.

"Well... I'm just gonna go to sleep you know...I've gotta be on it for the lads tomorrow."

"Can I just come back for a bit? I won't stay long honestly."

Is she coming on to me? I can't tell. Maybe she just likes me and wants to be my mate. Maybe she just doesn't want to go home. Fuckin' 'ell. I look at her. I'm a bit drunk. Actually, I'm fully drunk now that I'm standing up. She wants to come home with me. She's gorgeous. Shit.

Go home, child.

"Come on then. Just for a while, mind."

I figure I'll save on a taxi. Or something.

We head back to the ranch. I crack another bottle. We're back in the den and the CDs are everywhere. I'm playing her all my favourites and there's a bit of a Luke and Yoda thing going on. She loves everything I'm playing her...I think. Master and student. I've wandered off-script here but what the hell. I'm well smashed now and I'm dancing around the cellar to 'Cinnamon Girl' with an excited young girl who says "Oh my God!" a lot. I have to go to bed.

"I have to go to bed!" I exclaim loudly.

She's too fucked to drive now.

"Can I stay here? I just need a couple of hours and then I'll go."

Does she want to sleep with me? Or does she just want to go to sleep? I can't decide. I'm twatted.

I have to get up in a few hours. I'm not being professional at all. I think I'm on the verge of bedding a girl who I am supposed to be thinking about working with, if I ever get to hear her sing that is - Rule Number One: Don't shit where you eat, remember?

And I'm gonna turn up hungover for the session tomorrow.

"Come on then."

We go upstairs. My mother gives me a dirty look as we pass her in the hallway.

"There's a bed in the spare room just there, here's some water." I offer.

"Where do you go to sleep?" she asks, looking at me with Big Brown Eyes.

"In here."

I gesture towards the unmade bed behind me.

"I don't mind sleeping with you, you know? No funny business like."

"Like I would!" I chime.

I would.

She either trusts me or she's stupid. I don't know. I'm drunk. My perceptive powers have clocked off for the evening.

"Come on then."

I give her a Doors T-shirt and we climb in. She assumes fetal position and faces away from me. I put my arm around her and she holds on to it.

We go to sleep.

No, really.

I wonder if she can sing?

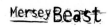

Mersey Beast

CHAPTER FORTY EIGHT

Goin' down
to a Spanish
town

I'm still thinking about recording the next album.

I've got enough songs but they all feel a bit like the continuation of the last one.

I'm waiting for a sign. A kick in the ass. A cough from God. Call up papers.

Anything. I write 'Unfinished Business In London Town (For Lee)', but I'm far too shy to play it to her - she might get the idea that I'm in love with her or something and we couldn't have that.

Easter's coming up and I'm despondent. I'm hanging out with Livia a lot. It's entertaining and maddening in equal amounts. She feels more like a daughter than a girlfriend.

I'm twenty years older than her.

I don't feel rich or famous enough to start dating what is effectively a child from my advancing years. People are wondering what's going on. "What's with Britney?" I introduce her to my friends and most of them seem to take an instant dislike to her - they inform me I'm being used. I inform them that she's young and wants to be rich and famous.

Whatever. It suits me for the time being. She makes me feel so young, she makes me feel like spring has sprung.

My ego's getting a good stroking. Every time I go out with her I seem to lose her within seconds as she talks and flirts her way

around the room. We usually end up back together at the end of the night - not always - and she comes home with me.

It seems every guy wants to fuck her and every girl hisses at her.

Guess I'm doing something right then. I still haven't heard her sing properly (apart from when we're wrecked at four in the morning and she's wailing along to the Carpenters with me).

I even took her to a party at Lee's one night to see if I got a reaction. I did - she told me to get out of her room and go and sleep with Livia.

I tell Livia I'm fed up one night after we go to see Jesse Malin play at the University, so she suggests we go away together. She keeps throwing her arms around me and kissing me and hugging me.

I dig it. I haven't been away with a woman for about twenty years - Hilary and I went to Tenby in South Wales for a week - it ended up in tears. She's keen so I go with the flow. I call up my mate Peter Crew who lives and works in Nerja on the Costa del Sol.

He owns a couple of bars there. I can get up and do a gig, maybe try out some of the new stuff.

Maybe the climate will encourage Livia to finally sing for me. Maybe I can find out if there's some future here or if I'm just being a dick.

McNabokov.

Off we go and it's fun. We get drunk, eat nice food, do all the usual stuff.

I finally get to hear her sing properly when she gets up on the karaoke in one of Peter's bars and attempts 'Like A Prayer'.

"Is that your new singer?" asks Sarah - the takes-no-shit Geordie lass who works behind the bar.

"Er, yeah!"

"She's fuckin' shite!"

(She wasn't - although I may not be the one to judge - I'd just been up and massacred 'The Air That I Breathe' in a key about three steps too high for me).

One night Livia nearly got us both murdered after we'd had a row. I wanted to go back to the apartment but she wanted to stay out longer. She was speaking French to some dodgy looking geezer in a gay bar we were in. We only had one set of keys - which meant I'd have to get out of bed when she eventually decided to return. I marched home alone, got lost for about an hour in a downpour, and eventually got to sleep after I'd locked the door and turned off my phone.

She'd pissed me off and would suffer the consequences. She banged on the door all night apparently but I was out cold. The next day she told me this guy was a drug dealer and she ended up going back to his place to do some coke.

He went to bed as he had to work early the next morning and left her alone in his living room. She thought about staying there but then got the jitters and split - but before she did she picked up half an eight-ball that was sitting on the table, thinking it would be a nice surprise for me. When she couldn't get in the apartment she had to go and sleep on the beach until I woke up.

She was quite remorseful and I suddenly felt guilty about locking her out. I was supposed to be looking after her after all.

I'd left her in a bar, drunk. The next night the guy turned up at the club I was playing in and started having an argument with her in French. It freaked me out and I thought we were done for. She told the guy I was her boyfriend (not strictly true) and I tried to look vaguely threatening.

I don't know how I got away with it but he buggered off. Later on when we were back at the apartment the guy rang her up and they started arguing again. Once again it was in French which made it even scarier.

I couldn't believe she'd given him her fuckin' phone number.

I made her hang up and turn it off. I toyed with the idea of making her give him his stuff back, but that meant a confrontation and Christ knows what would happen in that situation.

We lay in bed quivering in fear that he'd find us and burst in with a gang of shooters.

We're still here.

I was buzzed about the new songs after playing nearly all of them to a small crowd in a Spanish bar and decided to book time in Mike Cave's to get 'em down. Livia sang on 'Finally Getting Over You' and 'Western Eyes'.

I needn't have worried - she sounded great, just what I wanted. I recorded about ten tunes including 'People Don't Stop Believin', 'The New Me', 'The Lonely Ones', all acoustic. They all sounded great but it didn't feel like an album.

I decided to sit on them for a while and think about it.

Coldplay had been recording their second album at Parr Street. They were there for quite a while and we got to know each other fairly well.

Chris Martin kept his distance but spent a lot of time fawning over his hero Ian McCulloch, who was well chuffed with the attention.

The guitar player, Johny - was nice. Guy the bass player was full on rock 'n' roll.

One night we were all having a lock-in in the bar. Livia was ignoring me and sniffing round the superstars.

I got a cob on and split.

She followed me downstairs when she realised I was pissed off and asked me to play the piano for her in the studio, which I did for a little while. I had to leave soon however as I was scheduled to do a couple of numbers with Thea Gilmore in London the next night (I'd met Thea through Mike Cave who produced her records too).

Liv told me she was waiting for her sister to give her a lift home and she'd be leaving soon.

I got a cab home and went to bed. Ten minutes later I woke

up angry - knowing what was afoot.

I tried ringing Liv and she didn't answer. I called her sister who was still in the bar. She answered.

"Kat, where's Liv? I thought you were taking her home?"

Silence.

"Kat?"

"She doesn't deserve you. She can't see what she's got."

Kat liked me.

"Where is she?"

"She's just gone upstairs with Guy from Coldplay.

"Ian, I think you should come down here and have it out with her. She's so... wrong."

I put the phone down. Liv and I weren't officially together, but we carried on as though we were and everybody assumed we were an item by this point. Fact was she'd just made an idiot of me in front of most of my friends and associates in a place where I drank all the time.

This was a declaration of war in my drink-addled brain. I jumped out of bed in a drunken rage and demanded that Pat drive me to Parr Street immediately.

Bizarrely, she did. I jumped out of the car and bowled into reception.

Mac virtually rugby tackled me on the way in.

He dragged me off to a corner and told me: "Listen, you're a legend. Don't let some heft drag you down to this, she's not worth it. I don't like seeing you like this."

"Heft" was Ian's word for women. We all adopted it.

I wasn't interested. I pushed him off me and walked to the front desk and demanded that Johnny the night porter give me the key to the hotel floor. Bizarrely, he did. I jumped in the lift and turned the key. Within seconds I was pounding on Guy's door.

"Open the fuckin' door!"

I was behaving like a madman.

"OPEN THIS FUCKIN' DOOR! I MEAN IT! I'M NOT GOING AWAY!"

I hear noises and mumbled chatter. Eventually Liv opens the door. Fully clothed. She's freaked out.

"What are you doing? We're only watching a DVD!"

I fly past her and into the room. Guy is passed out on the bed, attire intact. I heard him say something before, through the door, so I reason that he's pretending to be asleep as this would be the safest course of action in his situation. I'm bigger than him and would have no trouble flattening him. None whatsoever in my current state.

I grab hold of Liv and drag her down to the street.

"You fuckin' lied to me! Don't you ever fuckin' lie to me!"

She's crying.

"I'm only twenty-one! Leave me alone! I'm twenty-one!"

She's right. She's twenty-one. What the fuck.

She comes home with me and we sleep as far away from each other as two people can in the same bed.

Twenty-one.

Get a fucking grip Ian - you silly old fart. You're making a show of yourself over a little girl.

The next morning I call Mike Cave to tell him I won't be coming to London to play with Thea as I had a late, stressful night. He tells me that when I went to the toilet in the restaurant that he, Liv and I were having dinner in the night before, she suggested that when I went home she and Mike should go back to his place and have sex, which he thoughtfully declined.

I'm beginning to understand what I'm dealing with.

Nothing new, just... disappointing.

I rang up Tom Lang who ran the bar at Parr Street and had her barred from the building. She wouldn't be preying on rock stars who came through the studios which I originally took her to every week on my sodding watch.

No fucking way, Jose.

Grow some funk of your own.

(Liv later thanked me for pulling her out of Guy's room. She also told me she fully intended to have him on the night in question.

Guy for his part apologised to me telling me that Liv simply referred to me as "my songwriter."

As far as he was concerned there wasn't anything more to our relationship than that. He was, from then on, very nervous whenever he saw me.

I reassured him that I had no beef with him and my anger was with the lady in question - or more precisely, myself).

This liaison was going to be different for sure. I could've just ended it there and then I guess.

What? And miss all the fun?

Fuck off!

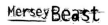

Mersey Beast

CHAPTER FORTY NINE

Mr. Atobe, and before all this

A Japanese guy was in Parr Street producing a local band for his own label back home.

His name was Mr. Atobe, and although he spoke appalling English, he tried to get into a conversation with me every time I bumped into him. After much trial and error and a lot of hand-signals and Origami sessions, I ascertained what he wanted to do was release *The Gentleman Adventurer* album domestically in his country.

He also wanted to promote a couple of McNabb solo shows over there. We struck a deal and I signed a contract (contracts are difficult to understand at the best of times, so you can understand how tough a Japanese one was to read. When I had it translated it made only slightly more sense). He would release the record the first week of November and I would fly out there to do two nights in a club in Tokyo.

I asked Steve Walter to come out with me. We could have fun and he could look after me. Travelling on your own is a drag. Geoff Dugmore would be out there at the same time, working with a Japanese artist, so a fun time could be had.

The date of leaving grew nearer and I was having trouble getting hold of Mr. Atobe in Japan. When I did get hold of him I had to have a three-way conference call - I asked a good friend of mine - Erica Yamashita – to translate.

Erica wrote for Japan's biggest music magazine *Rockin' On*. Eventually we worked out all the details and Steve and I flew from Manchester to Heathrow to catch a British Airways flight to Tokyo on the last day of October. Erica would also be in Japan for my shows, and would be a great help to me.

When we got to the B.A. check-in desk the tickets had yet to be paid for. Hasty phone calls were made to Erica who in turn tried to find Mr. Atobe.

When she eventually got hold of him, he told her to tell me to pay for the flights and he would reimburse me in cash when I landed. This was not ideal but Steve and I were here now, excited about the trip, and not anxious to turn around and go home.

I handed over my AMEX to the girl at the sales desk and she charged just short of fifteen hundred quid to my card.

When we landed, Mr. Atobe met us in arrivals. He told us he would have my money later that day as we took the long drive into Tokyo from Narita Airport.

He then checked us into our hotel, took us for lunch, and then left Steve and I to our own devices as we wandered around the shops and bars bleary-eyed and tired. I got back to my room and stuck the telly on.

The usual selection of whaling documentaries and shouty game shows. And the inevitable 'specialist' channel. Japanese porn is a little weird. Basically schoolgirls being chased through fields - screaming - and then effectively, raped. I assume it's all consensual and acted - a little unnerving though.

I look at the front of the latest Q magazine which features Britney Spears dressed in some form of school uniform which appears to be made out of leather.

I make a mental note to buy Livia a present. I have myself a little hand party and pass out listening to the Hollies boxset.

The next day I did some interviews with the Japanese media. At least Mr. Atobe had sorted that side of things out OK - or so

I thought. Erica later told me she had arranged the bulk of the interviews herself. We went down to the club in the late afternoon to soundcheck and make sure all the hired equipment was up to snuff.

It was.

The first gig was well attended and everything went swimmingly well. Mr. Atobe sold a lot of copies of my album at the back of the room.

Steve pressed him about the money he owed me and he assured him (through Erica) that everything was fine, but he hadn't had a chance to get to the bank due to all the preparations for the show tonight - but he would sort this out first thing tomorrow. After the gig we went out for food and drink with Geoff Dugmore.

Later on we went back to his hotel.

I asked him why he had bandages on both of his wrists. I assumed he had some sort of drummer straining injury.

He informed me that whilst he was in Japan he had received word that his wife was cheating on him with a much younger man, so he decided to slit his wrists. He delivered this news very matter-of-fact and then shrugged.

"Women eh?" He ventured.

"Yeah, man." I reply.

Steve and I eyeball each other as Geoff hunts for a CD in his case. Jesus. I'd spent a lot of time with Geoff and never thought he was wrapped that tight. Fuck.

"So, at what point did you change your mind and decide that er, y'know, killin' yourself wasn't a good idea?" I enquired.

"Oh... you know how it is. Fuckin' women. Can't live with them, can't kill 'em."

"Ha... yeah. Too true. Too true."

I prayed to myself I'd never find myself in that situation. I've had my moments but... so far so good.

The next day I do an in-store performance and signing session

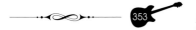

at one of the big record stores.

Mr. Atobe sells a lot of CDs. Steve taps him up about the cash again. Through Erica he promises that everything is well in hand but he still hasn't had a chance to visit his bank due to all the activity. Steve's leaning on him a bit harder now but - there really isn't too much he can do.

I could pull tonight's show, but that's letting fans down who only ever see me out here once in a blue moon. Mr. Atobe tells us not to worry.

The second night was even better than the first. It also happened to be my birthday. My second in Japan. We get walloped on Sake and Suntory Whiskey. The next day is a day off and Steve and I walk the length of the city and do lots of shopping. We are leaving early the next morning and Mr. Atobe has promised to make good with the cash tonight.

He owes me for my cut of the CD sales, my share of the gate, and of course the flights. We can't get hold of him all day.

He eventually shows up at the hotel at three a.m with an envelope. In it is the equivalent of about six hundred quid in Yen. Steve kicks off on him bigtime now but he assures us the rest of the money will follow in about a week.

He explains (once again through Erica) that he's a had a few problems but they will be sorted out very soon. He attempts to shake my hand as we enter the departure gate but I shoot him an icy stare and walk on.

He looks as if he is going to cry and I feel bad momentarily.

A month after we got home we were still trying to get hold of Mr. Atobe. He simply disappeared.

Also, he apparently had outstanding debts with HMV, the store I performed in, and they were now refusing to sell any stock he was involved with. Meaning: They cleared the racks of the Ian McNabb album which I had gone there to sell.

It's never too late in life to get burned. We should have turned around at Heathrow, but we wanted a little working holiday. I still haven't seen any money. I wonder where all those Japanese copies of my album ended up? I had a contract which was little use when the other party had simply vanished into thin air (Mr. Atobe also failed to pay the studio bill at Parr Street).

In January '04 I booked time at Parr St. to cut a bunch of electric stuff. I'd lived with the new songs I'd recorded for months and decided I would have an album that was half acoustic and half electric, something I'd never done before.

I'd written some new stuff, one number in particular sounded very commercial - 'Let The Young Girl Do What She Wants To' – written about an older gentleman's frustrations encountered whilst forging a relationship with a lady who is much younger than himself. I had to use a lot of imagination on that one.

I enlisted the talents of a hot young new drummer from Norwich by the name of Steve Barney, whom I'd met during his tenure with ace-but-unsuccessful Liverpool band Bullyrag. Myself, Roy Corkill and Steve set up and blasted away for a couple of days.

It was brilliant.

Mike Cave once again oversaw the recordings. We nailed '...Young Girl...' 'Lovers At The End Of Time', The New Me', 'Keeping Your Love Alive', 'The Lonely Ones', 'The Nicest Kind Of Lie'- and many others. I knew this would be my best album in ages. I got Livia to sing the harmony on Young Girl...' and 'Picture Of the Moon' - possibly the only time the subject matter has added vocals to a song written about them since Stevie Nicks added vocals to Lindsey Buckingham's 'Go Your Own Way' and 'Never Going Back Again'.

Well, the only time I'm aware of (I'm sure many of you will pull me on this once this book has been published).

I put the album together and sequenced it with great care. It dealt with my feelings about my brief experience with Lee and then gently changed colour as it became electrified and the subject matter eased into my fun and games with Livia (I got

her bar lifted at Parr Street about a week after it was implemented).

I was thrilled with it - if a little nervous about the way I'd revealed myself so openly.

It was incredibly personal and I felt a little uneasy about bareing my soul so clearly. Fuck it. It was a document about a time in my life that was pretty intense and - it was going to come out. It was fresh blood and it had a kick to it because of that fact. I'd harboured a fantasy about being with Lee, but she didn't want it and...that was that. You can't give an artist more inspiration to write or perform. It was amusing to me (and everyone else in the know) that the end of the acoustic 'side' which gave us 'Finally Getting Over You' (my cheerio to Lee - sung as a duet with Livia), gave way to the electric 'side' - which began with 'Let The Young Girl Do What She Wants To' (written about Livia and featuring her prominent vocals).

It was a masterpiece of sequencing and I was very proud. Everyone seemed excited by the album, if only for the fact that I was rocking out again. 'The Lonely Ones' in particular had turned into a balls-out affair that everyone wanted to kick the furniture around to (It's 'All Along The Watchtower' the wrong way around for those who care about such things - thanks - again - Mr. Dylan).

The album would be called *Before All Of This* and would be released a year after completion.

The reason for this being that I decided I should release an Ian McNabb 'Best Of' first to wake everybody up to the fact that I was still alive. I'd been making solo records for over ten years at this point, yet I'd still get people stopping me on street asking me what was I up to these days? It was very frustrating.

Many people assumed that I'd become a docker or something since the Icicle Works ceased to be, as they rarely heard me on the radio or saw me on the telly.

All they had to do was press 'search' on the internet and my world would be before them, but it seemed I'd slipped so far off their radar they never thought to do so.

Lazy bastards.

I put together a comprehensive selection of my solo work along with a bonus disc of rarities as a purchase incentive and released it that summer. I called it - *Potency: The Best Of Ian McNabb*.

Me and my trusty band of rockers consisting now of Mathew Priest (drums, vocals), Richard Naiff (keys), and Roy Corkill (bass, vocals) played many shows to promote it including a headline slot at Glastonbury which was filmed and shown live by the B.B.C.

The record got glowing reviews, sold very well, and did its job of re-introducing my catalogue in an easy-to-swallow package.

Paul Du Noyer, author of the definitive tome on Liverpool music - *Liverpool: Wondrous Place* - wrote very flattering liner notes for me to help my case along.

I found time to have a brief affair with an actress/supply teacher by the name of Laura (always the L's!) who decided she couldn't be with me because she was convinced she'd end up "An old-looking alcoholic, wheezing, drug-addict".

Oh dear. I took her to Glastonbury where Livia made a beeline for me as soon as she heard I was on site, ignoring Laura completely and giving the impression that we were still seeing each other.

As time progressed I would still date Livia when we were both on the same astral plane, or when she treated me with respect, instead of like her sugar-daddy - and I even still spent time with Lee when events transpired to throw us together.

It was never, ever, boring.

Bruce McKenzie of Townsend records (who sold my albums online), an old mate who had issued my *Best Of* album through his distribution deal with Universal, convinced me that I should attempt to have a hit single to introduce the new album.

After I'd stopped laughing I began to listen.

I hadn't been in the top forty for over twenty years and it seemed like a reasonable challenge. 'Let The Young Girl...' was as catchy as hell and it was worth a shot.

In May '05 I went out on the road opening for folk/jazz legend John Martyn and we released the single to tie-in. I asked my fans via my website to buy the thing in droves, and every town we hit, me and my crew raided the record shops and bought two each.

The fuckin' thing actually got to number thirty-eight and gave me my highest single chart entry since 1984.

Ian McNabb in the top forty in 2005.

Hilarious.

I waited for the ticker tape parade which never came, but I cracked a bottle of something cheeky and had a little chortle to myself. The album came out shortly after and got good notices and sold enough for me to carry on.

In July I was offered the opening slot on Brian Wilson's date at the Summer Pops, an event held every year by my one-time agent Chas Cole at C.M.P. It was fabulous.

I performed alone in front of five and a half thousand people and slayed 'em. I had them all singing along to 'You've Got To Hide Your Love Away'.

Just before he went on I went up to Brian and thanked him for letting me open the show.

He grabbed my hand firmly, stared me hard in the eye and said:

"Hello. GOODBYE!"

(This was not unusual apparently. Some time later I told this story to Mani from the Stone Roses/Primal Scream, and he told me he approached Brian a day earlier at Glastonbury, and introduced himself.

Brian freaked out and started yelling "SECURITY! SECURITY" to anyone who'd listen.)

'In the bleak mid-winter,
when the snow is on the ground,
I'll be thinking of you,
unfinished business in London town,
child, you were perfection,
so wild in autumn eiderdown,
I'll give you a ring for your finger,
unfinished business in London town,
now they say the heart has boundaries,
but I know that is not true,
for a heart could have no limits love,
if it should fall for you,
so, I gotta go now,
but I know just where you can be found,
and one day I promise to take care of,
unfinished business in London town.'

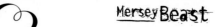

CHAPTER FIFTY

People
don't
stop believin'

There was a bunch of stuff left over from the BAOT sessions so I put them all together on an album.

I called it *People Don't Stop Believin'*, and sold it online to the fans.

Livia moved to London at the bequest of some hapless fool called Barnaby who was the trombone player in Jamie Cullum's band. The poor sod fell in love with her and asked her to move in with him where they could work on music and - a relationship together.

Nothing much happened on either front and she ended up moving out but staying in London to pursue her dream of being a singer.

He'd tried to clip her wings. She wasn't the kind of girl you could do this to. Part of the appeal. We continued to see each other regularly at sensible intervals. I dug being with Livia, I could feel her youthful energy and she was nearly as crackers/devious as me.

Nearly.

When it was good it was wonderful, and in a strange way I came to love her despite her questionable ways. Maybe even because of them. Christ, I was certainly no saint.

In the summer of '05 we went to see Oasis play at Milton Keynes Bowl. Zak was now playing drums for them, as well as playing with his childhood heroes the Who (it's one of the joys of my life to think that he broke his dream. Most people dream of playing with their idols but never manage it of course - Zak did just that. Amazing).

By the time we got called backstage by Lee - after virtually everyone had left the site, I was four sheets to the wind and nearly got ejected for singing Rutles songs at full volume into Liam Gallagher's ear. I know this only because I was told later on - I have no recollection.

Lee had moved into a new scene since Zak was now in the Oasis network, and because of this she met a lot of new people outside of her usual circle. One person she met she fell in love with - a very sweet American guy called Jay who played guitar in a band called Kasabian.

I was pleased she'd apparently found what she was looking for, and very interested to see what it was when she found it.

It's a rare thing to find the one.

People started reminding me that 2006 would be the twenty-fifth anniversary of the Icicle Works' first gig and perhaps I should consider doing a reunion tour. I left a message for Chris Sharrock with his wife Jo regarding this matter, but I never got a call back.

I wasn't going to push it and get the knockback and upset myself. I wasn't going to play with Chris L if Chris S wasn't on board (it would also mean splitting the money down the middle. Seeing as I'd kept the music alive for eighteen years since the split I didn't think that would be fair), but I decided to do the shows anyway, just using my touring band, who were more than up to the task. I was the singer and guitarist and the audience would hear everything they wanted to and more.

If anybody complained they had expected to see the original line-up and felt short-changed - they could have their money back. A tour was booked for the end of the year and ticket sales were rapid. It would be fun re-learning all the old tunes and seeing how I felt playing them after all these years.

I walked in to the rehearsal room at Crash and hugged all the guys in the band. We had five days to learn a two-hour-plus Icicle Works set. Mathew Priest had had much success with his own band Dodgy in the past. He was a great drummer, very excited (and perhaps just a little nervous) to be reproducing Chris Sharrock's brilliant, complicated drum parts.

Richard Naiff was the best keyboard player I'd ever worked with, a classically trained virtuoso whose favourite band was the Damned. Roy Corkill was the musician I would always choose to work with, A wonderful bass player, and a great friend - also a great foil for me on stage.

Never afraid of me - he would always (try) to keep me in my place.

We learnt many songs we'd never played together before, and many I hadn't played since the mid-eighties.

'Factory In The Desert', 'In The Cauldron Of Love', 'As The Dragonfly Flies', 'Nirvana', it was a strange feeling. ('Nirvana' had been recorded in this room. Crash Studios was once Square One - I was standing in exactly the same place I'd recorded my vocal in 1982). The shows were sold out and a great joy.

Once again the only voice of dissent was from Chris L who did an interview with the Liverpool Echo telling people they weren't getting the real deal. They turned out in droves and no-one asked for their money back. Chris turned up in Manchester, paid for a ticket and didn't attempt to come backstage.

I was told by several witnesses he danced the night away.

The night after the last gig I went to see Phil Sharrock's son's band play at the Cavern.

Chris S was there and had been hearing all about the tour and was genuinely pleased for me. He'd made a fortune playing in Robbie Williams' band and was at the top of the drummer's totem pole - a hard thing to achieve.

I still loved Chris.

His wife Jo was as icy with me as usual.

I've been doing this job for over thirty years now to varying degrees of success, but I always figured it wasn't about how big you got, but how long you got. I've watched the industry change.

These days recorded music doesn't seem that important anymore. A generation has sprung up who don't think it's cool to pay for it. But they have no problem buying concert tickets.

Live music is healthier than it's ever been as people can't download the experience of watching a great act do their thing on a brightly lit stage. This will last forever.

The worst thing that has happened recently is the 'unlocking' of albums. You can download individual tracks from the Internet without having to listen to a whole record. This has killed the artform.

It's like only reading certain passages from a book instead of digesting the whole story.

It's like watching the key points in a movie but not bothering with the scenes that set those moments up.

It's like having sex with someone without the wine, soft lights and the foreplay.

The glorious build up. The magic!

Me and my band are due to play a festival down south in a couple of weeks. I get my roadie to set my gear up in the celler so I can test my amps at full throttle and mark all the settings down.

I plug the Les Paul into the Acoustic head which is plugged into a Hiwatt 4x12 speaker enclosure.

I turn the amp up really high. I have a sip of tea, find a plectrum, and put my ciggie in the ashtray.

I hit an E chord hard and let it ring. It goes on forever. Suddenly I become aware of a banging noise two floors above me.

What is it? I hit an A chord this time.

More banging.

What the fuck? I can hear shouting now. It's my mother, screaming at me from her bed.

It's mid-afternoon, but we keep funny hours round here.

"IAN!"

"IAN!"

Christ.

"What?" . . .

"What?" . . .

"What is it?"

"WHAT ARE YOU PLAYIN' AT?!"

"I'm testing me gear! We've got a fezzie next week!"

"STOP TRYING TO DRAW ATTENTION TO YOURSELF!!!"

Bit late for that I reckon.

"I'm funky and I'm free,
this is how I plan to be,
I'm a rock'n'roll good-time boy,
and I can't contain my joy,
I can't contain my joy!"

I've pretty much always known what I've wanted.

Lucky bastard.

How about you?

Afterword

I showed this book to a few close friends before it went to print. I got differing reactions. Some of them are in it.

A couple of them weren't happy about the way they came across. One thought they appeared to be a bit player when they thought they would have a starring role. Another thought I wrote far too much about them and wanted a reduced part or... deletion.

Another thought I was too graphic about certain things and another thought details were sketchy.

Fact is it's MY book and we all see things differently.

There's a lot of stuff I don't remember the same way as they do because I saw it in a different light. It's not meant to be a reference book, it's meant to be an entertaining light read. I haven't tried to create a literary work for our times, I've tried to tell my story, fairly briefly, in an entertaining way.

If I've upset anyone I'm genuinely sorry, although plenty deserved what they got. You didn't think you'd got away with that shit did you? Really?

My suggestion is to write your own tome and balance will be achieved. No one will be interested of course because I'm a rock star and...you are?

There's plenty of stuff I left out as it was too hot and much of it too libellous. It will come out one day as this is the first sift. I have lots more to say and there will be another volume in the future. If you've been nice to me you really haven't got anything to worry about. I've enjoyed writing it immensely and found it very cathartic.

Things that seemed so important at the time now appear trivial and vice versa. It took me about two years off and on and some days words were flying out of me and others it was hard to get started. Just like songwriting. The only difference is I only write songs when I want to but this had to be finished by a certain time. I wanted it to come out in 2008 and I hit my target.

Lend it to your friends or better still get them to buy it too. Spread the word if you've enjoyed it. Get someone to nick one. Anyone can buy a book. Right? Make it interesting.

If you are a committed fan I thank you for your indulgence.

If you are not and my words have drawn you in to my little world, perhaps you'd like to check out the discography on my website and get stuck in.

Where the hell have you been?!

Ian McNabb
Liverpool July 2008
www.ianmcnabb.com
www.myspace.com/ianmcnabbtheicicleworks

This book is dedicated to my mum, Patricia Mavis McNabb.

d punksters selling
?) to teeming crowds at
ICA. Then there was Icicle
orks performing a blistering set
to a capacity crowd at the good ole
Town And Country Club at
Kentish Town. Finally, there was
derstanding Jane', a slab of
g, unashamedly-rock 'n' roll
which had shot into the Top

was a great day,
ugh just a few nights later
ouncers at Liverpool's charity 'Soap
id' concert savagely beat up Ian
McNabb and Chris Lay ne for trying
get in to their own — gig
ty! . . .

But to understa he Icicle
s you have to go rwards and
rds in time and understand
nery
he case
nutes

FRESH SQUEEZED ORANGE JUICE
100% PURE FROM FLORIDA
NO ADDITIVES
NO PRESERVATIVES

make people u
harder band th

At the time
Top 30 in the
deny them t'
excellent si
Broudie–v
in it—it is a
before ene
Icicle viny

And th
Icicle Wo
'Love Is
the arti
to Num
alread
almos
albu
vario
eme
M
ant
(ro
co
th
w

THE ICICLE WORKS
nchester
University

E ICICLES might neve
et the world on fire, but
hey're certainly warming
many hearts.

Sounding mildly like a
U2 or a Big Country, rather
than the Aztec Camera you
might expect, the Icicles
are hard but poppy. Ian
McNabb's voice just
mellowing around a
backdrop of persistent
drums and keys.

The group carry you
on their bobbing
dwagon of singles
ies and stirring
ems, occasional
ing into the owe
d guitar
generally y
ry nice indeed!

They're such ni
wearing their moo
uniform, thanki
everyone for co
owing. Very h
down to earth –
they've been li
that besweate
on the Ameri
prog.: "Reach
stars – but k
on the grou

And they
a huge loy
the proce
nowball
opery

■ ICICLE WORKS, CAMDEN PALA
LONDON

On the eve of their third album release, the Icicle
have taken to playing a selection of anti-heroin be
gigs. It's a cause they are all too familiar with in m
'Brookside' Land, as Ian McNabb. He's n on
ostensibly hooked on the soap that has gone a ng w
he reappraising the traditional image of smack t addi
he actually auditioned (and was turned down) for a pa
n 'Brookside' itself.

Like 'Brookside', the Icicle Works are a name kno
tter by reputation than experience. They unwitting
de a big mistake in 1983 by having a hit at pro
ped them in with the wimpering Lotus eaters
emember them?) of the world. Their creative lon
as been severely underestimated as a result, as this
exceptionally approachable set proved.

Almost every song played has been (or will be) a
at one time. From the starry-eyed 'Love Is A Wonder
Colour' to the more penetrating 'Understanding Jane'
should have been a classic collection of hits. Instead it w
a reminder that biggest is not always best.

Having now expanded to a four piece — with the
addition of keyboard player Dave Green — the Icicle
Works stand a greater chance of living up to their ow
ambitions. New songs like 'Little Girl Lost' and 'Starr
Blue Eyed Wonder' (allegedly about Waterboy Mike
Scott) were well received and indicate a more mainstre
approach that shouldn't compromise their position of
espect.

The Cause, though, was never long forgotten, and was
mmarised by the recent frostily received 'Up Here In
e North Of England'. "Children, don't put smack in
veins." McNabb warned, and then in the same br
rred back to 'Brookside'. "I'm only in a band becau
my own audition." Well, thank God he did.
Chris Twom

THE ICICLE WORKS

he Icicle Work

LIVE

ICICLE WORKS, TOWN AND COUNTRY CLUB, LONDON

Capturing the sound and style that is so reminiscent of all that is goth, the ... short set, which included the last single 'Happy Boy' and the chirpier enc... offering 'Away', was well received. They ended with the incongruous enc... cover of Michael Jackson's 'Billie Jean' — proving that it's not all black loc... serious moods.

The Icicle Works, on the other hand, are the epitome of the perfect guitar ... making up for anything they lack in image with a distinct, harmonious sound ... all their own.

Coming on to a tape of 'Brookside' (or so my soap viewing colleague info... me — never touch the stuff meself), they begin with the excellent 'Hollow H... With other great tracks like 'Love Is A Wonderful Colour', 'Seven Horses'... Daughter Of Her Father's House', you're quickly reminded just how many exce... songs they have in their repertoire. Add to that the new single — the plain... 'Understanding Jane' — and some really good new material like 'Who Do I... Want For Your Love' and 'Sweet Thursday', and you know that they have the tale... and tenacity to stay around for quite a while.

They've been criticised before for their guitar excesses, although these were ke... to a minimum, apart from on tracks like 'When It All Comes Down' they're b... when they're playing their pure and simple perfect guitar pop.

Nor are they without humour; "I saw Sammy Davis Junior do this once," quip... Ian McNabb before introducing a song for a friend, 'Starry Blue Eyed Wonder... No, not the song, smoking while he was singing. It's very anti-social but it sounds... better." Ian McNabb posing over mike, fag-handed, shrouded in light catching... ...ke, is a hysterical sight.

...e Icicle Works' sound knows no bounds; the audience loved them here, but... ...an image they'd be ... comfortable, just as good in some sweaty dive or... ...t of a stadium crowd. On stage for more than two hours, and it wasn't a... ...oo long.

Di Cross